T. H. Bertenshaw

Elements of music, harmony and counterpoint, rhythm, analysis and musical form

T. H. Bertenshaw

Elements of music, harmony and counterpoint, rhythm, analysis and musical form

ISBN/EAN: 9783742837585

Manufactured in Europe, USA, Canada, Australia, Japa

Cover: Foto ©Angelika Wolter / pixelio.de

Manufactured and distributed by brebook publishing software (www.brebook.com)

T. H. Bertenshaw

Elements of music, harmony and counterpoint, rhythm, analysis and musical form

LONGMANS' MUSIC COURSE
COMPLETE EDITION

ELEMENTS OF MUSIC,
HARMONY AND COUNTERPOINT,
RHYTHM, ANALYSIS, AND
MUSICAL FORM

WITH EXERCISES

BY T. H. BERTENSHAW, B.A., B.MUS.
ASSISTANT MASTER IN THE CITY OF LONDON SCHOOL

LONGMANS, GREEN, AND CO.
LONDON, NEW YORK, AND BOMBAY
1896

PREFACE.

THIS book contains a complete course, comprising the Elements of Music, Harmony and Counterpoint, and Rhythm, Analysis and Musical Form.

In Part I. will be found, besides the usual subjects included under Elements of Music, chapters on transcription from one time to another (*e.g.* from two-four to six-eight), on the variations in time produced by change of accent (*tempo rubato*), on enharmonics and enharmonic notation. Intervals are treated at great length, and there are chapters on Transposition, Grace Notes, and Musical Terms. Under this last head a section dealing with terms relating to Pianoforte technique is included. To each chapter is added a series of questions, many of which are taken from examination papers.

In Part II. I have tried to simplify the study of Harmony and Counterpoint for beginners. One great difficulty lies in the large amount of ground to be covered before the student is able to begin practical work. I have avoided this by breaking up the earlier parts of the subject into convenient sections. Thus, the rules for Part-writing are given as occasion for their use occurs in the exercises, and they are not presented in a body until the pupil has had some experience.

Every teacher knows that the beginner's greatest difficulty

lies in writing *successions* of chords. To overcome this I have confined the earlier exercises to chords which have one or more notes in common. Then, by degrees, chords without this connecting link are introduced. By this time the student has some idea of chordal succession, and he is ready to begin the systematic study of common chords.

The book embraces the complete system of Harmony as taught in modern text-books, but in apportioning the space I have had in mind more especially the needs of elementary students. Thus, common chords and their inversions, the chords of minor keys, the dominant seventh, &c., are treated with unusual fulness. No fewer than fourteen pages are given to suspensions, my experience being that that chapter is often the *pons asinorum* of Harmony.

Great pains have been taken to render the exercises interesting. They are all capable of being worked with a good melody, and they are all constructed on clear rhythmical lines.

I have added a chapter on Harmonising Melodies. This of necessity is short, but it points out a method which the intelligent student will have little difficulty in following. For convenience, this chapter is placed nearly at the end of Part II., *but the student is urged to take it in sections, as explained at the end of the several chapters on Harmony* (*vide* pp. 119, 129, 137, &c.).

The chapters on Counterpoint are very elementary, but it is hoped that they will be found useful.

Part III. is an attempt to deal with a large subject in a few pages. But though the subject is large, the underlying principles are few, and it is hoped on this account that the treatment will be found adequate from the beginner's point of view

The first four chapters deal with rhythm—the division of music into sentences and phrases, the lengthening and shortening of sentences. Particular attention is invited to Chapter LX., where the principles affecting the proper barring of music are explained.

Under the subject of Form I have given a good deal of space to song form, partly because it is the easiest way of approaching the subject for beginners, and partly because *the principles of form* (§ 861) can be learnt here just as well as in more elaborate movements. But the lion's share of the space is given to sonata form, and this will probably need no apology. As in the earlier books of this series, I have broken long chapters into sections for convenience of study.

I have paid more attention than is usual in books on form to the historical side of the question, and in particular I have written a long chapter on the history of sonata form. I feel sure that this new departure will add to the interest of the work and lighten the labours of teachers.

The exercises in analysis are very copious, and as they are carefully graduated it is hoped that they will be useful. I have given numerous models of what such analyses should be. It is very necessary that the student should examine the music of as many of the examples as possible. With this in view I have confined my quotations to compositions which are easily and cheaply obtainable. To induce students to procure the music referred to, I have in many cases used the same composition to illustrate more than one point. The references to Mozart's P.F. Sonatas are to Novello's edition, those of Haydn's to Peters' edition.

I gratefully acknowledge much assistance from numerous books, and in particular I mention as especially helpful in Part III. Professor Prout's *Musical Form* (Augener & Co.), a book which is so excellent that it cannot fail to become *the* book *par excellence* on this subject in English; Dr. Parry's *Art of Music* (Kegan Paul & Co.) and his various articles in Sir George Grove's *Dictionary of Music and Musicians* (Macmillan & Co.);

and Mr. Hadow's Essay on Form prefixed to his *Studies in Modern Music*, second series (Seeley & Co.).

I cordially thank my friends, Mr. Vice-Principal Barkby, B.A., Mr. G. F. Wrigley, M.A., Mus.Bac., and Mr. W. S. Desborough, Mus.Bac., for many valuable suggestions and much kindness in revising proofs.

CONTENTS.

PART I.
ELEMENTS OF MUSIC.

CHAPTER		PAGE
I.	Notes, Clefs, Leger Lines	1
II.	The Alto and Tenor Clefs; The Great Stave	3
III.	Origin of the Form of Clefs, Use of Clefs, Octaves	7
IV.	Shape and Length of Notes	10
V.	Accent and Time	13
VI.	Time-signatures	18
VII.	Accents, Beating Time, Rests, &c.	24
VIII.	Triplets, Syncopation	28
IX.	Semitones, Sharps, Flats, Naturals	35
X.	Major Scales	37
XI.	The Minor Scale	44
XII.	Keys	50
XIII.	Acoustics	52
XIV.	Diatonic and Chromatic Semitones	55
XV.	The Chromatic Scale	59
XVI.	Intervals	61
XVII.	Chromatic Intervals	66
XVIII.	Inversion of Intervals	69
XIX.	Transposition	73
XX.	Dots, Abbreviations, &c.	76
XXI.	Grace Notes	82
XXII.	Musical Terms	86

PART II.
HARMONY.

	Introductory Chapter—Intervals	93
XXIII.	Melody and Harmony	100
XXIV.	Common Chords in Succession	105
XXV.	Common Chords in Succession—*continued*	113

CHAPTER		PAGE
XXVI.	COMMON CHORDS IN MAJOR KEYS	117
XXVII.	FIRST INVERSIONS IN MAJOR KEYS	119
XXVIII.	SECOND INVERSIONS IN MAJOR KEYS	124
XXIX.	COMMON CHORDS IN MINOR KEYS	130
XXX.	INVERSIONS OF TRIADS IN MINOR KEYS	134
XXXI.	THE DOMINANT SEVENTH IN MAJOR KEYS	138
XXXII.	INVERSIONS OF THE DOMINANT SEVENTH IN MAJOR KEYS	144
XXXIII.	THE DOMINANT SEVENTH IN MINOR KEYS	148
XXXIV.	SECONDARY OR NON-DOMINANT SEVENTHS	151
XXXV.	RECAPITULATION OF THE LAWS OF PART-WRITING	156
XXXVI.	CADENCES	162
XXXVII.	SEQUENCES	166
XXXVIII.	MODULATION	169
XXXIX.	SUSPENSIONS	175
	SECT. I. THE SUSPENDED NINTH	176
	SECT. II. THE SUSPENDED FOURTH	181
	SECT. III. OTHER SUSPENSIONS	185
XL.	PASSING NOTES, AUXILIARY NOTES, ANTICIPATIONS, RETARDATIONS	189
XLI.	CHORDS OF THE NINTH	198
	SECT. I. THE DOMINANT NINTH	198
	SECT. II. INVERSIONS OF THE DOMINANT NINTH	201
	SECT. III. THE DIMINISHED SEVENTH, ENHARMONIC MODULATION	204
	SECT. IV. SECONDARY NINTHS	209
XLII.	THE DOMINANT ELEVENTH	211
XLIII.	THE DOMINANT THIRTEENTH	214
XLIV.	CHROMATIC CONCORDS	212
XLV.	CHROMATIC FUNDAMENTAL DISCORDS	222
	SECT. I. SUPERTONIC AND TONIC SEVENTHS	222
	SECT. II. SUPERTONIC AND TONIC NINTHS	225
	SECT. III. CHROMATIC ELEVENTHS AND THIRTEENTHS	227
	SECT. IV. FUNDAMENTAL DISCORDS AND THE CHROMATIC SCALE	230
XLVI.	THE AUGMENTED SIXTH	233
XLVII.	THE DISSONANT TRIADS	238
XLVIII.	PEDAL NOTES, ARPEGGIOS, GROUND BASS	240
XLIX.	MODULATION—*continued*	245
L.	HOW TO HARMONISE A MELODY	248

COUNTERPOINT.

LI.	INTRODUCTORY	261
LII.	LAWS OF PROGRESSION	263

CHAPTER		PAGE
LIII.	FIRST SPECIES OF COUNTERPOINT	267
LIV.	SECOND SPECIES OF COUNTERPOINT	271
LV.	THIRD SPECIES OF COUNTERPOINT	275
LVI.	FOURTH SPECIES OF COUNTERPOINT	278
LVII.	FIFTH SPECIES OF COUNTERPOINT	281
LVIII.	COMBINED COUNTERPOINT	283
	CANTI FERMI FOR EXERCISES IN COUNTERPOINT	287

PART III.
RHYTHM.

LIX.	SENTENCES AND PHRASES	289
LX.	THE METHOD OF BARRING MUSIC	299
LXI.	SECTIONS AND MOTIVES; THE RELATION OF SECTIONS	302
LXII.	HOW SENTENCES ARE LENGTHENED	309
LXIII.	HOW SENTENCES ARE SHORTENED	314
LXIV.	EXAMPLES OF RHYTHM	318

FORM.

LXV.	KEY-RELATIONSHIP	324
LXVI.	SECT. I. TWO-PART FORM.	325
	SECT. II. THREE-PART FORM	334
LXVII.	THE SONATA; SONATA FORM; CYCLIC FORM	340
	SECT. I. THE EXPOSITION	342
	SECT. II. THE DEVELOPMENT	349
	SECT. III. THE RECAPITULATION AND CODA	357
LXVIII.	THE SLOW MOVEMENT; MODIFIED SONATA FORM	364
LXIX.	THE MINUET AND TRIO; THE SCHERZO	368
LXX.	SECT. I. RONDO FORM	371
	SECT. II. THE MODERN RONDO OR SONATA-RONDO	375
LXXI.	THE HISTORY OF THE SONATA AND SONATA FORM	376
LXXII.	ORCHESTRAL MUSIC; CONCERTED MUSIC	383
	SECT. I. THE OVERTURE	383
	SECT. II. THE SYMPHONY	385
	SECT. III. THE CONCERTO	387
	SECT. IV. THE STRING QUARTET	389
LXXIII.	VARIATIONS; THE FANTASIA	390
LXXIV.	IMITATION; CANON AND FUGUE; FUGUE AND SONATA FORM COMBINED	391
LXXV.	THE SUITE; THE PARTITA; DANCE FORMS.	402
LXXVI.	VOCAL MUSIC	405
	GENERAL INDEX.	409
	LIST OF WORKS ANALYSED IN PART III.	414

ELEMENTS OF MUSIC

CHAPTER I.

NOTES. CLEFS. LEGER LINES.

1. Musical sounds differ from one another in **Pitch**. By the *Pitch* of a sound we mean whether it is high or low.

2. As regards pitch, musical sounds are named after the first seven letters of the alphabet—

A, B, C, D, E, F, G.

3. These seven sounds follow each other in *ascending* order of pitch, and if we take an *eighth* note in the same order it is so related to the first (A) that it receives the same name. As it is the *eighth* note from the first, it is called the **octave**[1] of the first (from the Latin word *octavus* = *eighth*).

4. Musical Sounds are represented by characters called **Notes**, which are written on, and in the spaces between, a series of five parallel lines called a **Stave** (or *Staff*).

Both *lines* and *spaces* are counted upwards. (Fig. 1.)

FIG. 1.

Lines   Spaces

5. To determine the *name* and *pitch* of notes written on staves, signs called **Clefs** are used.

The two chief clefs are the **G clef** or *Treble clef*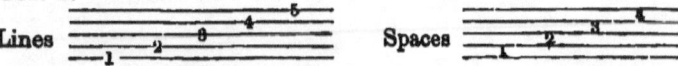

and the **F clef** or *Bass clef*

It will be seen that the G clef crosses the *second* line four times. It is said to stand on the *second* line, to which it gives the name G.

---

[1] It will be seen presently that the term *octave* is also applied to the whole series of eight notes in alphabetical order. (§ 25.)

6. Reckoning upwards and downwards from G on the second line the space above will be A, the space below will be F. Thus the names of the notes on the *Treble stave* will be as in fig. 2.

Fig. 2.

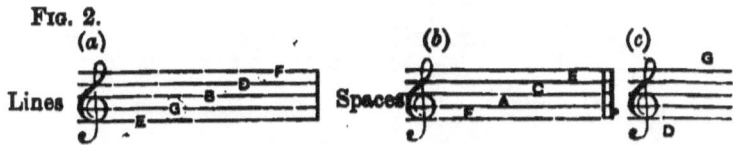

The note next *below* the treble stave will be D; the note next *above* will be G.

7. The *F clef* is placed on the *fourth* line, to which it gives the name of F. The names of notes on the *Bass stave* will be as in fig. 3.

Fig. 3.

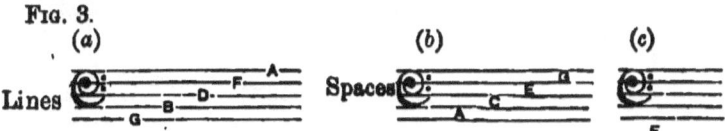

8. When it is necessary to represent notes of higher or lower pitch than can be shown on a stave, short lines called **Leger lines** (or *Ledger*) are used, above and below the stave.

Fig. 4.

9. The names of notes on and between these leger lines follow each other in alphabetical order. Thus:

Fig. 5.

NOTES. CLEFS. LEGER LINES.

EXERCISES.

Copy out the following and write underneath each note its alphabetical name.

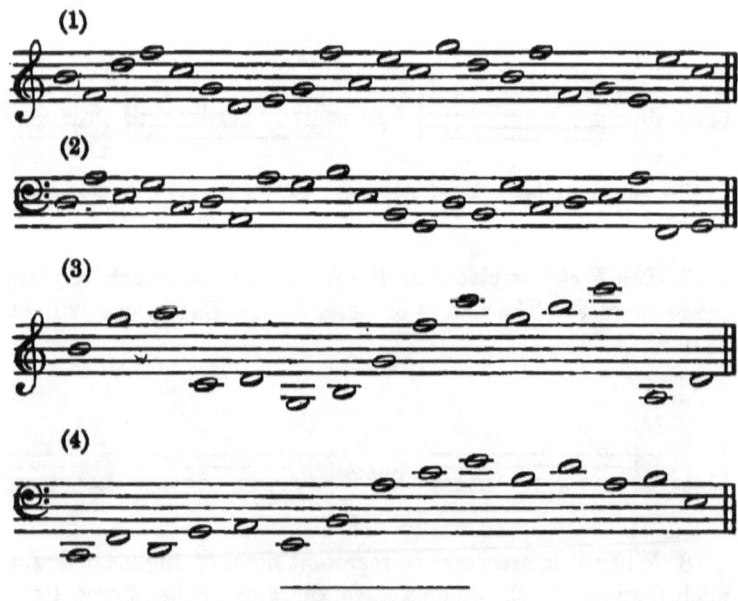

CHAPTER II.

THE ALTO AND TENOR CLEFS. THE GREAT STAVE.

10. If we place the *treble stave* above the *bass stave* we get the double stave used for pianoforte music.

FIG. 6.

11. Let us examine this pair of staves. The note below the treble stave is D; the note above the bass stave is B. There is then *one* step from the bass to the treble stave, and this can be filled up by using a *leger* line, the name of which will evidently be C.

FIG. 7.

12. We shall now be able to get a continuous series of notes beginning in the bass and continuing without break through the treble.

FIG. 8.

It will now be easy to specify more definitely the exact pitch of a note.

13. The note C written on the leger line *between the treble and bass staves* is called **Middle C**.

On a piano *Middle C* stands, roughly speaking, in the middle of the instrument; on a violin it is the C played in the first position by the third finger on the fourth string.

This *Middle C* is of great importance for reference, and the student should thoroughly understand its position on the double stave, on the treble stave, and on the bass stave. Thus the following are different ways of representing the same note:

FIG. 9.

14. When the treble and bass staves standing over each other are joined by a continued leger line, we get a stave of eleven lines. This is useful for reference and is called the **Great Stave of eleven lines** (*v.* § 245).

Fig. 10.

15. The treble and bass staves are merely sections of the *Great Stave*.

16. In order to avoid the use of a large number of leger lines other sets of five lines from the Great Stave are used.

To show this another clef, called the **C clef**, is used, or *It always denotes the* **Middle C**.

17. The five lines of the new stave may be made up in different ways.

Thus we may take *middle C* with two lines above (from the treble) and two below (from the bass). This stave is called the **Alto Stave**.

Or we may take *middle C* with one above and three below. This is called the **Tenor Stave**.

Or we may take *middle C* with four above, and this is called the **Soprano Stave**.

18. The relative position of all the staves will be seen from the Great Stave of eleven lines:

Fig. 11.

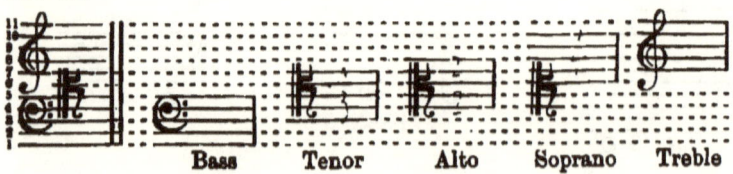

Bass   Tenor   Alto   Soprano   Treble

19. Two of these staves with the *C clef* are so important that we shall take them separately.

(a) The alto stave has the *C clef* on its middle line.
The names of the notes on the alto stave will then be:

Fig. 12.

(*b*) The tenor stave has the *C clef* on its fourth line. The names of the notes on the tenor stave are as follows:

Fig. 13.

20. It is important that the student should familiarise himself with the names of notes on all the staves. He should also be able to represent the *same* sounds on different staves.

Thus, suppose we are asked to re-write the following on the bass stave:

This can always be done by keeping in mind the middle C, and reckoning from that. Thus the first note is the G above the middle C, represented on the bass stave by the third leger line *above*. Similarly for the others. We therefore get the following:

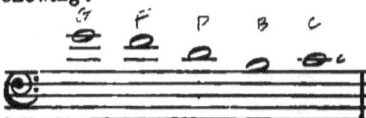

In the alto, tenor, and soprano the passage would stand

It is worth noticing that a note *on a line* with one clef will be on a line in any clef; so with notes in spaces.

THE ALTO AND TENOR CLEFS. THE GREAT STAVE

EXERCISE.

1. Rewrite the following, without altering the pitch, in the *bass clef*:

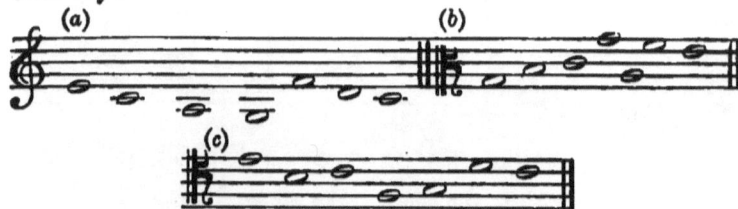

2. Rewrite the following in the *treble clef*:

3. Rewrite the following in the *alto clef*; and in the *tenor clef*:

CHAPTER III.

ORIGIN OF THE FORM OF CLEFS. USE OF CLEFS. OCTAVES.

21. The signs used for the G, F, and C clefs are merely corruptions of old forms of the letters G, F, and C. Thus, all the following shapes (with many others) are found in old music:

(a) G clef 𝕲, *i.e.* 𝄞.

(b) F clef 𝆑, 𝆒, 𝆓, ♦‖: , *i.e.* 𝄢

(c) C clef 𝄡, ‖: , ╫ , ⊏ , *i.e.* 𝄡.

8 ELEMENTS OF MUSIC

22. In writing for voices the *soprano* (highest voice of women), *alto*[1] (lowest voice of women), *tenor* (highest voice of men), and *bass* (lowest voice of men), were formerly indicated by the clefs bearing those names. Now[2] the treble *G clef* is used for soprano, alto, and tenor, and the *bass clef* for the bass. The *tenor part*, however, is written an *octave higher* than it is sung, and this is shown by writing *octave lower* (8ve lower) at the beginning of the tenor part.

The following extract from Handel's "Judas Maccabæus" will illustrate this: (*a*) is taken from an old edition; (*b*) is the same from a modern edition.

FIG. 14.

---

[1] The word *alto* really means *high*. Formerly this part was always sung by men (and it is still in most cathedral choirs), and so it meant the *highest* voice of men. It was also called *counter-tenor*. In modern music the part is sung by women, and is often called *contralto* (*v.* § 246).

[2] *I.e.* in England. In German editions of full scores the old clefs are still used for the four voices.

ORIGIN OF FORM OF CLEFS. USE OF CLEFS. OCTAVES

23. In music for *piano, organ*, &c., the *treble clef* is used for the higher notes, usually played with the right hand; the *bass clef* is used for the lower notes, played with the left hand.

The treble clef is further used for the *violin*, and for wind instruments of similar pitch, viz. *piccolo, flute, oboe, clarinet, cornet*, &c.

The alto clef is used for the *viola*,[1] and the *alto trombone*.

The tenor clef is used for the *tenor trombone*, and for the higher notes of the *violoncello*.

The bass clef is used for the *violoncello*, and *double bass*, and also for wind instruments of similar pitch, viz. *bassoon, bass trombone*, &c.

24. We have seen in Fig. 8 that there are several sets of notes (C, D, E, F, G, A, B) called *octaves*. It is convenient to give different names to the different octaves.

25. The octave beginning with the C on the second leger line below the bass is called the **Great Octave**. The next octave is called the **Small Octave**. That beginning with middle C is called the **Once-marked Octave**. That beginning with the C in the third space of the treble stave is called the **Twice-marked Octave**.

Note that each C begins a fresh octave.

Fig. 15.

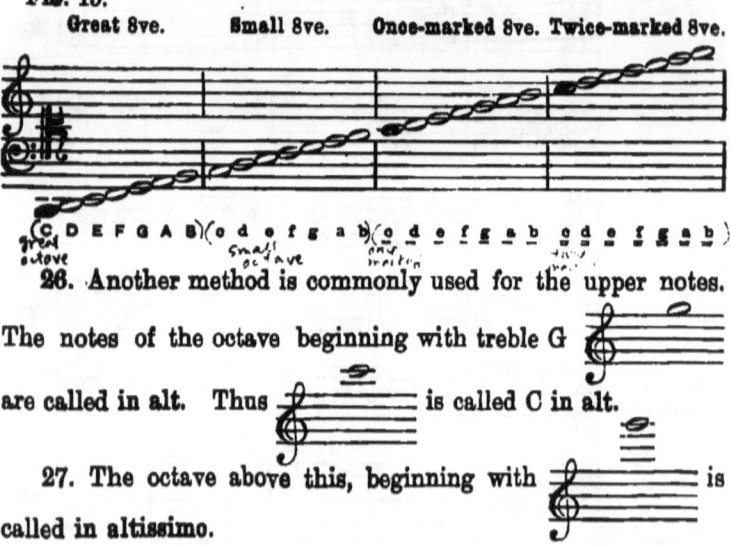

26. Another method is commonly used for the upper notes. The notes of the octave beginning with treble G are called in alt. Thus is called C in alt.

27. The octave above this, beginning with is called in altissimo.

---

[1] The *viola* is often called the *tenor violin*, but it plays from the *alto clef*.

28. Two other names should be noted: **the middle C (§ 13)** and the **tenor C** one octave below this:

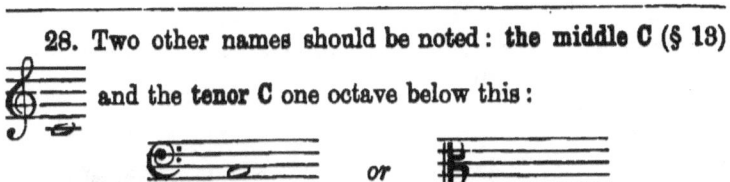

CHAPTER IV.

SHAPE AND LENGTH OF NOTES.

29. The relative duration of notes is indicated by their shape. The following are the chief shapes used in modern music:

    ◯ semi-breve.   ◗ minim.   ♩ crotchet.

    ♪ quaver.   ♬ semi-quaver.   ♬ demi-semi-quaver.

The *semibreve* is an open note; the *minim* is an open note with a stem: the *crotchet* is a black note with a stem; the *quaver* is a black note and its stem has a hook, while the *semiquaver* has two hooks, and *demisemiquaver* three.

30. In modern music the **semibreve is taken as the standard**, and in Germany it is therefore called the **whole note**. In the list below each note is equal in duration to two of that which follows. Thus, 1 semi-breve = 2 minims; 1 minim = 2 crotchets, &c. This will best be seen from the German names in the following table:

  ◯   semibreve or **whole note**.   ♪ semiquaver or **sixteenth note**.[1]

  ◗ ◗   minim or **half note**.

  ♩ ♩   crotchet or **quarter note**.   ♪ demisemiquaver or **thirty-second note**.[1]

  ♪ ♪   quaver or **eighth note**.

---

[1] *Semi-* and *demi-* both mean half.

SHAPE AND LENGTH OF NOTES

31. Stems may be turned up or down. When several *hooked* notes occur together they may be written in groups.

FIG. 16.

32. A **dot** placed after a note makes it half as long again.

Thus ♩· = ♩♩ or ♩♩♩.

A second dot adds half the value of the first dot. Thus:

♩·· = ♩♩♩.

33. Instead of using dots to increase the length of notes, a sign called a **tie** [1] (⌒) may be used. The *tie* indicates that the sound is to be continued for the total length of the notes joined.

Thus: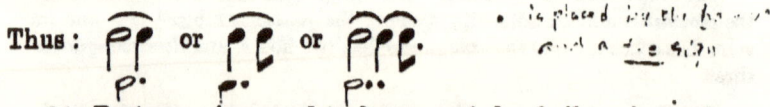

34. Rests are signs used to denote periods of *silence* in music. Each note shown above has a corresponding rest.

FIG. 17.

| Semibreve rest. | Minim rest. | Crotchet rest. | Quaver rest. | Semiquaver rest. | Demisemi- quaver rest. |

The *semibreve* and *minim* rests are alike in shape, but the *longer* rest hangs from the *higher* line, the *shorter* lies on the *lower* line. The *crotchet* and *quaver* rests are alike in shape, but the *longer* rest turns to the *right*, the *shorter* to the *left*. The *semiquaver* and *demisemiquaver* are easily distinguished by their hooks.

35. Owing to the similarity of the *crotchet* and *quaver* rests a **new crotchet rest** (written 𝄽) is now very generally used.

---

[1] Other uses of this sign will be shown later (§ 215).

86. Dots may be added to rests with just the same effect as when used with notes. Thus: ▮. = ▮ ▮

Except in certain cases, explained later (§ 72), dotted rests are not much used.

NOTE TO CHAPTER IV.

87. A note called a breve, equal to two *semibreves*, is occasionally used in Church music.

In instrumental music a **semi-demi-semi-quaver**,[1] equal in value to half a demisemiquaver, is sometimes used. These notes with their corresponding rests are shown below.

FIG. 18.

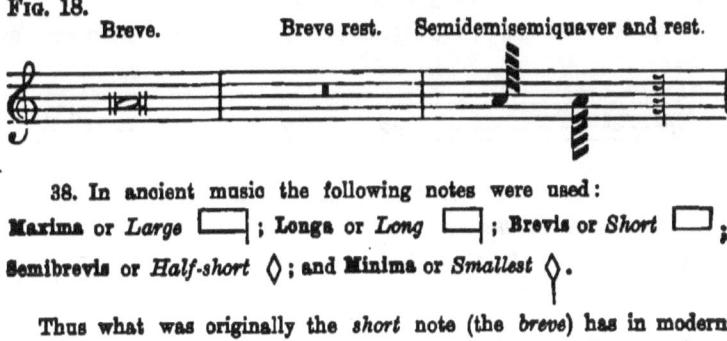

38. In ancient music the following notes were used:
Maxima or *Large* ▭ ; **Longa** or *Long* ▭ ; **Brevis** or *Short* ▭ ; **Semibrevis** or *Half-short* ◊ ; and **Minima** or *Smallest* ◊.

Thus what was originally the *short* note (the *breve*) has in modern music become the longest note used, and other shapes and names have been invented to indicate the shorter notes.

EXERCISE.

1. What single note is equal to 8 quavers; to 4 quavers; to 4 crotchets; to 8 semiquavers?

2. Express the following in *quavers*:—(a) ▮ ; (b) ▮▮ ; (c) ○.

3. Express the following in *semiquavers*:—(a) ▮ ; (b) ▮ ; (c) ▮▮▮.

---

[1] Occasionally in instrumental music a note with *five* hooks (half the length of the semi demi-semi-quaver) is found. *Vide* Beethoven's Piano Sonatas, No. 26, Andante Espressivo.

SHAPE AND LENGTH OF NOTES

4. How can a note equal to 6 quavers be written?

5. Write the *rests* corresponding to the following without using dotted rests:—(a) ; (b) ; (c) ; (d) ; (e) .

6. Rewrite the following, *halving* the value of each note and rest:

7. Rewrite the following, *doubling* the value of each note and rest:

8. Rewrite the following, making each note and rest four times greater in value:

CHAPTER V.

ACCENT AND TIME.

39. In a line like "Down the hill-side tripped the maiden" we pronounce some of the syllables with more emphasis than the others. Thus:

Down the hill-side **tripped** the **maiden**,

where the syllables in thick type are accented.

40. In music **Accent** means the *stress* or *emphasis* given to certain notes. We might represent the above line in music, marking the accent by the sign ʌ, thus:—

Fɪɢ. 19.

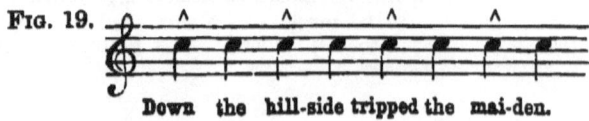

Down the hill-side tripped the mai-den.

41. In music the **accented note** is shown by placing *before it* an upright line called a **bar** or **bar-line.** Thus the above would be shown as follows:

FIG. 20.

Note: When the *first* note is accented the bar-line for that note is omitted.

42. The sign 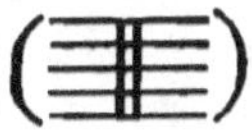  is called a **Double-bar.** It has nothing to do with accent; it merely indicates the end of a piece or of a section.

43. In the next example the first note is unaccented; the bar-lines would then stand as shown.

FIG. 21.

The way was long, the wind was cold.

44. It will be seen that the accent divides the notes into equal sets. These equal groups or sets are called **Bars**[1] or **Measures.** Thus the notes between any two bar-lines form a *bar* or *measure.*

45. Every bar can be divided into a certain number of equal lengths, called **Beats.**

Thus in (*a*) there are *two* beats; in (*b*) *three* beats.

FIG. 22.

46. In dividing bars into beats the following points must be kept in mind:

(1) The beats in each bar may be subdivided into notes of smaller value, or one note may be sustained for two or more beats. This, however, does not alter the *number of the beats.*

---

[1] Notice that the word *bar* is applied both to the upright line and to the contents of the measure.

FIG. 23.

Here each beat equals *one* crotchet, but in (a) some of the beats are divided into four semiquavers; others into two quavers. In (b) some of the notes are held for two beats (*i.e.* one minim).

(2) The unit note may be of any value without altering the number of beats. In (a) fig. 24 each beat = one *crotchet*; in (b) one *quaver*; in (c) one *minim*; but in each case there are *three* beats in a bar.

FIG. 24.

(3) Rests may make up some of the beats.

FIG. 25.

(4) If the first bar is incomplete the last bar of the *section* must also be incomplete, so that the first and last incomplete bars make up a complete bar. The bars marked (a) and (b) together make a complete bar. If the first bar is complete the last bar must also be complete. In both these cases rests must be added to the last bar if necessary to make up the completeness.

FIG. 26.

47. Time is the grouping of notes into regular sets by means of accents.

Time depends upon the number of beats in a bar.

When there are **two** beats in a bar it is called **Duple** time.
When there are **three** beats in a bar it is **Triple** time.
When they are **four** beats in a bar it is **Quadruple** time.

48. Very often the term *Common Time* is applied to all music having an *even* number of beats, but as the term *common* is still more frequently applied to one special time (§ 59), it seems better to use the terms *duple*, *quadruple*, &c.

49. Time is further subdivided into **Simple** and **Compound**.
When the value of each beat is equal to a simple undotted note the time is said to be simple.

When the value of each beat is equal to a **dotted note** the time is said to be compound (v. § 247).

Fig. 27.

Both of these are *duple* time, because there are *two beats* in a bar.
In (a) each beat is equal to a *crotchet*, therefore (a) is **simple duple**.
In (b) each beat is equal to a *dotted crotchet* therefore (b) is **compound duple**.

Similarly (c) is **simple triple**; (d) is **compound triple**.

Fig. 28.

ACCENTS AND TIME

Exercise.

1. Represent *each syllable* in the following by the note ♩ ; mark the accented note ; add bar-lines, and say whether the time is *duple* or *triple*.

   (a) But amid my broken slumbers
   Still I heard the magic numbers.
   (b) In happy homes he saw the light
   Of household fires gleam warm and bright.
   (c) Under the willows the streamlet runs murmuring.
   (d) The pride of his country, the hope of his nation.
   (e) With the accents of wildest despair in her voice.

2. Rewrite (a) and (b), making the beat equal to a *crotchet*; (c) and (d), making the beat equal to a *quaver*.

3. Add a rest (or rests) to each of the following, so as to make each bar equal to four crotchets.

4. Correct, by adding rests or lengthening the notes, the bars marked *. [*Vide* § 46 (4).]

CHAPTER VI.

TIME-SIGNATURES.

50. The **time** used in a piece of music is shown by a sign called the **time-signature**, which is placed at the beginning of a piece immediately after what is called the *key-signature* (explained in Chapter X.).

51. The time-signature shows the time-value of one bar. It is most conveniently written as a *vulgar fraction*, on the understanding that **a semibreve = 1**.

Thus a *minim* is the *half* of a semibreve: therefore if each beat equals *one minim* we say that each bar contains so many *halves* of a semibreve. Two minims in a bar = $\frac{2}{2}$; three minims = $\frac{3}{2}$, &c. Similarly, as a crotchet = $\frac{1}{4}$ of a semibreve, two crotchets in a bar = $\frac{2}{4}$; three crotchets = $\frac{3}{4}$, &c.

52. When each beat = 𝅗𝅥 the lower figure is 2
 ,, ,, ,, = ♩ ,, ,, 4
 ,, ,, ,, = ♪ ,, ,, 8
 ,, ,, ,, = 𝅘𝅥𝅯 ,, ,, 16
 ,, ,, ,, = 𝅘𝅥𝅰 ,, ,, 32

These figures show what fraction of a *semibreve* each beat is (*v.* § 80).

TIME-SIGNATURES

53. To find out the upper figure of the time-signature we must distinguish carefully between *simple* and *compound* time (§ 49).

54. When the time is **simple**[1] the *upper* figure shows the number of beats in each bar; the *lower* figure shows the *value* of each beat.

Thus in *duple* time we should write $\frac{2}{2}$, $\frac{2}{4}$, or $\frac{2}{8}$ according as each beat is worth a *minim*, a *crotchet*, or a *quaver*.

Triple time would similarly be $\frac{3}{2}$, $\frac{3}{4}$, $\frac{3}{8}$, &c.

55. In **compound time** the *upper* figure does *not* show the number of beats. The lower figure shows the kind of note which equals one-*third* of the beat; the upper figure shows how many of such notes make up a bar.

Thus in *compound duple*, when the beat = ♩• or ♫♫♫, the lower figure will be 8, denoting quavers; the upper figure will be 6: *i.e.*

| ♩• ♩• | = $\frac{6}{8}$.

If each beat = ♩• we should get

| ♩• ♩• | = $\frac{6}{4}$.

56. If we wish to find out what *compound* time corresponds to a given *simple* time we proceed as follows: Suppose the given simple time is $\frac{3}{4}$; it means there are *three* beats of one crotchet each. The corresponding compound time would have *three* beats of one dotted crotchet (= three quavers) each. Therefore each bar would contain nine quavers, and the signature would be $\frac{9}{8}$. This gives us the rule: multiply the upper number by 3 and the lower by 2. $\frac{3}{4} \times \frac{3}{2} = \frac{9}{8}$.

57. When the number of notes in a bar is 6 or 12, we must notice carefully how they are accented.

FIG. 29.

---

[1] There are occasional exceptions to the rule in the case of $\frac{2}{4}$ time. Thus, in Mendelssohn's 'I waited for the Lord' there are *four* distinct beats of *one* quaver each: its signature ought to be $\frac{4}{8}$; but this signature is not often used. So we find $\frac{2}{4}$ in its place.

We may accent this passage with *three* beats in a bar, each beat = ♩ when it is clearly simple time ¾ (*a*). Or we may have two beats in a bar, each beat = ♩. when it is compound time 6/8 (*b*).

FIG. 30.

58. Besides the fractional time-signatures two other signs are used : C and ₵.

59. C means four crotchets in a bar, and therefore is just the same as 4/4. It is frequently called **common time**—a term which therefore means four crotchets in a bar (§ 48).

Formerly *triple* time was called *perfect* time, and was indicated by a circle, O. Time with an even number of beats was then called *imperfect*, and was indicated by an imperfect circle C, which has since become the letter C.

60. ₵ is called **Alla Breve**[1] time (or better, *Tempo a Cappella*, from the fact that it is much used in church [=*cappella*] music). It means two minims in a bar (2/2) with two beats in a bar.

The sign ₵ is very frequently used in the final section of a chorus which begins in C time (with *four* beats and *two* accents), and which changes to ₵ (with *two* beats and *one* accent). It generally implies an increase in the pace of the movement, and sometimes the words **Doppio movimento** (=*double the pace*) are added. This means that the section marked ₵ is to be twice as fast as that marked C : *i.e.* the *beat* remains the same, but a *minim* (= one beat) of the section marked *Doppio movimento* occupies just the same time as a *crotchet* (= one beat) in the section marked C. See Mendelssohn's "Elijah," last chorus.

---

[1] The term *alla breve* is commonly applied to 2/3 or ₵ time, but this is nevertheless quite an error. *Alla breve* really means *breve* time, *i.e.* where each bar = four minims or one breve, *i.e.* 4/2 ; sometimes the sign ₵ is used instead of the signature 4/2.

TIME-SIGNATURES

Table of Time-signatures.

	SIMPLE	COMPOUND
Duple	₵ or 2/2 ♩♩	6/4 ♩. ♩.
	2/4 ♩♩	6/8 ♪. ♪.
	2/8 ♪♪	6/16 ♫. ♫.
Quadruple	4/2 ♩♩♩♩	12/4 ♩. ♩. ♩. ♩.
	C or 4/4 ♩♩♩♩	12/8 ♪. ♪. ♪. ♪.
	See p. 19, footnote	12/16 ♫. ♫. ♫. ♫.
Triple	3/2 ♩♩♩	9/4 ♩. ♩. ♩.
	3/4 ♩♩♩	9/8 ♪. ♪. ♪.
	3/8 ♪♪♪	9/16 ♫. ♫. ♫.

Exercises.

1. Add time-signatures to the following, stating whether they are simple or compound:

2. Complete each of the following bars by adding *one* note at the end:

3. Add bars to each of the following according to the time-signature. Each begins on the first beat of a bar:

4. Bar the following notes in as many different ways as you can, adding time-signature in each case:

5. Add bar-lines and time-signatures to the following:

6. State exactly the time-signature of the following, giving your reasons:

7. Add missing bar-lines and time-signatures to the following:

CHAPTER VII.

ACCENTS. BEATING TIME. RESTS, ETC.

61. Accents. We have so far only spoken of *one* accent in a bar. When there are more than *two* beats in a bar there will be more than *one* accent. The *first* beat of a bar has the strongest accent, while a secondary accent will fall on every alternate beat.

Thus in *duple time* there is *one* accent, on the first beat; in *triple* and *quadruple* time there is a *strong* accent on the first beat, and a *secondary* accent on the third beat.

In *simple triple* time the second accent only occurs when the pace is slow.

62. When the pace is slow and each beat is subdivided it is usual to accent the first note of each beat, the first note in the bar still keeping the strongest accent.

63. Compound time is accented exactly like simple, *i.e.* on the alternate *beats*, or, if the beats are subdivided, on the first note of each beat.

ACCENTS. BEATING TIME. RESTS, ETC.

64. In Counting time we count *one* for each *beat*. If, however, the pace is slow, we may consider each beat subdivided, *e.g.* a crotchet into two quavers, a dotted crotchet into three quavers, &c.

FIG. 31.

65. In counting a half beat it is convenient to use the word "and," thus:

FIG. 32.

66. Beating time. When a number of persons are performing music together, a conductor "beats the time," *i.e.* marks the beats, or the divisions of the beats, with a *bâton*. There are many ways of doing this, the following being one of the commonest. The strong accent is shown by the thick type, the secondary accent by capitals. For *duple time*, **Down**-*up*; for *triple time*, **Down**-*left*-UP; for *quadruple time*, **Down**-*left*-RIGHT-*up*.

67. When the music is slow it is sometimes necessary to divide the beats. This is done by beating twice (or, in compound time, three times) in each direction; thus for *simple triple* time: **Down**—*down*—LEFT—*left*—UP—*up*. 6/8 time is often beaten **Down**—*left*—*left*—RIGHT—*right*—*up*.

The Use of Rests.

68. The sign for a *whole bar's* rest in any kind of time[1] is the **semibreve rest.**

---

[1] Except in 4/2 time, where the breve rest is used (*v.* p. 20 note.)

Fig. 33.

69. In expressing a rest which lasts through several bars, the *breve* rest is used to mean *two* bars' rest. This may be doubled in length (when it means *four* bars' rest) or combined with the semibreve rest. In all cases it is usual to write the number of bars over the sign. Very often, especially when the number of bars' rest is great, a long stroke is drawn, and the number of bars' rest written above it.

Fig. 34.

70. In writing rests, care should be taken to show that *each beat* is complete in itself. Thus, the following are *incorrect*:—

Fig. 35.

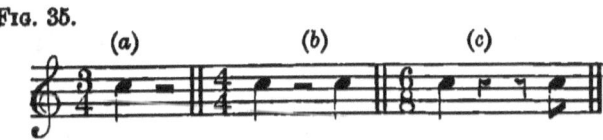

At (*a*) and (*b*) each beat equals a crotchet, and therefore a minim rest cannot be used. At (*c*) each beat is a dotted crotchet, and the first beat must be shown by adding a quaver rest, letting a crotchet rest and the quaver make up the second beat. Corrected, these examples would stand as below:—

Fig. 36.

71. In quadruple time a minim rest may be used to denote half a bar's rest, *provided it occurs at the beginning or end* of the bar, and not in the middle. Thus:—

Fig. 37.

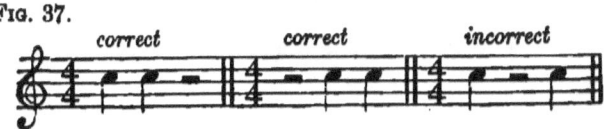

ACCENTS. BEATING TIME. RESTS, ETC.

✓ 72. In *compound time*, a sound which occupies a whole bar may be written as one note (*a*), In all other cases the notes must be grouped so as to indicate the *beats* (*b*).

Since the beat in compound time always equals a dotted note, it is clear that a *dotted rest* corresponds to a beat. Dotted rests may, therefore, be used in compound time. (*c*) (§ 36).

FIG. 38.

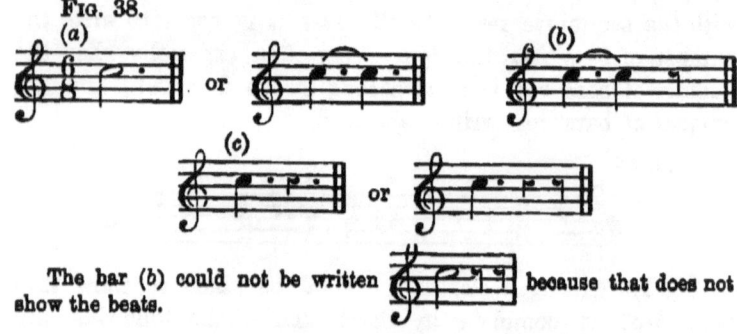

The bar (*b*) could not be written because that does not show the beats.

EXERCISES.

1. Write a bar of music in common time and one in 9/8 time, and mark the accents in each case.

2. Express by means of the breve and semibreve rests a rest for seven bars; for six bars; for ten bars. Express in any way you like a rest of thirty bars.

3. Correct the rests used in the following example, giving reasons:

4. How ought the following notes and rests to be written to be in strict accordance with a time-signature?

5. In what kind of time is the *minim* rest unavailable?

CHAPTER VIII.

TRIPLETS. SYNCOPATION.

73. Three notes played in the time of two form a **triplet**.

FIG. 39.

Here the second half of the second bar is equal to *two* crotchets. *Three* are put in place of the *two*, and the figure 3 is added to make this clear.

Rests may form part of a triplet, or two notes of the triplet may be sustained and written as one note (*v.* § 249).

FIG. 40.

When several sets of triplets follow each other, very often only the first set has the sign ⌒₃, the grouping being sufficient to indicate the meaning in the other cases.

74. Sometimes in compound time a beat (which is usually divided into *three*) is divided into *two*; thus *two* notes are played in the time of *three*. This is shown by the figure 2. The group is called a **duplet**, or, where *four* are written for *six*, a **quadruplet**.

FIG. 41.

75. A beat or part of a beat may be divided into any irregular number of notes. The number in a set is shown as in the case of the triplet. The terms **Quintuplet** (*i.e.* group of *five* notes), **Sextuplet** (*six* notes), &c., are used.

FIG. 42.
(a)   Beethoven.

At (a) the fourth beat has five semiquavers instead of four; at (b) the first beat (four quavers in a bar: v. § 54, *note*) has twelve semidemisemiquavers instead of eight; the first half of the second beat has six instead of four; the last half of the last beat has seven instead of four.

76. The use of the triplet is practically confined to simple time, where a few beats are divided into three instead of into two. But sometimes a movement in simple time has triplets throughout, so that the effect is just the same as if written in compound time. The following from Mozart is of that kind:

FIG. 43.

This might clearly be written in $\frac{9}{8}$ time, when each beat would be a dotted crotchet. The treble would stand as below:

FIG. 44.

77. Music which is written in *simple* time may also be expressed in *compound* time, and *vice versâ*.

For example, rewrite the following passage in $\frac{2}{4}$ time:

Fig. 45.

We have to produce the same effect in $\frac{2}{4}$ time. This will be done by representing a beat of $\frac{6}{8}$ time by a beat of $\frac{2}{4}$ time, and by indicating where necessary the subdivision of the beats.

In $\frac{6}{8}$ time a beat = ♩•; in $\frac{2}{4}$ time a beat = ♩ ; each *dotted crotchet* (*i.e.* $\frac{6}{8}$) will therefore be represented by a crotchet (*i.e.* $\frac{2}{4}$) In bars two and three the beats are divided into *three* parts. In $\frac{2}{4}$ time a beat is usually divided into two parts, and it can only be divided into three by writing the notes as triplets. The passage then would stand as follows:

Fig. 46.

78. Sometimes a double time-signature is used, *e.g.* $\frac{6}{8} \frac{2}{4}$ This means that some parts of the movement are in $\frac{6}{8}$ time; others in $\frac{2}{4}$ time.

79. **Syncopation.**—When a note is begun on an *unaccented* beat and continued over an *accented* beat, the accent is given to the beginning of the note. This is called **Syncopation**.

Fig. 47.

80. When a note begins in one bar and is *continued* into the next, a tied note must always be used (a). Formerly this was not the rule. Such a note used to be written *on* the bar line as at (a) below; or with a dot placed at the beginning of a bar (b).

Fig. 48.

81. When a note begins on the *half* beat (§ 62), and is continued over the next beat, there is syncopation.

Fig. 49.

82. Syncopated notes are always played with an increased emphasis, and this is very often indicated by the signs > or — or *sf*. (*Vide* § 239.)

83. An effect very similar to syncopation is produced when an unaccented beat receives a special emphasis, although the note is not prolonged.

This is usually indicated by the signs >, &c.; but sometimes, as at (*a*), the grouping of the notes by means of slurs alone shows that the accent is displaced:

Fig. 50.

84. We have seen (§ 47) that time depends on the **regular recurrence of accents**, and also that sometimes the accent is taken from its usual place and given to a beat usually unaccented.

Now if the **displaced accent** is made to recur **regularly**, the effect will sound like a change of time.

Fig. 51.

This example is in $\frac{3}{4}$ time, but in the third bar the accent is given to the second beat and then it is made to *recur on every other beat*. The part in brackets is therefore practically in $\frac{2}{4}$ time.

85. Changes of time like this are usually indicated by signs like >, &c., but very often the grouping of the notes by means of slurs is sufficient. Occasionally the same effect is produced by means of rests, as in the following example from Schumann's Pianoforte Concerto.

FIG. 52.

If the student will play this carefully he will find that the notes group themselves as regards accent in the way indicated. Each beat is clearly equal to two crotchets, and the strong accent occurs on every third beat. The time is then three beats of two crotchets (= one minim), or $\frac{3}{2}$ as shown below.

FIG. 53.

86. As a rule such changes of time occur (though this is not so in the above example) when several parts are being performed together. Then one part changes its time while the original time is kept up by the remainder. We thus get two different kinds of time played together: *e.g.*

FIG. 54.   *F. Chopin.* Op. 42.

Here the bass is clearly in $\frac{3}{4}$ time. But the upper stems of the right hand show that the melody has two *dotted crotchets* to the bar—*i.e.* the melody is in $\frac{6}{8}$ time.

TRIPLETS. SYNCOPATION. 33

87. Cases of the alternation of different kinds of time are not infrequent.

Brahms has written variations on a Hungarian song which consists of bars in $\frac{3}{4}$ and $\frac{4}{4}$ time alternately. The slow movement of Chopin's Sonata, Op. 4, is in $\frac{5}{4}$ time (*i.e.* five crotchets in a bar), with the first and third beat accented. This is equivalent to bars of $\frac{2}{4}$ and $\frac{3}{4}$ combined.

Schumann (*Carneval*) interpolates a single bar of $\frac{4}{4}$ time in a piece which is in $\frac{3}{4}$ time. Such an interpolation is usually a question of rhythm, and the subject is best studied under that head.

These various methods of changing the time in a movement prevent monotony and add to the interest.

EXERCISES.

1. Write examples of triplets in $\frac{2}{4}$ time and $\frac{3}{8}$ time.

2. Rewrite the following in $\frac{3}{4}$ time:

3. (*a*) In the following extract (from S. Heller), what other time-signature might be used, and what trifling alteration would then be necessary to make it strictly correct? (*b*) As it now stands, what is omitted which would have made the meaning clearer?

FIG. 55.

4. Rewrite the following in $\frac{6}{4}$ time:

D

5. Rewrite the following examples of syncopation (from Mozart) as they would probably be written now:

6. What effect (as regards *time*) is produced by the grouping of the notes in the following? Explain your answer fully.

7. Explain the effect (as regards time) of the following:

8. In what other time might the following be written and still produce the same effect? Would any alteration become necessary?

R. Franz. Op. 2, No. 5.

CHAPTER IX.

SEMITONES. SHARPS, FLATS, NATURALS.

88. If we examine the notes C, D, E, F on a pianoforte keyboard, we see that a *black* key comes between C and D, and also between D and E; but there is nothing between E and F.

The reason for this is that the musical distance from C to D, *or* from D to E, is twice as great as from E to F. The black key represents a note half way between C and D. The musical distance or *interval* from E to F is called a **Semitone** (*i.e. half* tone); that from C to D is called a **Tone**, and two semitones make a tone.

FIG. 55.

Further examination of the keyboard will show that a similar semitone occurs between B and C.

89. Sometimes it is necessary to raise the pitch of a note by making it a semitone higher. This is shown by writing the sign ♯ (called a **Sharp**) before the note: *e.g.*

 = C sharp.

90. Sometimes it is necessary to raise a note already sharpened. This is shown by the sign × (called a **Double Sharp**).

A *double sharp* means that a *natural* (§ 98) note has been raised *two* semitones.

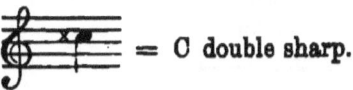 = C double sharp.

91. The sign ♭ (called a **Flat**) means that a note before which it stands is lowered a semitone in pitch.

 = D flat.

92. When it is necessary to make a note already flattened a semitone lower, the sign ♭♭ (called a **Double Flat**) is used. A *double flat* means that a *natural* note has been lowered *two* semitones.

 = D double flat.

93. When a note which has been made *sharp* or *flat* returns to its original pitch, it is indicated by the sign ♮ (called a **Natural**).

94. When a *double sharp* note is to be lowered a semitone (*i.e.* made only a single sharp), it is indicated by ♮ ♯ (sometimes by ♯ alone).

95. When a *double flat* note is to be raised a semitone (*i.e.* made a single flat), it is indicated by ♮ ♭ (sometimes by ♭ alone).

96. When any of these signs (♯, ♭, ×, ♭♭, ♮) are used, they apply to the same note *throughout the bar*, unless they are contradicted.

Fig. 56.

At (*a*) each C in the bar is meant to be *sharp*, though only the first is marked. If we wish the other C's to be natural the sign ♮ must be used, as at (*b*).

97. If the last note of a bar is raised or lowered, and the first note of the next bar is the same note, the sign ♯, ♭, &c., may be omitted, though it is better to use the sign in the fresh bar.

SEMITONES. SHARPS, FLATS, NATURALS

EXERCISES.

1. Rewrite the following notes, (*a*) making each note one semitone *lower*; (*b*) making each note one semitone *higher*, *using the same lines and spaces*:

2. Rewrite the following, making the notes in (*a*) one semitone lower; the notes in (*b*) one semitone higher, using the same lines and spaces:

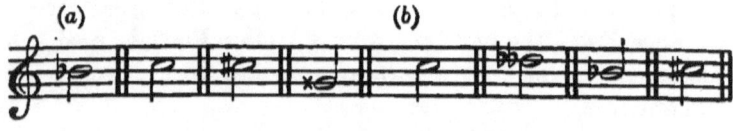

CHAPTER X.

MAJOR SCALES.

98. We have seen that in the series of notes C, D, E, F, G, A, B, C, semitones occur, between E and F *and* B and C.

This is seen clearly when we exhibit the series in the form of a ladder:

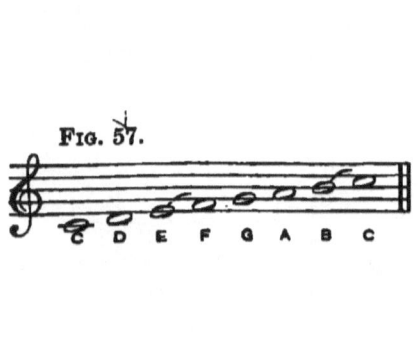

FIG. 57.

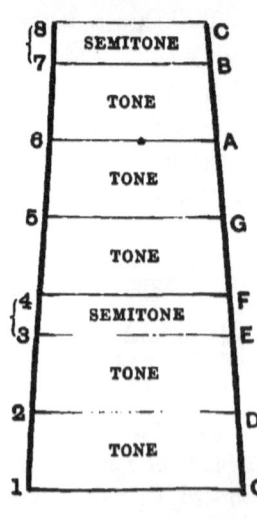

We have here a series of *eight* notes following each other in alphabetical order; there are *five* tones and *two* semitones: the semitones occur between the 3rd and 4th *and* the 7th and 8th degrees.[1]

99. This series of notes is called the **Major Scale of C**, and the note it starts from (*i.e.* C) is called the **Keynote** or **Tonic** of the scale.

We can now give some definitions.

100 (1). A **Scale** (Lat. *scala*, ladder) is a series of notes arranged in alphabetical order.

101 (2). A scale which is made up chiefly of **tones** is called a **Diatonic Scale**.

The term diatonic means *through the tones*. The scale shown above has five tones and two semitones.

The term *diatonic* is used to distinguish this scale from one (to be presently described) called a *chromatic* scale, which is made up entirely of *semitones*. There are two kinds of *diatonic* scales, *major* and *minor*. (§ 120.)

102 (3). A **major scale** is a *diatonic scale* proceeding by five tones and two semitones, having the semitones between the 3rd and 4th and the 7th and 8th degrees.

103. We might have a succession of eight notes in alphabetical order beginning with some other note than C; *e.g.*

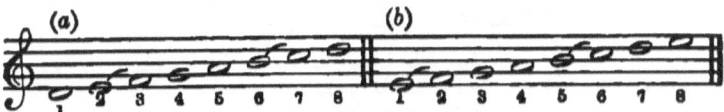

(*a*) is a scale beginning on D, and (*b*) is one beginning on E. They are both *diatonic* scales, but they are neither of them major scales, because their semitones do not occur between the 3rd and 4th *and* 7th and 8th degrees. We can make them into *major scales* by altering the pitch of some of the notes so as to make the semitones fall in the right places. We shall best understand this, however, by looking at the scale of C again.

104. Any major scale can be divided into two exactly equal halves.

---

[1] Each step or note of the scale is called a *Degree*.

MAJOR SCALES

Thus C—F consists of *four* notes with the intervals *tone, tone, semitone*; G—C consists of *four* notes with the intervals *tone, tone, semitone*. Each of these halves is called a **Tetrachord**.[1]

105. If we begin with the upper tetrachord of the scale of C and continue it to the G above, we get a scale beginning on G. But while the semitone of the lower tetrachord is in its right place (between 3rd and 4th), that of the upper tetrachord is between the 6th and 7th. To make this semitone fall between the 7th and 8th (as in the scale of C), we must raise the 7th note a semitone by sharpening it.

Thus by sharpening every F we get a major scale on G exactly resembling the major scale on C.

Fig. 58.

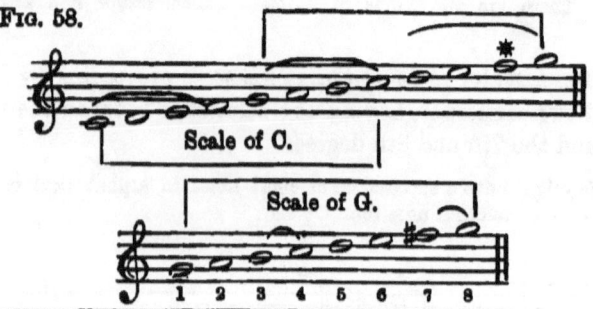

[1] A **tetrachord** (*tetra*, four, *chorde*, string), is a series of *four* notes in alphabetical order, and comprising two tones and one semitone. The semitone does not always occur as in the tetrachord shown above. Thus

is a tetrachord having the order *tone, semitone, tone*.

When two tetrachords overlap, *i.e.* the last note of one is the first note of the other, they are called **Conjunct** tetrachords.

When the two tetrachords are distinct from each other, *i.e.* where there is a tone between the last note of one and the first of the other, they are **Disjunct** tetrachords.

106. By taking the upper tetrachord of G, and continuing it, we get the scale of D. And here again the 7th note (C) would have to be sharpened. Continuing this process, we should get a series of major scales, each new scale beginning on the *fifth* note *upwards* of the previous scale; the *seventh* note of the new scale being sharpened.

FIG. 59.

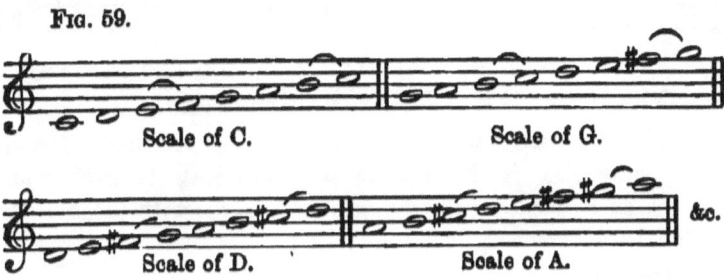

107. The sharps thus used in scales are not written every time each note occurs, but are placed *once for all* at the beginning of every stave. These together are called the **Key Signature**, and it is understood that every note in a piece of music is to be played according to the signature, unless altered in the course of the movement.

108. Each fresh sharp added is a **perfect fifth**[1] (§ 186) higher (or a *perfect fourth lower*, § 185) than the preceding one. Thus: F♯, C♯, G♯, D♯, A♯, E♯, B♯.

These are written in the signature in a definite order, in such a way as to get them symmetrically on the stave. Each fresh sharp is added to the *right* of those previously standing. Starting with F♯, the other sharps are either a fourth below or a fifth above, no leger lines being used.

109. The scales are named after their keynote or according to the number of sharps or flats in the signature. Thus we speak of G or one sharp, &c. The scale of C is often called the *Natural Scale*, because no notes of it are sharp or flat.

---

[1] The musical distance from one note to another is called an *interval*. Intervals are named according to the *number* of notes included: *e.g.* C-G is called a **fifth**. When a fifth consists of *three* tones and *one* semitone it is called a **perfect fifth** (*v.* Chap. XVI.)

MAJOR SCALES

110. Table of key-signatures of keys with sharps.

Fig. 60.

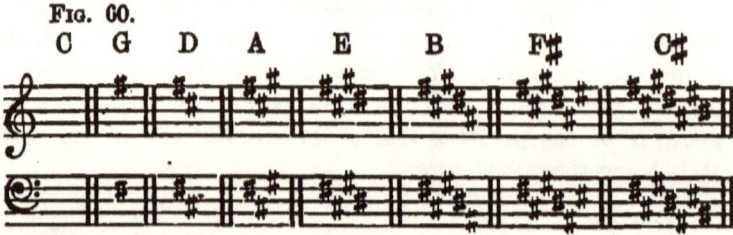

111. In major keys with *sharps* the **keynote** is always a semitone above the last sharp of the signature.

112. By taking the *lower* tetrachord of the natural scale and continuing it downwards, we get a scale beginning and ending on F, but to make the semitones agree with those of the natural scale we must make the B flat.

Fig. 61.

113. Continuing the process, we get a series of *major scales* with flats.

Each new flat scale begins a *perfect fifth below* the old one, and each new flat scale has its fourth note flattened. Thus:

Fig. 62.

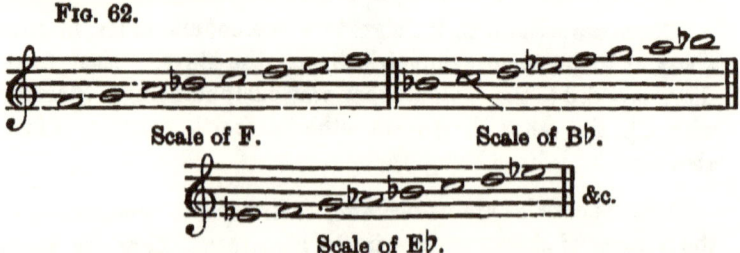

114. The flats used follow each other a **fifth** below (or a *fourth above*), *i.e.* B♭, E♭, A♭, D♭, G♭, C♭, F♭.

As in the case of scales with sharps, the flats of a scale are written as a key-signature at the beginning of each stave, each new flat being placed out to the right, alternately a fourth above and fifth below.

115. Key signatures of keys with flats.

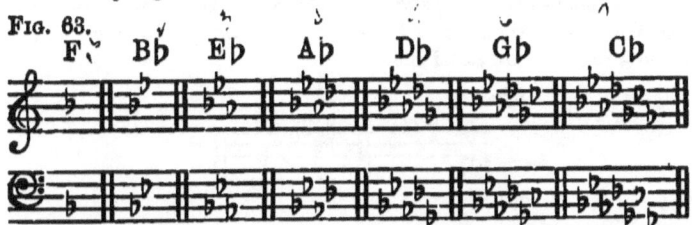

116. In major keys with flats the last added *flat* is always the *fourth* note of the scale, and therefore the **keynote is three notes below the last added flat.**

117. Summary.—The following **major scales** are used in music:

(1) The **natural scale** of C, without sharps or flats.

(2) *Seven* scales with **sharps** in the signature. The **sharp** keys follow each other in the order of the number of sharps required, each new scale beginning **a perfect fifth above** the last one.

Thus (starting from C) G, D, A, E, B, F♯, and C♯, are the keynotes.

(3) *Seven* scales with **flats** in the signature. The **flat** keys follow each other in the order of the number of flats required, each new scale beginning **a perfect fifth below** the last one.

Thus (starting from C) F, B♭, E♭, A♭, D♭, G♭, C♭ are the keynotes.

118. We have used the terms *Key* and *Scale*. It is necessary to distinguish between them.

A **scale** means notes arranged *in alphabetical order*.

A **key** means all the notes of a scale, but *not taken in alphabetical order*.

Thus the following consists of notes from the scale of F. It is in the *key* of F; but it is not the *scale* of F.

FIG. 64.

Note on Key-signature.—When in the course of a piece the key changes, it is usual to correct the sharps or flats of the first key by *naturals* before writing the proper signature. Thus, a piece beginning in A major and modulating to E♭ would stand thus:—

FIG. 65.

EXERCISES.

1. Write out the major scales beginning on E, on B, on F♯, adding the sharps as required. Mark the position of the semitones (by the sign ⁀).

2. Write out the major scale having *four* flats for signature, (*a*) making each note flat as required; (*b*) with a key-signature.

3. Write the signatures (on the bass stave) for the following keys: F, E, E♭, D♭, B.

4. Add sharps or flats to the following to make the scales of (*a*) D; (*b*) A♭; (*c*) E.

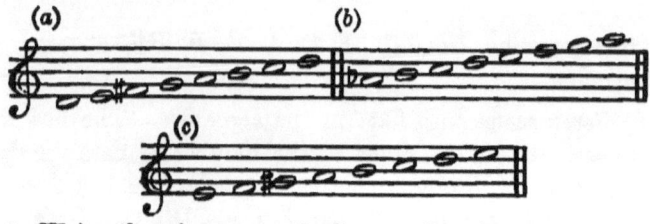

5. Write the signatures (in bass and treble staves) for the major scales of B♭, A♭, D, D♭, A.

6. Rewrite the following signatures, placing the sharps and flats in the usual order. Write underneath each the keynote of the scale represented.

7. Add any sharps or flats that may be necessary to make the following melody in the key of E♭. Add the signature.

44   ELEMENTS OF MUSIC

8. Write below each of the following the name of the major key it indicates.

CHAPTER XI.

THE MINOR SCALE.

119. There is another diatonic scale, which differs from the major. The pattern scale is that beginning on A, using only natural notes.

FIG. 66.

120. This is one form of the scale of **A minor**; it is a diatonic scale, having its semitones between the 2nd and 3rd, 5th and 6th.

121. The chief difference between a *major* and a *minor* scale lies in the first three notes. In a major scale (*e.g.* C), the distance from the *first* note to the *third* (C—E), is *four* semitones, or a major third; in the case of a *minor* scale (*e.g.* A—C), it is *three* semitones, or a minor third. This is the reason for the names *major* (= greater), and *minor* (= less).

122. In the above scale the 7th note is a tone below the 8th. This has an unsatisfactory effect, and the 7th note of a minor scale, like that in fig. 66, is raised a *semitone* in order to make it only a semitone below the octave.

FIG. 67.

This produces an interval (F—G♯) larger than a tone, called an *augmented* second (§ 197). As that interval used to be considered difficult to sing, the 6th note of the minor scale was also *raised* a semitone in *ascending*. In *descending* there is no objection to the 7th being a tone below the 8th, so both the 6th and 7th notes have their pitch as in fig. 66.

Fig. 68.

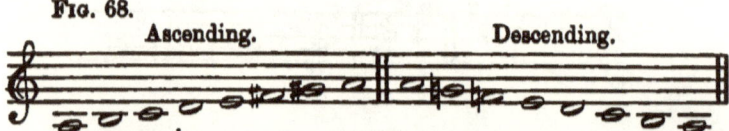

123. This form is called the **Altered Diatonic** minor scale. As it is chiefly used in melodic progressions, it is sometimes called the **Melodic** minor scale. Note that the *ascending* form differs from the *descending*.

124. The form of the minor scale most used in modern music is that which has only the *seventh raised*. As this form is convenient for purposes of harmony (*i.e.* the harmonies of the minor scale are built up from the notes of this form), it is often called the **Harmonic** minor scale. It is also called the **Chromatic** minor scale, because it contains an interval between the 6th and 7th notes called a *chromatic interval* (*v.* § 181). This form of the scale is the same ascending as descending.

125. There are then *three* forms of every minor scale.

I. **Diatonic** minor scale.

Fig. 69.

II. **Altered**[1] diatonic minor scale.

III. **Harmonic** or **Chromatic** minor scale.

[1] The altered diatonic minor scale is also found with the raised 6th and 7th in descending, especially in Bach and Handel.

46   ELEMENTS OF MUSIC

I. The diatonic *natural* minor is the same *ascending* and *descending*.

II. The altered *melodic* diatonic has the sixth and seventh notes raised a semitone in *ascending*; in *descending* the sixth and seventh notes are restored to the same pitch as in the diatonic minor.

III. The harmonic form has only the seventh note raised both ascending and descending, and it contains a *chromatic* interval between the 6th and 7th degrees.

126. If we compare the *major* scale of C and the *minor* scale of A in its original diatonic form, we shall see that they are both made up of exactly the same notes, the only difference being that they each have a different starting-point.[1]

127. Two scales which contain all (or nearly all) the same notes are said to be **related**.[2]

The scale of **A minor** is called the **Relative minor** of *C major*.

The scale of **C major** is called the **Relative major** of *A minor*.

128. In the same way every *major* scale has a **relative minor**, which begins a **minor third** (*i.e.* three semitones) **below** the major.

The relative minor of A major begins on F♯; the relative minor of E♭ major begins on C, &c.

129. Every *minor* scale has a **relative major**, which begins a **minor third above** the minor.

The relative major of F minor begins on A♭; the relative major of C♯ minor begins on E.

---

[1] Major and minor scales are sometimes spoken of as diatonic scales *major mode* and diatonic scales *minor mode*. The word *mode* means *manner*. Both scales, major and minor, use the same notes, but each in different *manner* or *mode*.

[2] Another way of expressing this is, by reference to tetrachords: *Two scales which have a tetrachord in common are said to be related*. Thus (fig. 58) the upper tetrachord of C is the lower tetrachord of G. The scales of C and G have a tetrachord in common: they are therefore related.

THE MINOR SCALE

FIG. 70.

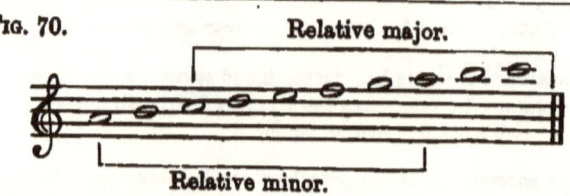

Relative major.

Relative minor.

130. The alterations (§ 122) in the minor scale are not shown in the key-signature, but are indicated by the signs ♯, ♭, &c., each time they occur in the course of the music.

131. The signs ♯, ♭, ♮, &c., used, not in a signature, but in the course of a composition, are called *Accidentals*.

132. The key-signature of relative *major* and *minor* scales, therefore, is the same.

133. Table of major and minor keys, with key-signatures.

134. Every *signature*, therefore, stands for two keys. We have already shown (§§ 111, 116) how to find the *major* key from the signature and, knowing the major, § 128 tells us how to find the minor.

135. In writing out minor scales care must be taken to use the proper sign for raising and lowering the sixth and seventh notes. If, according to the signature, these are *flat*, a *natural* will raise them, as in C minor below. If they are *sharp*, a *double sharp* will be necessary. (§ 90.)

C Minor.

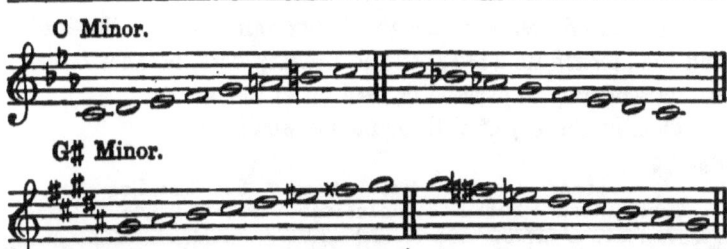

G♯ Minor.

136. A *major* and a *minor* scale beginning on the *same* note are called respectively **Tonic Major** and **Tonic Minor**: *e.g.* C major and C minor.

137. To change any tonic major scale into the tonic minor it is necessary to lower the 3rd and 6th notes a semitone. This will give us the harmonic form of the minor scale, from which either the melodic or diatonic forms can be got by §§ 120–5.

Fig. 71.

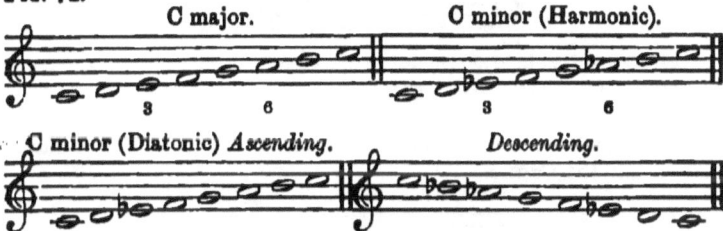

188. The degrees of every diatonic scale receive certain names.

The **first** note is called the **Tonic**. The **fifth** note, from its importance in harmony, is called the **Dominant** (or *ruling*-note). The third note, being *midway* between *tonic* and *dominant*, is called the **Mediant**.

Reckoning from the tonic a fifth *downwards*, we get to the octave of the *fourth* note of the scale, and as the fifth *upward* is called the *dominant*, the *fourth note* is called the **Subdominant** (or *lower* dominant). The *sixth* note is midway between *sub-dominant* and *tonic* (or octave of tonic), and it is called the **Sub-mediant**.

THE MINOR SCALE

The *second* note is called the **Supertonic** (*i.e. over* the tonic), and the *seventh* note is called the **Leading-note**, because it has a strong tendency to proceed or lead up to the octave.

Thus in the key of C these names would be:

FIG. 72.

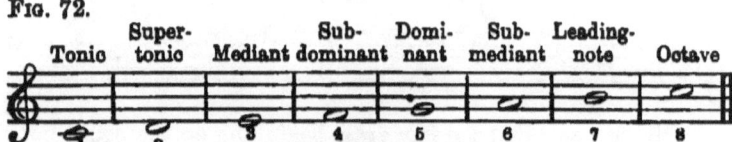

NOTE TO CHAPTER XI.
French and German Names of Notes, &c.

139. In French the notes C, D, E, F, G, A, B are called respectively ut, re, mi, fa, sol, la, si. The sign ♯ is called *dièse*; the sign ♭, *bémol*; *majeur* and *mineur* respectively mean *major* and *minor*.

140. In German the letter names are used as in English, but B always means B♭; the name for B natural is H.

Bach wrote a series of fugues on the name B A C H.

141. When a note is sharpened or flattened its German name is obtained by adding -is (= *sharp*), -es (= *flat*) to the letter name: *e.g. Dis* = D sharp, *Des* = D flat.

Schumann has a melody founded on the name A S (= *es*) C H (*v. Harlequin*, &c., in the *Carneval.*

142. The terms for *major* and *minor* are respectively *dur* and *moll*.

143. Examples of names of keys in English, French, and German:—

English.	French.	German.
F minor	Fa mineur	F moll.
C♯ major	Ut dièse majeur	Cis dur.
E♭ major	Mi bémol majeur	Es dur.

EXERCISES.

1. Write out, in the three forms, the minor scales beginning on F, D, and E.

2. What form of the minor scale is the following? Why is it so called? What interval characterises it?

50 ELEMENTS OF MUSIC

3. What alteration is necessary to make the following scales into harmonic minor scales? How would the alteration be made?

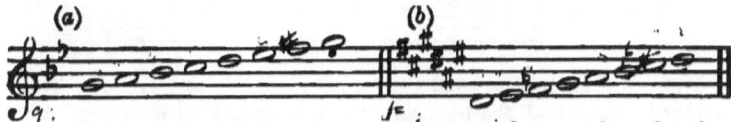

4. What are *related* scales? Give several examples of pairs of related scales.

5. What are the *relative minors* of E, G, F, and D major? What are the relative majors of F♯, C♯, G, and A♭, minor?

6. Add accidentals which will make the following major scales into *tonic minor scales*, Harmonic form.

7. Write *above* the following the name of the major scale to which they belong, and *below* the name of the minor.

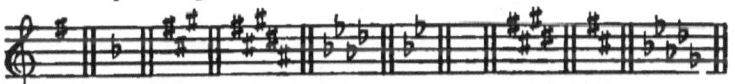

8. What note is the dominant in each of the following scales: E maj.; B min.; B♭ maj.; F maj.; F minor? What is the leading-note in B♭, C, F, F♯, B, D, and A major?

9. What is the mediant, and what is the submediant in F, G, B♭, C♯, A♭, E.

CHAPTER XII.

KEYS.

144. A piece of music rarely remains very long in the same key. The signature, however, is not changed every time a change of key occurs, but notes which differ from the signature have accidentals.

KEYS

145. To recognise what key any part of a composition or any melody is in it will be necessary to examine the accidentals used, keeping in mind the sharps and flats which characterise each key (§ 117). This will best be seen from examples.

146. I.

FIG. 73.

The first sharp present is D ♯—the *fourth* added sharp (§ 117). This in itself indicates four sharps, unless there is something to contradict it. The order of the sharps in the major keys is F ♯, C ♯, G ♯, D ♯. All these are present in the above melody except G ♯, and as G does not occur at all in this melody there is no reason for assuming that it would not be G ♯ if it did occur. We may therefore conclude that the key is E major (four sharps).

147. II.

The first accidental is F ♯, which would suggest a key with sharps, but we soon find flats, which suggest a key with flats.

It must be here remembered that the leading note (7th) of a *minor* key with flats often has the sign ♯. The F ♯ is then probably the raised seventh, in which case the tonic is G, and when we remember that G minor has two flats, B♭ and E♭, we shall soon see that the key here is G minor (two flats).

148. It will help the student if he remembers that practically all melodies *end* either on the *tonic*, on the *mediant*, or (rarely) on the *dominant*.

EXERCISES.

1. Say what key each of the following melodies is in; rewrite it with a key-signature.

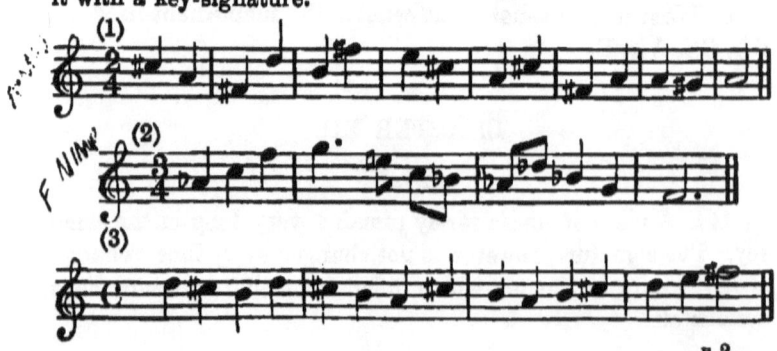

2. In the following cases say what is the key, taking into consideration the signatures and accidentals; rewrite with proper signature.

CHAPTER XIII.

ACOUSTICS.

149. The science which investigates the laws of sound is called acoustics, from a Greek word *akouo*=I hear.

150. All sounds are the result of vibrations. When the vibrations are regular, the sound is musical; when the vibrations are irregular, the sound ceases to be musical and becomes mere noise.

151. The pitch of a sound depends on the number of vibrations in a given time. The greater the number of vibrations the higher the pitch.

Thus, middle C is produced by 256 vibrations in a second; the D above by 288 vibrations, &c. On this principle, if we *double* the number of vibrations we must get a note twice as high. Therefore, the octave of a note is produced by exactly *twice* as many vibrations as the note itself: *e.g.* the C above the middle C would have 512 vibrations; that below the middle C, 128, &c. The lowest sound used in music is that produced by

---

* Whatever the signature may be, the sign ♯ or ♭ now always means a note altered from its *natural* state, not from its condition according to the signature. Here G♯ means a semitone higher than G♮. On the contrary, a natural (♮) always means that a note is changed from its condition according to the signature or to some previous accidental.

16 vibrations per second. This note is the C *four* octaves below middle C, produced by an open organ pipe 32 feet long.[1]

The highest sounds used in music have between 4,000 and 5,000 vibrations; such are those produced by the highest notes of a piano, piccolo, &c.

The standard of 256 vibrations for middle C is called the philosophical standard, but it is not the one in general use. Indeed, owing to a variety of circumstances, the standard pitch has gradually been raised since Handel's time. English concert-pitch is now about 264 vibrations for middle C. French standard (normal) pitch is in general use on the Continent; it has about 435 vibrations for the A above middle C. This gives middle C 261.

152. The *relative* pitch of sounds is expressed by the ratio of their vibration numbers: *i.e.* by placing their vibration numbers as a vulgar fraction.

Thus C = 256; D = 288; the relation of D to C is $\frac{288}{256}$, or reducing to lowest terms $\frac{9}{8}$.

153. The **intensity** or *loudness* of a sound depends on the *amplitude* (*i.e.* size) of the vibrations.

This may be proved by plucking a violin string: the further we pull it aside the wider the vibrations and the louder the sound.

154. Vibrating bodies possess, in a greater or less degree, the following natural property, best explained by a vibrating string:

If a stretched string, fastened at both ends, is made to vibrate, not only does the string vibrate as a whole, but also in *halves, thirds, quarters, fifths,* &c., at the same time.

The vibrations of the different parts of the string each produce their own notes at the same time, so that the total sound heard is a *compound sound* made up of a series of sounds produced by the whole string and its different parts. The shorter the same string is made, the higher the note produced: therefore the notes produced by the subdivisions of the string are higher than the note of the whole string.

The sound produced by the whole string is called the **Fundamental** or **Generator**; the upper notes are called **Harmonics** or **Overtones**.

These harmonics exist practically in all sounds, even when they cannot be detected by the unaided ear; and if a low note on the piano be struck, by carefully listening we shall be able to detect some of the overtones.

155. The whole of the notes produced by a fundamental note —*i.e.* the fundamental note and its overtones—are called the **Harmonic Series**.

---

[1] This is only found in the largest organs, the lowest note of most organs being the C, *three* octaves below middle C, produced by 32 vibrations. The lowest note (A) in the modern piano has 27 vibrations.

Thus for the note 🎼 the first twelve overtones would be as shown below. The fraction below each note shows the *part* of the string producing that particular note.

Generator

The note marked * is a little flatter than B♭; that marked + is definitely sharper than F♯.

The notes here exhibited are heard together, and the total result is the compound tone spoken of in § 154. As might be expected, the overtones are much fainter than the generator; indeed, they cannot often be heard by the unaided ear, although it is easy to prove their existence even in that case. The effect of the overtones, therefore, is, not to hide the generating tone, but merely to modify it in *quality*. Those sounds are richest in quality which have most overtones in addition to the generator.

156. We are now able to explain the cause of the differences of quality in musical sounds. We have said that all vibrating bodies produce overtones, but some bodies naturally produce more than others. The quality or **timbre** of a musical sound depends mainly on the number and force of the overtones included in the sound.

157. **Resonance.** When any sound is produced, the vibrations producing that sound have the power to set other bodies in vibration, provided those bodies produce the same note (or one of its harmonics) as the original sound. This is called **Resonance**.

If, after gently raising the dampers of a piano, I sing the note C, the vibrations produced by my singing set in motion the strings of the piano which produce C or its harmonics, and I hear distinctly the note I sang, reproduced on the piano. If, again, with raised dampers, I cough or shout near a piano, I am able to set up vibration in a great number of strings, which produce a confused noise. This will make it clear why the so-called loud pedal in a piano is, besides being a sustaining pedal, really a *loud* pedal; for if a chord is struck while the dampers are up, all similar notes in the piano are set in vibration and the chord is reinforced and made louder.

158. We can now fully explain the quality of musical sounds. If we make a stretched string vibrate, the quality of the sound

ACOUSTICS   55

will depend on its overtones, which again depend on the quality of the string. If now we place this string on a violin and make it vibrate, the vibration of the string will by resonance cause the air in the instrument to vibrate, and also the wood of the instrument. Therefore the quality of the *sound* will depend on the quality of the string, the quality of the wood, and the perfection of the shape and make of the instrument.

CHAPTER XIV.

DIATONIC AND CHROMATIC SEMITONES.

159. We have already seen that the intervals B-C and C-C♯ are each called a semitone, but *theoretically* the two examples are not exactly equal. This requires explanation.

160. A semitone occurring between two notes with different letter-names is called a **Diatonic Semitone** [fig. 74 (*a*)].

Such semitones are *diatonic*, because they can occur in diatonic scales.

161. A semitone occurring between any note and the same note raised or lowered by an accidental is called a **Chromatic Semitone** [fig. 74 (*b*)].

Chromatic semitones can only occur in a chromatic scale (§ 174).

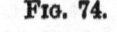
Fig. 74.

(*a*) Diatonic semitones.   (*b*) Chromatic semitones.

162. We might express the difference by means of the *ratio of vibration* (§ 152). The *ratio* for a *diatonic semitone* is $\frac{16}{15}$; the ratio for a *chromatic semitone* is $\frac{25}{24}$. As a *diatonic* semitone is greater than a *chromatic* semitone, the *diatonic* is sometimes called a **major semitone** and the *chromatic* a **minor semitone**.

163. We see then that the semitones C to C♯ and D to D♭ are both chromatic. If we raise C to C♯, and lower D to D♭, according to the ratio for chromatic semitones, the two notes C♯ and D♭ are *not alike*. In other words, **theoretically** there are *two* intermediate notes between C and D, *i.e.* C♯ and D♭.

164. Formerly organs were occasionally made which had different keys for C♯ and D♭. But as to be perfectly accurate it would be necessary to have similar pairs of keys for G♯ and A♭, &c., it is easy to see that such a plan would make instruments like the organ or piano extremely complicated. It is therefore necessary to set aside *theoretical* semitones in tuning pianos and organs, and this is done as follows:—

165. The octave is divided into **Twelve equal semitones**, so that in *practice* C to C♯, D to D♭, E to F, B to C are all equal.

As the semitone thus obtained is smaller than a diatonic and larger than a chromatic, *i.e.* it lies between them, it is called a **mean semitone**.

A violinist produces semitones by moving his fingers up or down the string, and as he is able to move them at will he is able to make the difference between chromatic and diatonic semitones. So also is a good singer. But in all cases where the note is played by a fixed key, as in the piano, &c., the mean semitone is used.

166. Since on instruments of the piano kind there is no difference between C♯ and D♭ &c., it makes no difference in effect whether C♯ or D♭ is written, the same key of the instrument being used in both cases.

167. When two notes with different names have the same sound, *i.e.* are played by the same key on a keyed instrument, they are said to be enharmonic[1] to each other.

Thus C♯ and D♭ are **enharmonics**; so also G♯ and A♭.

If C♯ occurred in a piece of music, and the next note was D♭, *i.e.* D♭ written instead of C♯ a second time, it would be called an **enharmonic change**.

168. By means of enharmonic change every note on the piano (except G♯=A♭) can be written in three ways. Thus C may be also called B♯ or D♭♭, each of the three notes being played by the same *key* on a piano.

Fig. 75.

169. Enharmonics are useful as offering a convenient means of simplifying *written* music for *keyed* instruments.

170. If we compare the keys of seven flats (C♭) and five sharps (B) we find the notes played on a piano identical. As it

---

[1] There is another use of the word. A scale which provided for the two notes C♯ and D♭, &c., would be called an *enharmonic scale*.

is easier to play with fewer altered notes we often find where a piece has *modulated* (*i.e.* changed its key) into the key of C♭ the notes are written as if in B (*i.e.* five sharps). Similarly, seven sharps (C♯) and five flats (D♭) use just the same keys on a piano, and the key of D♭ is often used instead of C♯.

The first movement of Beethoven's "Moonlight Sonata" is in C♯ minor (signature four sharps). The second movement is in the *tonic major* (§ 136), *i.e.* C♯ major (seven sharps), but it is written enharmonically in *five flats* (D♭).

171. When a change of this kind only lasts for a few bars the signature is not altered, but the enharmonic change is indicated by accidentals. Sometimes an enharmonic change is made for convenience of modulation. Thus the following example (Mozart's "Fantasia e Sonata" in G minor) modulates at ✱ into C♭ (seven flats), but as it changes into G major in a few bars, it is simpler to approach this by writing in B major (five sharps) instead of seven flats.

Fig. 76.

If this were written without enharmonic change it would stand thus:

Fig. 77.

172. If we continued the series of scales described in § 117 we should get scales having more than seven sharps or flats in their signature.

For example: a major scale beginning on G♯ (the next fifth above C♯) would be the same as that on G with every note made a semitone higher. That is, every note would be sharp, and as F was already sharp (in the key of G), it would now be double sharp. The signature for G♯ would then be eight sharps, thus

173. Keys requiring more than seven sharps or flats are never indicated by signature, but not infrequently music modulates into such keys. If the change into the key with more than seven flats or sharps only lasts a few bars, accidentals are used; if a longer section occurs the key is enharmonically changed. Two examples from Schubert will make this clear.

No. 1 is from the Trio in Op. 78. The movement begins in five sharps, as shown in the signature, but presently it modulates into G♯ major (eight sharps). As this only lasts for two or three bars, accidentals are used.

FIG. 78.

That this is in G♯ major is seen from the fact that all the notes used are made sharp, and the leading note is F×.

No. 2, 'Moments Musicaux,' No. 6, in four flats modulates at the end of the second section to eight flats (F♭ major). The third section is written enharmonically in E major (four sharps).

FIG. 79.
End of Section 2.   Beginning of Section 3.

DIATONIC AND CHROMATIC SEMITONES

Exercises.

1. What is the difference between a diatonic and a chromatic semitone? Give examples in musical notation.

2. What other names can the following keys on the piano bear? C♯, F, B♭, G♯.

3. By what notes on a piano are the following played? B♯, F♭, G×, G♭♭, C♭, B♭♭.

4. What does the term enharmonic mean? Give examples. Of what use are enharmonics?

5. What would be the key-note of a scale having nine flats? Write its signature. How could it be represented enharmonically?

CHAPTER XV.

THE CHROMATIC SCALE.

174. A Chromatic¹ Scale consists entirely of semitones.

As pointed out in § 165, the chromatic scale consists of *twelve* equal semitones, and, counting the upper octave as well, there are thirteen notes.

There are two ways of writing the chromatic scale.

175. I. The Harmonic Chromatic Scale is the same ascending and descending. The notes between the tones of the ordinary scale are obtained by *lowering* the upper one (*e.g.* between C and D is called D♭), except that between the fourth and fifth, which is always written as the **sharpened fourth**.

Harmonic Chromatic Scale of C (ascending or descending).

Fig. 80.

This form of the chromatic scale is called "*Harmonic*" because, as will be seen later, it is the most convenient for purposes of *harmony*. If the *harmonic series* described in § 155 were continued far enough we should find that it contained all the notes used in the above scale.

---

[1] The word *chromatic* is derived from the Greek *chroma* = colour.

176. II. In the **arbitrary chromatic scale** the semitones are written as follows: The *fourth* is **always raised**; the *seventh* is always *lowered*. The other semitones are raised in *ascending*, lowered in *descending*.

Arbitrary Chromatic Scale.

Fig. 81.

The reasons in favour of this scale are that, though it is not *theoretically correct*, it is easier to read and requires fewer accidentals than the harmonic form.

The note marked (*a*) is sometimes written A♯ in ascending. Great composers like Mozart and Beethoven have used both forms. Sometimes they begin a chromatic scale in the harmonic form and then continue it (in a second octave) in the arbitrary form. Their principle apparently was to use whatever form best suited their immediate purpose.

177. NOTE.—Great care must be exercised in selecting the proper accidentals for *lowering* and *raising* the notes of the chromatic scale. Thus in the harmonic form of A♭ the second note must be B♭ lowered a semitone, *i.e.* B♭♭. Thus:

Fig. 82.

Note on writing the Chromatic Scale.

Suppose we have to write the chromatic scale of D. First write the major scale of D, leaving a space between the *tones* of the scale and marking the semitones[1] by slurs thus:

---

[1] It is obvious that *no notes can be added between the notes forming semitones*.

THE CHROMATIC SCALE

Next insert the intermediate notes according to §§ 175-6. Thus if we are writing the *harmonic* (§ 175) *chromatic*, (1) the *fourth* note must be *raised*; in all the other cases the upper note of each pair must be lowered thus:

(2) between D and E is E♭
(3) „ E and F♯ is F♮
(4) „ A and B is B♭
(5) „ B and C♯ is C♮

When the chromatic scale is written, count the notes. There should be eight in the major scale with five added notes, *i.e.* thirteen in all.

Exercises.

1. Write the chromatic scales (harmonic form) in the following keys: D, B, A; C♯; F, B♭, D♭.

2. What are the reasons in favour of the arbitrary chromatic scale as against the harmonic? Write out in both forms any chromatic scale which you think specially illustrates the point.

CHAPTER XVI.

INTERVALS.

178. An **Interval** is the difference in pitch between any two notes. Intervals are named according to the number of degrees of the staff included.

Thus C to D is called a *second*; C to E a *third*, &c., as seen from the following table:

Fig. 83.

Intervals are always counted *upwards* unless the contrary is expressly stated.

179. Intervals up to and including the 8th are called *Simple Intervals*. Beyond the 8th they are called *Compound Intervals*, being merely an octave added to a simple interval, *e.g.* a 10th is an octave added to a third.

 = tenth.

With the exception of the 9th, 11th, and 13th, compound intervals are not used in harmony, and the simple name is usually applied however many octaves may be added to a simple interval: *e.g.* each of the following would be called a 3rd in harmony:—

FIG. 84.

180. The **name** of the interval depends entirely on the **number of degrees included**. C to D and C to D♭ are both seconds. It is clear then that different *kinds* of intervals must be distinguished.

181. Intervals which occur between any two notes of an *unaltered* diatonic scale are called **diatonic intervals**.

Intervals which can only occur in a chromatic scale are called **chromatic intervals**.

E.g. the interval E to G is *diatonic*, because it can occur in the scales of C, D, &c.

The interval C♯ to B♭ is *chromatic*, because it cannot occur in any unaltered *diatonic* scale. It occurs in D minor, but only when the diatonic form of D minor has been altered by the raising of the 7th to C♯ (§ 124).

DIATONIC INTERVALS.

182. If we examine all the intervals of the second in the scale of C major we find that some contain *two* semitones (*e.g.* C to D; G to A &c.); others contain only *one* semitone, *e.g.* B to C; E to F. Those containing two semitones are called **major seconds**; those with *one* are **minor seconds**.

183. In the same way there are *major* and *minor* **thirds**; **major thirds** (*e.g.* C to E; F to A) have four semitones; **minor thirds** (*e.g.* D to F; E to G) have three semitones.

183 (a). Similarly, **sixths** may be *major* or *minor*; **major sixths** (*e.g.* C to A) have nine semitones; **minor sixths** (*e.g.* E to C) have eight semitones.

184. Again, **sevenths** may be *major* or *minor*; **major sevenths** (*e.g.* C to B) contain eleven semitones; **minor sevenths** (*e.g.* D to C) contain ten semitones.

185. The *fourth, fifth,* and *octave* of any major scale reckoning from the tonic are called *perfect.*

All the fourths of a major scale (*e.g.* C to F; D to G, &c.), with one exception, contain five semitones and they are called **perfect fourths.**

The exception is the *fourth* from F to B *upwards* (*i.e.* from the *subdominant* to the *leading note*), and it is larger than a perfect fourth. It contains six semitones, and is called an **augmented**[1] **fourth.**

As the *augmented fourth* consists of six semitones or *three tones,* it is often called the *tritone* or the tritone fourth.

186. All the *fifths* of a major scale (*e.g.* C to G; D to A, &c.), with one exception, contain seven semitones, and they are called **perfect fifths.**

The exception is the *fifth* from B to F *upwards* (*i.e.* from leading note to subdominant), and it is smaller than a *perfect fifth.* It contains six semitones, and is called the **diminished fifth** (or the *imperfect fifth*).

187. The *augmented fourth* and the *diminished fifth* occur only once in each major scale, on the fourth and seventh degrees respectively.

FIG. 85.

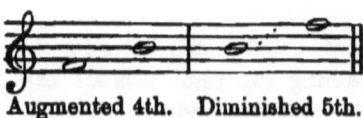

Augmented 4th.   Diminished 5th.

---

[1] This 4th is sometimes called the *pluperfect* 4th, and its companion, the diminished 5th, is then called the *imperfect* 5th. Those who use these names do so because these intervals are *diatonic,* and they prefer to reserve the names *augmented* and *diminished* for *chromatic* intervals (*v.* §§ 192–4).

In the Harmonic form of the minor scale each of these intervals occurs *twice*—viz., *augmented* 4ths on the 4th and 6th degrees ; the *diminished* 5th on the 2nd and 7th.

188. Summary of Diatonic Intervals :—

Seconds, thirds, sixths, and *sevenths* are either *major* or *minor.*
Fourths are *perfect* or *augmented.*
Fifths are *perfect* or *diminished.*

189. Table of Diatonic[1] Intervals.

NO. OF SEMITONES	SECONDS		THIRDS		FOURTHS	
	MINOR	MAJOR	MINOR	MAJOR	PERFECT	AUGMENTED
	2	2	3	4	5	6

	FIFTHS		SIXTHS		SEVENTHS		OCTAVE
	DIMINISHED	PERFECT	MINOR	MAJOR	MINOR	MAJOR	PERFECT
	6	7	8	9	10	11	12

190. To find the exact name of any interval proceed as follows. First see how many *degrees of the staff* are *included* ; then count the number of semitones.

(a) Includes D, E, F ; it is a *third*, therefore, because there are *three* degrees. Now count the semitones thus : D to D♯ = 1 ; to E = 2 ; to F = 3 ; therefore it is a minor third.

---

[1] It must not be supposed that all the intervals in this table occur in the *same* diatonic scale, though they all occur in *some* diatonic scales.

(b) Includes A, B, C, D; it is a *fourth* because there are *four* degrees. Counting the semitones we get A to A♯ = 1; to B = 2; to C = 3; to C♯ = 4; to D = 5; to D♯ = 6; *i.e.* it is the augmented fourth.

The result obtained by the above method may be tested as follows :—

190 (a) The intervals from the tonic up to each note of every major scale are either **major** or **perfect**, *i.e.* the 2nd, 3rd, 6th, and 7th, are *major*; 4th, 5th, and 8th are perfect. Thus in the key of C:

Major 2nd. Major 3rd. Perfect 4th. Perfect 5th. Major 6th. Major 7th. Perfect 8ve.

Refer any interval to the **major scale** which has the lower note of the interval for tonic; thus in § 190 :

(a) D-F is referred to the major scale of D. If this were in D major, D to F♯ would be the *major 3rd*, and since D to F♮ is one semitone smaller, it must be a **minor third**.

(b) A-D♯ is referred to A major. A to D♮ would be the *perfect fourth*, and as A to D♯ is one semitone larger it must be the **augmented fourth**.

EXERCISES.

(1) Write underneath each of the following intervals its exact name :

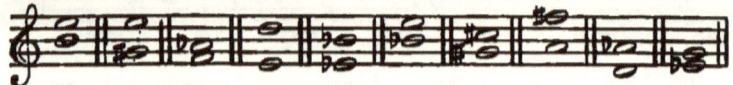

(2) To (a) add a *perfect 5th* above each note; to (b) add a *minor 6th* above :

(3) What two differently named intervals of the major scale contain the same number of semitones? Write them in the key of F and give their exact names.

(4) Write above each note of (a) a *diminished fifth*; above each note of (b) an *augmented fourth*:

(a)   (b)

(5) Write underneath each of the following intervals its exact name:

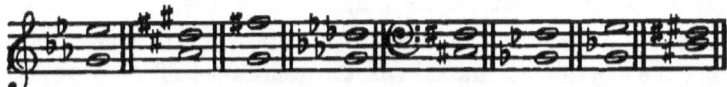

(6) Write the *harmonic* minor scale of A, and point out between what notes the interval of the *augmented fourth* occurs.

CHAPTER XVII.

CHROMATIC INTERVALS.

191. Chromatic intervals can only occur in a *chromatic scale* (§ 174), or in the Harmonic form of a minor scale.

192. The chromatic intervals are obtained by chromatically (§161) raising or lowering one of the notes of a diatonic interval.

Intervals so altered are called either *augmented* or *diminished*.

193. When a *major* or a *perfect interval* is increased it is called an **augmented interval**.

FIG. 86.
Major 2nd. Augmented 2nd. Perfect 5th. Augmented 5th.

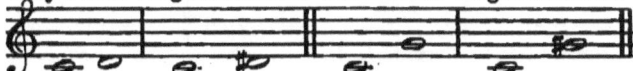

194. When a *minor* or a *perfect interval* is lessened it is called a **diminished interval**.

FIG. 87.
Minor 3rd. Diminished 3rd. Perfect 5th. Diminished 5th.

It should be noted that an interval may be *augmented* by raising the upper note or by lowering the lower; similarly, an interval may be *diminished* by raising the lower note or by lowering the upper, *e.g.*:

CHROMATIC INTERVALS

Fig. 88.

(a) Is diminished by raising the C to C♯.
(b) Is diminished by lowering E♭ to E♭♭.

195. All *augmented* and *diminished* intervals are *chromatic* except the augmented fourth[1] and the diminished fifth[1] (§ 187) which can occur in diatonic scales.

196. Theoretically all intervals may become *diminished* or *augmented*, but only the following are used in harmony:

Intervals which can be **augmented**: 2nds and 6ths.
Intervals which can be **diminished**: 3rds and 7ths.
Intervals which can be both **augmented** and **diminished**: 4ths and 5ths.

197. Table of Diatonic and Chromatic intervals:

NO. OF SEMITONES	UNISONS[2]		SECONDS		
	PERF.	AUGM.	MINOR	MAJOR	AUGM.
	0	1	1	2	3

	THIRDS		FOURTHS			FIFTHS		
DIMIN.	MINOR	MAJOR	DIMIN.	PERF.	AUGM.	DIMIN.	PERF.	AUGM.
2	3	4	4	5	6	6	7	8

[1] The augmented 4th and diminished 5th may be either diatonic or chromatic according to the key in which they occur. Thus if, in the key of C, F is made sharp by an accidental and there is no modulation, C to F♯ would be in the chromatic scale of C, and therefore a chromatic interval. But if the same interval occurs in G it is clearly diatonic, because, in the key of G, F♯ is part of the diatonic scale.

[2] The **unison**, *i.e.* two notes of the same name, is not, strictly speaking, an interval, but it is usually included in a scheme of intervals.

SIXTHS			SEVENTHS			OCTAVE
MINOR 8	MAJOR 9	AUGM. 10	DIMIN. 9	MINOR 10	MAJOR 11	PERF. 12

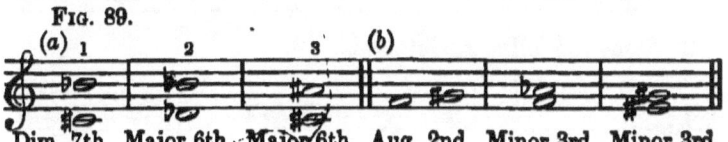

198. Either of the notes forming a *chromatic interval* may be enharmonically altered, *i.e.* altered in name but not in pitch (§ 167). Such alteration changes the *name* of the interval and makes it diatonic.

FIG. 89.

Dim. 7th. Major 6th. Major 6th. Aug. 2nd. Minor 3rd. Minor 3rd.

The three intervals at (*a*) are all alike in pitch; the first is the chromatic diminished 7th; by writing D♭ for C♯ we get a major 6th (2); by keeping C♯ and writing A♯ for B♭ we again get a major 6th. Similarly the three at (*b*) are all alike in pitch but different in name.

199. Further examples of naming intervals [§ 190 (*a*).]

(*a*) C♯ to B♭ is referred to the scale of C♯; C♯ to B♯ is a major 7th; C♯ to B♭ is two semitones smaller, therefore *diminished 7th*.

Or thus: If C were natural we should refer to C major, when C♮-B♮ is a major 7th; C♮-B♭ a minor 7th; C♯-B♭ is one semitone smaller than minor; therefore *diminished 7th*.

(*b*) D♭-B♭ referred to scale of D♭. The interval is the *major 6th*.

(*c*) F-G♯ referred to scale of F; F to G♮ would be major 2nd; this is one semitone larger; therefore an *augmented 2nd*.

CHROMATIC INTERVALS

(*d*) E♯–G♯. As there is no scale beginning on E♯ refer to scale of E ; E to G♯ major 3rd ; therefore E♯ to G♯ is a *minor* 3rd.

(*e*) E♭–B♭♭ referred to scale of E♭ ; E♭ to B♭ is perfect 5th. This is one semitone smaller ; therefore *diminished* 5th.

(*f*) F♯–C× referred to scale of F♯. F♯ to C♯ is a perfect 5th. This is one semitone larger ; therefore an augmented 5th.

EXERCISES.

1. Add to (*a*) an augmented 2nd above ; to (*b*) a diminished 7th.

2. Name the following intervals :

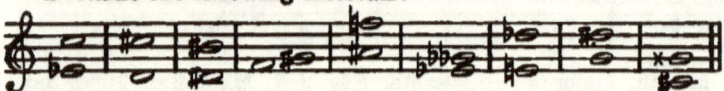

3. Name the following intervals ; change one of the notes enharmonically and then name the interval :

4. Copy each of the following notes and add *above* each a diminished 5th, *below* each a diminished 3rd.

CHAPTER XVIII.

INVERSION OF INTERVALS.

200. When the lower note of an interval is placed above the upper, or, *vice versâ*, the interval is said to be inverted.

FIG. 90.

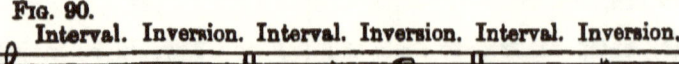

201. The numerical name of an interval subtracted from the number *nine* always gives the numerical name of the *inversion,* *e.g.* a 3rd becomes a 6th (9—3); a 4th becomes a 5th.

Fig. 91.

2nd 7th   3rd 6th   4th 5th   5th 4th   6th 3rd   7th 2nd   8th unison.

The interval and its inversion together make up *an octave, i.e.* eight degrees, but one note of the interval is counted twice, *e.g.* C to D and D to C; therefore the total number is nine.

202. Most intervals when inverted change their quality.

{ **Major** inverted becomes **minor**.
  Minor   ,,   ,,   **major**.

{ **Augmented** inverted becomes **diminished**.
  Diminished   ,,   ,,   **augmented**.

But **perfect**   ,,   remains **perfect**.

If we examine fig. 91 we shall see this: *major* 2nd becomes *minor* 7th, &c., *perfect* 4th becomes *perfect* 5th.

203. Consonance and dissonance.

A **consonant interval** is a combination of two notes which sounds complete and satisfactory in itself.

If we play the following intervals on the piano we notice the completeness.

Fig. 92.

A **dissonant interval** is one which sounds incomplete and unfinished; it requires other notes to follow it, to make a satisfactory effect.

Fig. 93.

If we play these intervals the incompleteness is evident. They require to be followed by other notes to complete them, as shown in figure below; this is called **resolving** the dissonances.

INVERSION OF INTERVALS

FIG. 94.

204. The *consonant* intervals are perfect unisons and octaves, perfect fifths, perfect fourths, major and minor thirds, major and minor sixths.

Major or minor 2nds, or 7ths, and all *augmented* and *diminished* intervals, are dissonant.

The *consonant intervals* are subdivided into *perfect consonances* (unison, octave, perfect 4th and 5th), and *imperfect consonances* (major and minor 3rd and 6ths).

205. The *perfect* intervals cannot be made larger or smaller without becoming *dissonant*; the major 3rd and 6th can be changed to minor and *vice versâ*, and still remain consonant. This is one difference between perfect intervals and others (*v.* also § 202).

206. In using intervals it is important that the student should know in what key or keys they may occur. The following examples will show the method to be pursued. Bear in mind throughout the signatures of the major and minor keys (§ 133) and the order in which the sharps and flats are added.

To find the keys in which any given intervals may occur:

(*a*) This evidently occurs in a key with sharps. F♯ is the first added sharp; D♯ is the fourth (F♯, C♯, G♯, D♯). The interval then occurs in four sharps (E major). It could also occur in keys with more than four sharps, *e.g.* in B, F♯, and C♯ major.

Since D♯ is the raised 7th of the harmonic minor scale on E (§ 124), it is clear this interval might occur in E minor also.

(*b*) This must be in a key with flats. The order in which flats are added is B♭, E♭, A♭, D♭, G♭, C♭, F♭. This interval containing F♭, then, can only occur in seven flats in C♭ major, and in its relative minor (§ 128).

(*c*) G♯ being the third added sharp suggests three sharps (A major); but C♮ cannot occur in A major. The G♯ must then be the raised seventh of A minor and the key is A minor.

This interval is the *augmented fifth*, and it occurs on the *mediant* of every minor scale (harmonic form). Here are examples of the *augmented fifth* in other keys:

(d) B♭ suggests one flat (F major). C♯ cannot occur in F major. C♯ is the raised seventh of D minor, the relative minor of F.

(e) A double sharp never occurs in a signature; it can only occur as the *raised seventh* of a minor scale, and as the tonic is one semitone above the raised seventh the key is G♯ minor.

EXERCISES.

1. Give the name of each of the following intervals; then write the inversion and name of inversion.

2. In what key or keys can each of the following intervals occur?

3. Write the following interval in every major and minor key in which it could occur, giving key signatures:

4. In what form of the minor scale can the augmented 5th and the diminished 7th occur, and between what notes?

CHAPTER XIX.

TRANSPOSITION.

207. It is sometimes necessary to alter the pitch of a piece of music. A melody in a given key may be rewritten in a *higher* or a *lower* key. This is called **transposition**.

RULES FOR TRANSPOSING.

208. I. *When there are no accidentals.*

(*a*) Write the new key-signature.

(*b*) See whether the new key is higher or lower than the old one ; then find out by what *interval* it is higher or lower.

It is only necessary to ascertain the *numerical name* of the *interval*, not whether it is major, minor, &c.

This will be done by comparing the *tonics*[1] of the two keys, *e.g.* to transpose a melody in F to the key of A. A is a third above F.

(*c*) Raise or lower each separate note the required interval.

Example :—Transpose the following melody into the key of G :—

(*a*) The new key is G major, *i.e.* one sharp signature.

(*b*) G major is a **fourth higher** than D major (the original key).

(*c*) Every note must therefore be **raised a fourth**.

The melody then stands as below :—

209. II. *When there are accidentals.*

Proceed first as if there were no accidentals (by § 208), and put them in afterwards, on the following plan :—

---

[1] Unless otherwise stated, that tonic of the new key which is nearest to the old tonic is meant ; thus in F to A, the A a third *above* F is meant, *not* a sixth *below*.

74   ELEMENTS OF MUSIC

(a) Examine separately each accidental in the original: notice whether the accidental *raises* or *lowers* the note from its condition according to the key-signature.

(b) Then add an accidental, which will produce the same effect, taking into account the new key-signature.

EXAMPLE 1.

Transpose the following into the key of E major:

Proceeding as in § 208, the new key (E) has *four sharps* for signature, and it is a **second lower** than the original F. Each note must then be written a **second** (*i.e. one note*) lower, leaving out accidentals.

To add **accidentals**:

(1) The B is *flat* by the signature; the *natural* **raises** it a semitone. The corresponding note in the transposed melody is *natural* according to the signature; to *raise* it a **sharp** is necessary.

(2) The *flat* here restores the B to its original state; to restore the A♯ to its original state a **natural** is wanted.

(3) E♭ is *lowered* a semitone from the signature. In the transposed melody D is *sharp* according to the signature; to lower it a **natural** is wanted.

(4). In C♯ the *sharp* raises the note a semitone; a sharp similarly raises B.

EXAMPLE 2.

Transpose the following into F minor:

This is in C♯ minor; the new key F minor has four flats for signature, and F is a *fourth* higher than C.

To add **Accidentals**.

(1) F according to the signature is *sharp*; the *double sharp* (x) then

merely raises it a semitone. In the transposed melody the corresponding note (B) is flat by the signature; a *natural* will raise it a semitone.

(2) The *natural* lowers D (sharp by the signature) a semitone; the corresponding note (G) is *natural* by the signature, and will require a flat to lower it.

(3) The *sharp* raises B a semitone; the *natural* raises E (which is flat by the signature).

Exercises.

1. Transpose the following melody (*a*) into A♭, (*b*) into G, (*c*) into B, (*d*) a minor third [1] lower.

2. Transpose (*a*) into D; (*b*) into A; (*c*) into E♭.

3. Transpose (*a*) into C; (*b*) into B♭; (*c*) into D.

4. Transpose (*a*) into E minor; (*b*) into C minor; (*c*) into F♯ minor; (*d*) a *major third* higher:

---

[1] In cases of this kind proceed as follows: The melody is in E♭; the new tonic will be a *minor third* lower, *i.e.* C. The question then means transpose into C.

ELEMENTS OF MUSIC

5. Transpose the following into the key of F major:

CHAPTER XX.

DOTS, ABBREVIATIONS, ETC.

210. Dots placed to the *left* of a double-bar (§ 42) mean that the music is to be repeated, either from the beginning of the piece, or from a previous double bar,  or

When the repetition is from a previous double-bar, dots are often placed to the *right* of that double-bar:

211. Sometimes, in repeating, a different ending is necessary for the second time. This is indicated by marking the endings 1st time, 2nd time, or simply 1, 2, or *Prima volta, Seconda volta*.

FIG. 95.

The first time we play to the double-bar and repeat; this time we omit the bar marked 1*st time* and play in its stead the bar marked 2*nd time*.

212. Da Capo (= *from the beginning*) or **D. C.** placed at the end of a piece means that we are to begin again *from the beginning*, and to continue until we reach a double-bar marked by the sign ⁀ called a *pause*, or by the word **Fine** (= *end*).

DOTS, ABBREVIATIONS, ETC. 77

When such a repetition is not absolutely from the beginning a sign 𝄋 indicates the exact note from which the repeat is to be made. The words to denote repeat in this case are **Da Capo al Segno** or **Dal Segno** (= *from the sign*), or simply the sign 𝄋 is used.

213. When a short passage (a few bars) occurring in the middle of a section has to be repeated it is enclosed in a bracket or a slur, and the word **bis** (=twice) is written.

FIG. 96.

214. The sign ⌢ called a **pause** is used in two ways.

(a) Placed over a *note* or a *rest*, it means that the note or rest is to be prolonged beyond its written value.

When the pause is to be very long the words *lunga pausa* are written. In all cases the length of a pause depends on the taste of the performer.

(b) A pause placed over a double-bar denotes the final end of a piece which has been repeated (§ 212).

FIG. 97.

215. The **slur** ⌢ used with two (or more) notes of the same pitch means that the second is not to be struck, but that the two are to be sustained without break, just as if their total length were written in one note (§ 83).

In this case the *slur* is often called a *tie*.

The **slur** used with notes of different pitch means that they are to be played as *smoothly* as possible, one note following another without break.

This smooth way of playing is called *legato*, and when a whole passage is to be played so the word *legato* is used with or without slurs.

FIG. 98.

In music for the voice the *slur* means that the notes so joined are to be sung to *one* syllable. In instruments like the violin each group of notes slurred is played with the same stroke of the bow.

When notes are slurred in *twos* the second of each pair is made slightly shorter than its real value in order to show the grouping more definitely by separating each group of two from its neighbours. The first note of such a pair is accented slightly.

Fig. 99.

216. The word **staccato** means that the notes are to be played short and crisp, and well separated from each other. This is indicated by **dashes** (׳ ׳) or by **dots** (. . .) placed over the notes. When *dashes* are used the notes are to be played as *staccato* as possible (ᵃ); *Dots* (ᵇ) indicate a moderate staccato, sometimes called *mezzo-staccato* (*mezzo* = half). A third degree of staccato is marked by *slurs and dots*; this indicates a staccato less marked than when dots alone are used (ᶜ).

On instruments like the violin this staccato (ᶜ) means that each group so marked is to be played with the same up or down bow, with a fresh impulse for each note but *without the bow being taken off the strings*.

Fig. 100.

216 (a). When the staccato is long-continued, the first bar only is marked, and the word **simili** (= *similarly*) is added.

217. The sign ⁻ or ⁒ placed over a note or notes means that each note is to be held its full length, and is to be played with a firm but gentle pressure.

218. 8va (*ottava alta*) written over a passage means that each note must be played an octave *higher* than it is written.

The continuance of 8*va* is shown by dots, or by a wavy line. When 8*va* is to be contradicted, and the notes played as written, the word **loco** (=*in the place, i.e.* as written) is added.

Fig. 101.

219. 8va (*ottava bassa* or *ottava sotto*) used *below* a passage means that each note is to be played an octave lower than written.

Sometimes the figure 8 (*not* 8va) is placed *over* or *under* a note. It means that the octave above or below is to be played *with the note, i.e.* in octaves. This is sometimes indicated by *con 8va* (*con* = with).

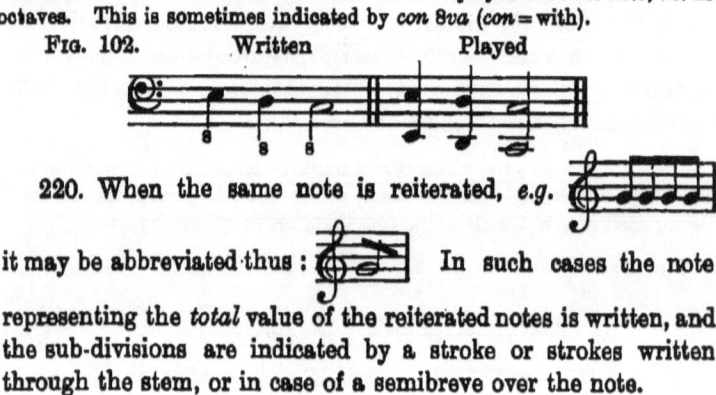

Fig. 102.

220. When the same note is reiterated, *e.g.* it may be abbreviated thus: In such cases the note representing the *total* value of the reiterated notes is written, and the sub-divisions are indicated by a stroke or strokes written through the stem, or in case of a semibreve over the note.

Fig. 103.

(a) *A semibreve* (= 8 quavers) is divided into *quavers*; (b) a *minim* (= 8 semiquavers) is divided into *semiquavers*; (c) *crotchets* (= 2 quavers) divided into quavers; (d) *dotted crotchets* (= 6 semiquavers) divided into *semi-quavers*.

FIG. 104. (e)

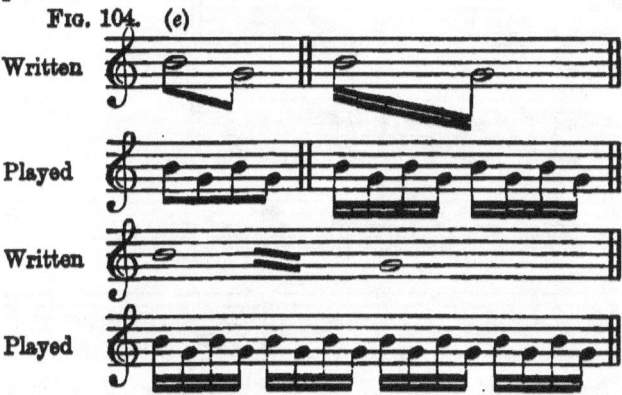

When as at (e) a group consists of *two* notes it requires two notes to write it, but the total value in all such cases is only *one* of the notes, *i.e.* bars 1 and 2, each equal one minim in length; bar 3 equals one semibreve.

221. When notes are to be repeated very quickly indeed the word **tremolo** or **tremolando** is written, and generally as many repetitions as can be got in the time of the note are played.

The manner of playing the *tremolo* on the pianoforte and violin is shown below.

FIG. 105.

DOTS, ABBREVIATIONS, ETC.   81

222. Repetitions of groups of notes are shown by writing ━, or ☰, or ⁙, or by the use of the word *simili* [§ 216(*a*)].

Fig. 106.

228. The notes of a *chord*, *i.e.* a combination of several notes sounded together, are usually struck all at the same time. A chord is then said to be a **firm chord**. If a chord has a *wavy line* or a curve at its left side, the notes are to be played as quickly as possible one after the other, beginning with the lowest. This is called an **arpeggio**, because on a harp (Italian *arpa*) chords are so played.

Sometimes the notes are written as they are to be played, as at (*b*).

Fig. 107.

Exercises.

1. Explain the following terms: *bis, simili, lunga pausa, dal segno, mezzo-staccato*.

2. Rewrite the following passages as they are to be played.

3. Express in abbreviated form, using the note G:

G

(*a*) 6 quavers; (*b*) 8 semiquavers; (*c*) 16 semiquavers; (*d*) 16 quavers; (*e*) 12 semiquavers; (*f*) 8 demisemiquavers.

4. Write out in full the following abbreviation:

5. Write two bars of music, using signs to make one bar staccato and the other legato.

CHAPTER XXI.

GRACE NOTES.

224. A melody may be ornamented by the addition of *grace notes*. The chief grace notes used in modern music are the *appoggiatura, acciaccatura, turn, shake, mordent.*

225. The **appoggiatura** (from *appoggiare*, to **lean upon**) is written as a small note before a principal note. It takes its time from the principal note, and is usually *half* the length of an undotted note, *two-thirds* the length of a dotted note.

Appoggiatura means the note leaned upon, and therefore it always takes the accent instead of the principal note. It should be written as a *crotchet, quaver, &c.*, according to its length.

Fig. 108.

Written

Played

Written

Played

In modern music the appoggiatura is almost always written as an ordinary large note.

226. The *acciaccatura* (from *acciaccare*, to crush) is written as a small note with a stroke through its stem (). It should be played just *before* the principal note, but as close to it as possible.

The principal note—*not* the acciaccatura—takes the accent.

227. When an acciaccatura is a semitone *below* a note it is sometimes called a beat.

228. Several grace notes played before a principal note are sometimes called a *double appoggiatura*. They are played as quickly as possible, never take the accent and take their time from the previous note or beat.

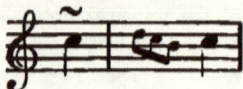

229. The **turn** consists of a principal note with the note above and the note below.

When the note above the principal note comes first, the *turn* is said to be **direct**, and the sign for it is ∾.

230. The **inverted turn** (written ?) has the note below the principal note first.

The notes of the turn will be according to the key in which they occur. If it is necessary to modify this, accidentals are written above or below. Thus, a turn with a sharp below it means that the lower note is to be made sharp, &c.

Fig. 109.

281. When the principal note is to be played before the turn begins, the sign ought to be placed a little to the right (*a*). If a turn occurs on a dotted note, the principal note is first played, and the turn is made to terminate with the principal note on the dot (*b*). The speed of the turn will depend on the character of the music.

When a turn stands immediately *over* a note, it should begin with the note above the principal note, and then the turn will consist of four notes, played in the time of the note over which the turn is written (*c*).

Fig. 110.

282. The **shake** (or *trill*) consists of a principal note, and the note above it rapidly alternated. It is written ⁕ or ⁕⌇⌇⌇ Generally the principal note comes first. When the upper note is to come first it is usually indicated in modern music by a small note (*appoggiatura*) (*b*).

Before the last recurrence of the principal note, the note below is often taken, thus forming a *turn* at the end of the shake. This is indicated in modern music by two small notes as at (*c*), and, as a rule, a shake should only end with a turn when these small notes are written.

The length of the shake is the value of the principal note, as many notes being played as can be got distinctly in the time.

GRACE NOTES

Fig. 111.

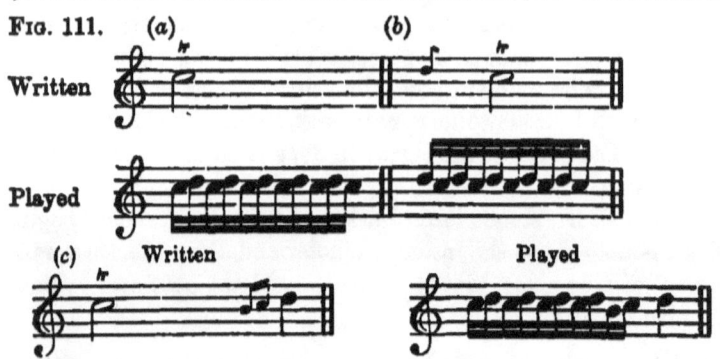

As in the case of a turn, the note above the principal note may have an accidental which is written above the sign for the shake, *e.g.* ♭.

233. A shake may occur in two (or three) notes at the same time. This is a double (or triple) shake.

Sometimes a series of shakes occurs on notes following each other stepwise. When the series ascends each shake will finish with a turn.

234. The *mordent*,[1] written 𝍩, consists of a principal note, and the note above taken *once* very rapidly, and followed by the principal note.

235. An *inverted mordent* (𝍪) has the principal note and the note below.

Exercises.

1. Explain clearly, with examples, the difference between *appoggiatura* and *acciaccatura*.

2. Write in full each of the following ornaments as it is played:

---

[1] In Germany the sign 𝍪 is called *praller* or *pralltriller*, while 𝍩 is called a *mordent*. The signs, however, are interpreted as in §§ 234-5, so that the difference is merely in the *names*.

CHAPTER XXII.

MUSICAL TERMS.

286. Many words, mostly Italian, are used to indicate pace, force, style, &c.

287. I. Terms denoting pace (beginning with the slowest, and going upwards to the quickest):

Grave	very slow.
Adagio	slowly, leisurely.
{ Largo	slow.
{ Larghetto[1] . . .	rather slow.
Lento	slow.
{ Andante	going, slow but graceful.
{ Andantino[1] . .	rather slower[2] than Andante.
Moderato	moderate.
{ Allegro	merry and fast.
{ Allegretto . . .	not so fast as Allegro.
{ Presto	fast.
{ Prestissimo[3] . .	very fast.
{ Tempo comodo . .	at a convenient pace.
{ Tempo giusto . .	in exact time.
{ Tempo ordinario .	in ordinary time.

Some of these words also convey an idea of style as well as of pace. Thus *largo* means not only slow, but also broad, large in style.

---

[1] The ending *-etto* or *-ino* is called a diminutive, and it diminishes the force of the meaning of a word to which it is applied, *e.g. larghetto* is not so slow as *largo*; *allegretto* not so quick as *allegro*.

[2] Unfortunately there are two exactly opposite meanings attached to *andantino*. As *andante* means " going," *andantino* should mean *less going*, *i.e.* not so fast as *andante*. Some composers, however, taking *andante* as meaning *slow*, make *andantino* mean *less slow*, *i.e.* faster than *andante*.

[3] The ending *-issimo* is a superlative, and corresponds to our word *most* or *very*.

These words usually apply to a whole movement or section, and they are to be considered in force until contradicted by some other term.

288. II. Terms denoting a temporary alteration in pace:

Accelerando or *accel.*	increasing the pace.
Ad libitum or *ad lib.*	} at pleasure.
A piacere	
A tempo	} after a modification to return to original time.
Tempo primo	
Calando[1]	decreasing the pace.
Rallentando or *rall.*	} gradually slower.
Ritardando or *rit.*	
Slentando	
Stringendo	pressing or hurrying the pace.
L'istesso tempo	at the same pace; used when there is a change of time, *e.g.* $\frac{2}{4}$ to $\frac{6}{8}$; it means that the *beat* in the new time is to be just the same as the beat in the previous time; *i.e.* the dotted crotchet of $\frac{6}{8}$ to be the same length as the crotchet of the $\frac{2}{4}$.

289. III. Terms relating to degrees of loudness, softness, or force:

Piano, p	soft.
Mezzo piano, mp	moderately soft.
Pianissimo, pp	very soft.
Forte, f	loud.
Mezzo forte, mf	moderately loud.
Fortissimo, ff	very loud.
fp	loud and then soft immediately.
Crescendo, cres. or <	{ gradually louder. increasing in loudness.
Decrescendo, decres.; *Diminuendo, dim.* >	} decreasing in loudness.
Morendo	} gradually softer; dying away.
Perdendosi	
Dolce	softly, gently, sweetly.
Sforzando, sf, > or ∧	} strongly accented or emphasised.
Forzato, fz	
Sforzato, sf	

240. IV. Terms relating to style. The words marked * are used with others to form phrases.

---

[1] *Calando* also implies gradually more softly.

Affetuoso	with feeling.
Agitato	agitated.
Alla or *all'*	like, according to.
e.g., *alla marcia, alla breve.*	
Amoroso	lovingly.
Animato or *con anima*	animated.
Appassionato	impassioned.
*Assai	enough or very.
e.g., *Allegro assai.*	
*Ben (e.g., *ben marcato*)	well.
Brillante	brilliantly.
Cantabile	in a singing style.
Colla voce	with the voice part.
Comodo	convenient, without haste.
*Con	with.
Con brio	with spirit.
Con energia	with energy.
Con espressione	with expression.
Con forza	with emphasis.
Con fuoco	with fire.
Con grazia	gracefully.
Con moto	with movement, spirited.
Con spirito	in a spirited manner, lively.
Con tenerezza	with tenderness.
Dolente	in a plaintive style.
Espressivo	full of expression.
Grazioso	gracefully.
Legato	smoothly.
Leggiero	lightly.
*Ma	but.
e.g., *ma non troppo*	but not too much.
Maestoso	majestically.
Marcato	well marked, emphasised.
Marziale	like a march.
*Meno	less.
*Mezzo	half.
Mezzo voce	with half the power of the voice.
Mosso	moved.
*Molto	much, very.
*Non	not.
Pesante	heavily, each note to be played with great firmness, but not staccato.
*Più	more.
*Poco	little.
Poco a poco	little by little, gradually.

*Quasi	as if, like.
Risoluto	boldly.
Scherzando	lightly, playfully.
Tanto	so much.
Troppo	too much.
Segue	placed at the end of a movement

means that the next movement is to follow without break.

*Sempre	always, throughout.
*Senza	without.
Smorzando	fading away.
Soave	delicately.
Solo	a part performed by one person.
Sotto voce	subdued in tone.
Sostenuto (applied to a passage)	each note held its full length.
Tempo rubato . . .	lit. *robbed time*, means—(a) not

in strict time, *i.e.*, occasionally accelerating or retarding the pace for the purpose of *expression*. (b) The effect of a change of time caused by change of accent (§ 84).

Tenuto or *ten* (applied to a single note) . . .	to be sustained its full length.
Tutti	to be performed by full band or
chorus (v. *solo*).	
*Vivace	lively.
Vivo	briskly.

241. **V. Terms applying to pianoforte technique.**

Sometimes it is necessary to indicate which hand shall be used for certain notes. This is done by using **R. H.** (*right hand*), or **M. D.** (*main droite*, French; *mano destra*, Italian), for the right hand; and **L. H.** (*left hand*), **M. G.** (*main gauche*), or **M. S.** (*mano sinistra*), for the **left hand.**

242. **Pedals.**—Modern pianos have two pedals—the **right pedal** or sustaining pedal, the **left pedal** or soft pedal.

The use of the **right pedal** is indicated by the word ped., and the pedal is kept down until the sign ✻ or ⊕ is reached.

The strings corresponding to each note of the piano (except the highest octaves) are touched by an arrangement for deadening the sound, called a *damper*. When a note is struck the same action raises the *damper*, thus allowing the strings to vibrate freely, and when the note is left the *damper* falls on the strings and stops their vibration. The *right pedal* raises all the *dampers* in the piano at once, and thus allows full and free vibration after a note is left (§ 157).

These *dampers* are called **sordini** (= mutes), and we sometimes find **senza sordini** (= without dampers) when the dampers are to be raised, *i.e.* **ped.**, and **con sordini** (= with dampers) when the dampers are to be lowered, *i.e.* ✳ or ⊕, *v.* Beethoven's Sonata XIV., first movement.

243. The use of the **left pedal** is indicated by the words **una corda** (=one string), and the pedal is to be kept down until the words **tre corde** (= three strings) are reached.

To most of the notes of a piano there are three strings (all of the same pitch) to increase the volume of tone. The action of the left pedal is to move the hammers in such a way that only *one* string is struck. This, of course, diminishes the loudness of each note. Instead of *una corda* we often find *mit Verschiebung* (= with shifting) in German music.

244. The terms for the indication of pace (§§ 237-40) can, of course, only give a rough idea of the intentions of the composer. He may, however, accurately indicate the pace by reference to a contrivance called Maelzel's **Metronome**. This is a piece of clockwork to which is attached a pendulum with a sliding weight. By moving the weight the pendulum can be made to swing more quickly or more slowly. The pendulum is graduated, and the divisions are numbered on the principle of the number of beats *per minute*. Thus, when the weight is fixed at 60, the pendulum beats 60 times in a minute; fixed at 100, the pendulum beats 100 times in a minute.

M. M. ♩ = 60 means that when the metronome weight is fixed at 60 each beat of the pendulum gives the time of a crotchet. M. M. ♩ = 80 means that fixed at 80 each beat is the time of a minim, &c.

It must not be imagined that all music marked with the same Italian word for pace would have the same metronome mark, for the Italian word is used to roughly describe many degrees of pace. The following then must only be considered as roughly indicating the possible metronome marking:

Andante M. M. ♩ = 60; *Adagio* ♩ = 54 to 50; *Moderato* ♩ = 90; *Allegro* ♩ = 110 to 135; *Presto* ♩ = 135 to 160, &c.

EXERCISE.

1. Explain the following terms:—*Doppio movimento, largo, quasi, pesante, soave, maestoso, senza sordini, allegro assai.*

MUSICAL TERMS

1. In what key is this?
2. Does it keep in the same key throughout?.
3. For what other key does this signature stand?
4. Is the time simple or compound?
5. What signs are used here for altering the pitch of the notes? Explain them.
6. Explain all the uses to which the *dot* (.) and the *slur* are put in this extract.
7. What does ⌜1⌝ ⌜2⌝ mean?
8. Explain the following signs and terms occurring here: *con moto, legato, mf*, >, *cres*, <*f* > *p*.
9. What *clefs* are used here?
10. Transpose the extract a semitone higher.

245. The Stave.—The number of lines used for the *stave* has varied greatly at different periods, and it was not until the invention of printing that the number was fixed at *five*. In mediæval music staves with from *three* to *fifteen* lines were used. In some of these only the spaces were used; while in others the spaces were not taken into account, only the *lines* being written upon.

Even at the present time a stave of four lines is used for the *Gregorian Tones*, *i.e.*, the traditional chants of the Early Christian Church.

In music for the *organ* there are usually three staves (of five lines each) bracketed together—two used for the notes to be played by the two hands, and the third for the part played by the feet.

246. Names of Voices.—Originally the part we now call *Tenor* always sang or held the melody—hence its name (from *teneo*, I hold). The part below was called *Bass*, a word meaning *low*. The part immediately above the *tenor* was called *alto*, as explained in § 22. The word *treble* means *third*, and thus it was applied to the third part above the tenor (compare the word *triple*). The word *soprano* means *highest*, and *mezzo-soprano* means lower than soprano (v. mezzo in § 240.)

247. Compound Time.—Each bar in *Compound Time* may be regarded as consisting of two, three, or four bars of *simple triple* time. Thus ⁶⁄₈ is compounded of two bars of ³⁄₈.

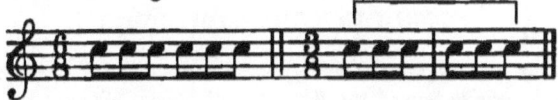

Similarly, ⁹⁄₈ is compounded of three bars of ³⁄₈ ; and ¹²⁄₈ is compounded of four bars of ³⁄₈.

On this principle ⁴⁄₄ time is always considered in Germany as compound, *i.e.*, made up of two bars of ²⁄₄.

The grouping of *bars* into equal sets or groups constitutes **Rhythm** (*see* Part III.).

248. The Origin of the Sign ♭.—The B at first used in music was only a semitone above A, and from this the letter *b* in time was used to denote the lowering of a note by a semitone. The letter *b* eventually was corrupted into the sign ♭. (Compare § 140.)

249. In the eighteenth and the beginning of the nineteenth centuries it was not the custom to write two of the parts of a triplet as one note, *e.g.* The plan was always to have *three* characters to represent the triplet, either three notes, or two notes and a rest, or two notes and a dot. Instead of we find incorrectly . An example like (*a*) below occurring in music of the period referred to must be played as at (*b*):

MUSIC COURSE

PART II.
HARMONY AND COUNTERPOINT

HARMONY.
INTRODUCTORY CHAPTER.

THE student who begins the study of *Harmony* should be conversant with what is usually termed the Elements of Music. We shall, therefore, assume that the reader is familiar with the shape and value of notes and rests, time, keys, scales, &c. Certain other elementary subjects which form the immediate groundwork of Harmony it will be convenient to recapitulate.

250. Each note of every diatonic scale receives a technical name.

The *first* note is called the **Tonic**; the *eighth* note is called the **Octave**. The *fifth* note, from its importance in harmony, is called the **Dominant** (or *ruling*-note). The *third* note, being *midway* between *tonic* and *dominant*, is called the **Mediant**.

Reckoning from the tonic a fifth *downwards*, we get to the octave of the *fourth* note of the scale, and as the fifth *upward* is called the *dominant* the *fourth note* is called the **Subdominant** (or *lower* dominant). The *sixth* note is midway between *subdominant* and *tonic* (or octave of tonic), and it is called the **Submediant**.

The *second* note is called the **Supertonic** (*i.e. over* the tonic), and the *seventh* note is called the **Leading-note**, because it has a strong tendency to proceed or lead up to the octave.

Thus in the key of C these names would be:

FIG. 112.

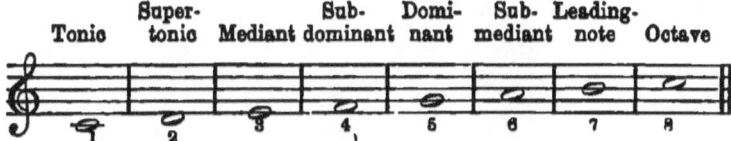

INTERVALS.[1]

251. An **Interval** is the difference in pitch between any two notes. Intervals are named according to the number of degrees of the staff included.

Thus C to D is called a *second*; C to E a *third*, &c., as seen from the following table:

FIG. 113.

Intervals are always counted *upwards* unless the contrary is expressly stated.

252. Intervals up to and including the eighth are called *Simple Intervals*. Beyond the eighth they are called *Compound Intervals*, being merely an octave added to a simple interval, *e.g.* a tenth is an octave added to a third.

FIG. 114.

---

[1] For fuller details see Pt. I., pp. 61-72.

With the exception of the ninth, eleventh, and thirteenth, compound intervals are not used in harmony, and the simple name is usually applied however many octaves may be added to a simple interval—*e.g.* each of the following would be called a third in harmony:—

Fig. 115.

253. The smallest[1] interval used in music is the semitone. Semitones are of two kinds. A semitone occurring between two notes with different letter-names is called a **diatonic semitone**—*e.g.* B to C, C to D♭, &c.

A semitone occurring between any note and the same note raised or lowered by an accidental is called a **chromatic semitone**—*e.g.* C to C♯, A to A♭.

254. The **name** of the interval depends entirely on the **number of degrees included.** C to D and C to D♭ are both *seconds.* It is clear then that different *kinds* of intervals must be distinguished.

255. Intervals which occur between any two notes of an *unaltered* diatonic scale are called **diatonic intervals.**

Intervals which can only occur in a chromatic scale, or in the Harmonic form of a minor scale, are called **chromatic intervals.**

DIATONIC INTERVALS.

256. Reckoning upwards from the tonic of any major scale, the *second, third, sixth,* and *seventh* are called **major,** the *fourth, fifth,* and *octave* are called **perfect.**

Fig. 116.

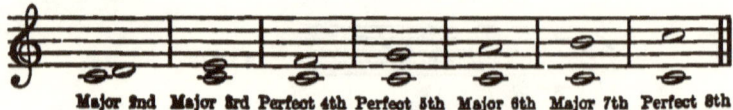

Major 2nd   Major 3rd   Perfect 4th   Perfect 5th   Major 6th   Major 7th   Perfect 8th

[1] See, however, Pt. I., §§ 163–5.

257. We see from fig. 116 that C to D is a *major second*, and it contains *two* semitones (C to C♯, = 1, to D = 2). Some of the *seconds* in this scale are smaller than C to D; thus E to F has only *one* semitone. This is called a **minor second**, and it contains *one* semitone.

258. In the same way there are **minor thirds** (E to G), **minor sixths** (E to C), **minor sevenths** (D to C); each *minor* interval being *one semitone less* than the corresponding *major* interval.

259. All the *fourths* found in the major scale are **perfect** (C-F, D-G, &c.), with the exception of that from the *subdominant* upwards to the *leading-note*, *i.e.* F-B. This is one semitone larger than a perfect fourth, and is called an **augmented fourth**.[1]

As the augmented fourth consists of six semitones or *three tones*, it is often called the tritone fourth or the tritone.

260. All the *fifths* found in the major scale are **perfect** (C-G, D-A), except that from the *leading-note* upwards to the *subdominant*. This is one semitone less than a perfect fifth, and it is called a **diminished fifth**.[1]

The *augmented* fourth and the *diminished* fifth occur only once in each major scale, viz. on the fourth and seventh degrees respectively (*a*). In minor scales (Harmonic form) the *augmented* fourth occurs on the fourth and sixth degrees; the *diminished* fifth on the second and seventh (*b*).

FIG. 117.

(*a*) C major   (*b*) C minor
Aug. 4th   Dim. 5th   Aug. 4ths   Dim. 5ths

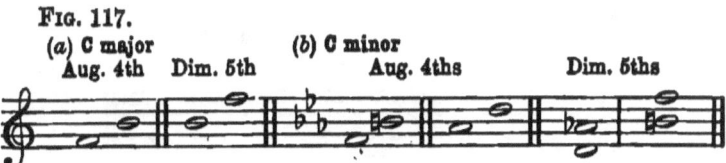

261. Summary of diatonic intervals:

{ Seconds, thirds, sixths, and sevenths are either **major** or **minor**.
Fourths are either **perfect** or **augmented**.
Fifths are either **perfect** or **diminished**.

---

[1] This fourth is sometimes called the *pluperfect* fourth, and its companion the diminished fifth is then called the *imperfect* fifth. Those who use these names do so because these intervals are diatonic, and they prefer to reserve the names *augmented* and *diminished* for *chromatic intervals*, v. § 262.

CHROMATIC INTERVALS.

262. Chromatic intervals are obtained by chromatically [1] raising or lowering one of the notes of a diatonic interval.

Intervals so altered are called either *augmented* or *diminished*.

263. When a *major* or a *perfect interval* is increased it is called an **augmented interval**.

FIG. 118.

Major 2nd.   Augmented 2nd.   Perfect 5th.   Augmented 5th.

264. When a *minor* or a *perfect interval* is lessened it is called a **diminished interval**.

FIG. 119.

Minor 3rd.   Diminished 3rd.   Perfect 5th.   Diminished 5th.

It should be noted that an interval may be *augmented* by raising the upper note or by lowering the lower; similarly, an interval may be *diminished* by raising the lower note or by lowering the upper, *e.g.*:

FIG. 120.

                               Diminished 3rd.
        Minor 3rd.   (*a*)   or   (*b*)

265. All *augmented* and *diminished* intervals are *chromatic* except the **augmented fourth** [2] and the **diminished fifth**,[2] which can occur in diatonic scales.

---

[1] *I.e.* by using an accidental, *v.* § 253.
[2] The augmented fourth and diminished fifth may be either diatonic or chromatic according to the key in which they occur. Thus if, in the key of C, F is made sharp by an accidental and there is no modulation, C to F♯ would be in the chromatic scale of C, and therefore a chromatic interval. But if the same interval occurs in G it is clearly diatonic, because, in the key of G, F♯ is part of the diatonic scale (*v.* § 593).

98   *HARMONY*

266. Theoretically all intervals may become *diminished* or *augmented*, but only the following are used in harmony:

  Intervals which can be **augmented**: seconds and sixths.
  Intervals which can be **diminished**: thirds and sevenths.
  Intervals which can be both **augmented** and **diminished**: fourths and fifths.

We now give a complete table of all intervals, showing the number of semitones in each.

267. Table of **Diatonic and Chromatic** intervals:

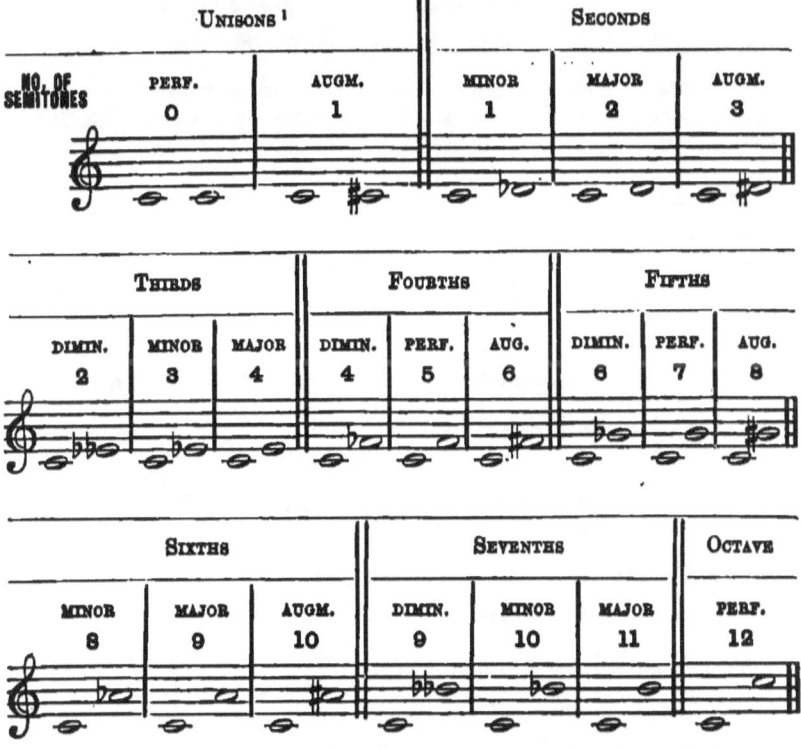

[1] The unison—*i.e.* two notes of the same name—is not, strictly speaking, an interval, but it is usually included in a scheme of intervals.

INVERSION OF INTERVALS.

268. When the lower note of an interval is placed above the upper, or *vice versâ*, the interval is said to be inverted.

FIG. 121.

Interval
Inversion
Interval
Inversion
Interval
Inversion

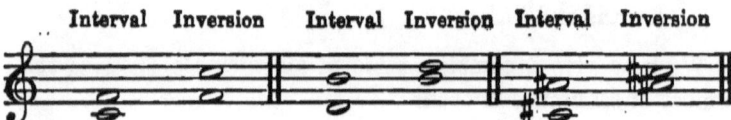

269. The numerical name of an interval subtracted from the number *nine* always gives the numerical name of the *inversion*—*e.g.* a third becomes a sixth (9 – 3); a fourth becomes a fifth.

The interval and its inversion together make up *an octave—i.e.* eight degrees; but one note of the interval is counted twice—*e.g.* C to *D* and *D* to C; therefore the total number is nine.

FIG. 122.

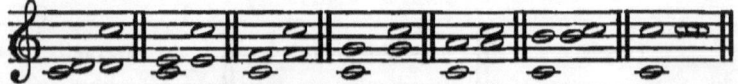

2nd 7th
3rd 6th
4th 5th
5th 4th
6th 3rd
7th 2nd
8th unison

270. Most intervals when inverted change their quality.

{ **Major** inverted becomes **minor.**
{ **Minor** „ „ **major.**

{ **Augmented** inverted becomes **diminished.**
{ **Diminished** „ „ **augmented.**

But **Perfect** inverted **remains perfect.**

Thus, a major second becomes a minor seventh, &c.

271. Consonance and dissonance.

A consonant interval is a combination of two notes which sounds complete and satisfactory in itself.

If we play the following intervals on the piano we notice the completeness.

Fig. 123.

A **dissonant interval** is one which sounds incomplete and unfinished; it requires other notes to follow it to make a satisfactory effect.

Fig. 124.

If we play these intervals the incompleteness is evident. They require to be followed by other notes to complete them, as shown in fig. 125; this is called **resolving** the dissonances.

Fig. 125.

272. The *consonant* intervals are **perfect unison and octave, perfect fifth, perfect fourth; major and minor thirds, major and minor sixths.**

Major or *minor seconds*, or *sevenths*, and all *augmented* and *diminished* intervals, are **dissonant**.

The *consonant intervals* are subdivided into *perfect consonances* (unison, octave, perfect fourth and fifth), and *imperfect consonances* (major and minor thirds and sixths).

CHAPTER XXIII.

273. **Melody** means sounds of different pitch heard *in succession*.

Harmony means sounds of different pitch heard *in combination*.

MELODY AND HARMONY

When each combination consists of *two* notes the music is said to be in *two parts*, fig. 126 (a).

When each combination consists of *three* notes the music is in *three parts* (b).

When each combination consists of *four* notes the music is in *four parts* (c).

Fig. 126.

(a) Harmony in *two* parts.

(b) Harmony in *three* parts.

(c) Harmony in *four* parts.

274. A part means what is performed by one voice or one instrument.

Thus, in fig. 126 (a) the treble voice would sing the upper notes: these are called the *treble part*. Similarly, the lower notes are called the *alto part*, &c.

275. Three or more notes sounded together are called a **Chord**.[1]

---

[1] Though a chord is built up of at least *three* notes, one of these notes is sometimes omitted in using the chord.

In *Harmony* we study the way in which chords are built up, and the relation of chords one to another—*i.e.* the way in which one chord may follow another.

276. **Chords are built up by adding successive thirds above a given note.** The note from which the chord is built up is called the **root** of the chord.

FIG. 127.

At (*a*) the note C is the root. Above C is added a *third* (E), and then another *third* (G). At (*b*) we have three *thirds* added above the *root* C; at (*c*) we have four *thirds* added.

277. **Triads.** When a *chord* consists of two thirds placed one above the other, it is called a **triad**, because it consists of *three* notes. Fig. 127 (*a*).

278. **Common Chords.**[1] When the interval from the root to the upper note of a triad [2] is a *perfect fifth*, the chord is called a **Common Chord.**

A common chord, then, consists of any note with the **third and perfect fifth** above it.

If the *third* is *major* the chord is a **major common chord.**
If the *third* is *minor* the chord is a **minor common chord.**

FIG. 128.

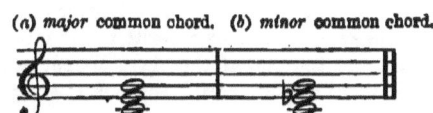

(*a*) is a *major* common chord because C–E is a *major* third.
(*b*) is a *minor* common chord because C–E♭ is a *minor* third.

---

[1] Some writers only apply the term *common chord* to a chord in four parts (§ 280).
[2] When the fifth of a triad is diminished and the third is minor, the chord is called a **diminished triad** (*a*) (§ 640). When the fifth is augmented and the third is major, the chord is an **augmented triad** (*b*) (§ 642).

FIG. 129.

RULES FOR DOUBLING

279. Music is written in two, three, four, five, or more *parts*; but the most convenient method of studying Harmony for beginners is to practise Harmony in *four* parts.

280. Since a *common chord* consists of three notes, it is evident that if common chords are used in four-part harmony, one of the notes of each chord must be used twice. This is called **doubling** [1] a note.

FIG. 130.

(a) The common chord on C.
(b) The same common chord with the *root* (C) *doubled*.

281. Rules for Doubling. (a) The **Root** of a chord is the best note to double, and the next best is the **fifth**.

(b) When the *third* of a chord is *minor* it may be doubled. When the *third* is *major* it should not, as a rule, be doubled, though sometimes, as will be seen later, this cannot be avoided.

(c) *Never* double the **leading-note**.

282. Sometimes it is necessary to omit a note of a common chord. The *third should never be omitted*, for without the third it is impossible to say whether the chord is major or minor. The *fifth* is the best note to omit.

283. In fig. 131 (a) the common chord on C is given with the doubled root in the upper part. The same chord may be written with either the *third* or *fifth* in the upper part. **If the root of the chord is kept in the Bass**, the position of the other notes may be varied without altering the nature of the chord.

FIG. 131.

---

[1] The note *doubled* may be the same note in unison or one or more octaves higher.

Each of these chords is the same; each consists of the bass note C, with E, G, and the doubled C. In (b) the third (E) is put an octave higher than at (a), but because the chord (b) has the same bass note unchanged the chord is the same.

284. When the three upper notes of a chord in four-part harmony lie close together, the chord is said to be in *close* harmony or in a close position (a).

When the parts are further apart from each other, the chord is said to be in extended harmony, or in an **extended position** (b).

FIG. 132.

(a) Close Harmony.　　　(b) Extended Harmony.

285. The best position of a chord is when the parts are about equally distant from each other. If this is not possible, then the widest interval should be, as far as possible, between the lower parts.

FIG. 133.

(a) Good.　　　(b) Bad.

(a) The position of each of the chords here is good; the notes are about equally distant, and in almost every case the largest interval is between the two lower parts.

(b) Each of the chords here is in a bad position; the notes are unequally distributed, and the widest interval is *not* between the lowest notes.

COMMON CHORDS IN SUCCESSION 105

EXERCISES.

1. Write a common chord (of three notes) on each note of the scale of C major (except the leading-note), and state which chords are major and which minor.

2. Write a major common chord in four parts on each of the following bass notes, doubling the root in each case.

[Each chord is distinct from its neighbours; use accidentals where necessary.]

3. Write, as in Question 2, a minor common chord, doubling the third.

4. Write on two staves common chords (in four parts) on the following notes (according to the key), double either *root*, *fifth*, or the *third* (when it is minor).

CHAPTER XXIV.

COMMON CHORDS IN SUCCESSION.

286. There are three ways in which the notes of chords may move:—

(*a*) When two parts are both moving in the same direction, they are said to be in **similar motion**.

(*b*) When two parts are moving in opposite directions, they are in **contrary motion**.

(*c*) When one part remains stationary—*i.e.* on the same note —while the other moves up or down, we have **oblique motion**.

Fig. 134.

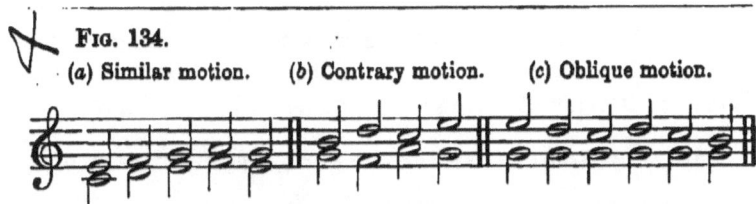

(a) Similar motion.   (b) Contrary motion.   (c) Oblique motion.

287. In using successions of chords it is best to vary as much as possible the kind of movement. Thus, after two parts have moved in similar motion, it is best to let them then move in contrary or oblique motion.

We must now consider how common chords can follow each other.

288. One chord most easily follows another when the two chords contain one or more *notes in common*.

For example, the common chord on C (*i.e.* C, E, G) can easily be followed by the common chord on G (*i.e.* G, B, D), because each chord contains the note G. Similarly, the common chords on C (*i.e.* C, E, G) and F (*i.e.* F, A, C) each contain C.

289. When two chords following each other have a note in common, it is best[1] as a rule to keep that note *in the same part or voice*.

Fig. 135.

(a)   (b)   (c)

(a) The chord on C (with root doubled) followed by chord on G (with root doubled), the note G is kept in the alto.

(b) The note C kept in the treble.

(c) Here the two chords have *two* notes in common. Both C's are kept in the treble ; both E's are kept in the tenor.

---

[1] When a rule states that such and such a course is 'best,' it implies that it is not absolutely imperative, but that sometimes, owing to circumstances, it may be necessary to disregard it.

COMMON CHORDS IN SUCCESSION

290. The notes of a chord in moving to the notes of the next chord should do so with **as little leaping as possible.** When possible they should move to the note next above or below.

At (*a*) fig. 185, C moves *one* step to B; E moves *one* step to D.

291. When the bass-note of a common chord (or its octave) is repeated monotony is avoided by letting two of the parts alternately take the third and fifth of the chord, the two parts moving in contrary motion.

FIG. 136.

In writing harmony certain rules [1] must be followed.

292. The parts must not cross or overlap.

Each part must be kept distinct from the others, *e.g.* the treble must not go to a lower note than the alto of the previous chord, and *vice versâ*.

FIG. 137.

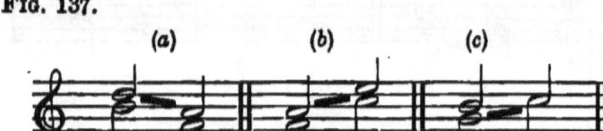

At (*a*) the treble D goes to A, which is lower than the alto B of the previous chord.

At (*b*) the alto goes to C which is higher than the previous treble A.

---

[1] These rules are given by degrees as the necessity for them arises in the exercises. In Chapter xxxv. the complete list will be found. The student is urged to keep to all the rules here given. There is scarcely a rule of Harmony which is not broken some time or other by the greatest writers, but the beginner should recognise that they only can be trusted to break rules who know thoroughly how to keep them.

293. No two parts may move at the distance of a **perfect fifth** in two consecutive chords.

This fault is called **consecutive fifths**.

FIG. 138.

At (a) the bass and tenor of each chord make a *perfect fifth*.
At (b) the bass and alto of each chord make a *perfect fifth*.
At (c) the treble and alto of each chord make a *perfect fifth*.

294. It must be clearly understood that *perfect fifths* are only disallowed when they occur between the same parts. Thus in fig. 139 there are *perfect fifths* between the bass and tenor of the first chord, and between the tenor and alto of the second, but this is perfectly correct because the fifths are *not between the same parts*.

FIG. 139.

295. Nor again are there *consecutive fifths* when two parts are merely repeated. *Consecutive fifths* are only objectionable between parts which are both moving.

FIG. 140.

PROGRESSION OF THE LEADING-NOTE

✗ 296. No two parts may move at the distance of a **perfect octave** or **unison** in two consecutive chords, a fault called **consecutive octaves.**

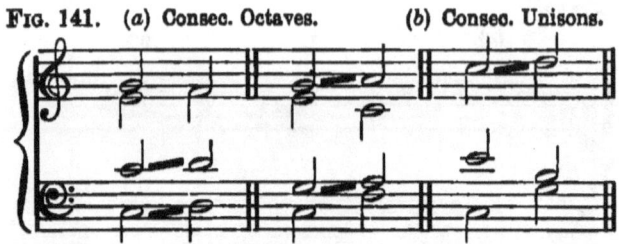

FIG. 141.   (a) Consec. Octaves.   (b) Consec. Unisons.

297. Every exercise will conclude with the common chord on the *tonic*, and most frequently the chord immediately before it is the common chord on the *dominant*. This ending with the *tonic common chord* preceded by the *dominant common chord* is called a **perfect cadence** [1] (*v.* ch. xxxvi).

FIG. 142.   Perfect Cadence.

298. The third of the dominant common chord is always the *leading-note*. The leading-note (called by the French the *sensitive* note) must be very carefully handled, and we now give the rules for its treatment:

(*a*) The **leading-note** must **never** be doubled.

(*b*) When the **leading-note** occurs in a **perfect cadence** it must **always rise** to the **tonic.**

(*c*) When the leading-note is *not* in a perfect cadence it is *better* for it to rise; but it may rise to any note, not necessarily to the tonic (*v.* § 433).

---
[1] The word *cadence* means *falling*. The music, we might say, *falls* to a close.

299. Note on perfect cadence.

When, as in fig. 143, the *treble* in a perfect cadence has the *fifth* of the dominant chord going to the *tonic* of the final chord, this final chord will consist of the root used three times and the third, the fifth being omitted. For the bass goes to the *root*, the treble goes to the *root*, and the leading note (§ 298) goes to the *root*. As the third of a chord cannot be omitted, we must omit the fifth (§ 282).

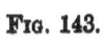

Fig. 143.

300. In writing exercises in four parts it is best to consider the parts as *treble, alto, tenor,* and *bass* voices respectively. The upper part (treble) should therefore never exceed the usual compass of the treble voice, and so for each of the others.

The compass of each voice is shown below :—

Fig. 144.

301. The early exercises should be written on two staves bracketed together as in fig. 145. The treble and alto stand on the upper stave, the bass and tenor on the lower. To distinguish between the two parts on the same stave, the upper part of each stave has the stems turned upwards, the lower, downwards (*a*). If two parts on the same stave have the same note, one head is written, and two stems, one upwards and one downwards (*b*). If the note is one without a stem the two notes are written overlapping as at (*c*).

In writing notes with stems place stems which turn upwards to the *right* of the head; those which turn downwards to the *left*.

Fig. 145.

METHOD OF WRITING EXERCISES

302. The method of writing four parts on two staves is called **short score** or *pianoforte score*. Sometimes each part is written on a separate stave, when the *music* is said to be in open score or simply in score. When exercises in Harmony are written in *open score* it is customary to use the alto and tenor clefs for those voices (Part I. § 16). The student who intends to carry his musical studies into the highest branches should familiarise himself as early as possible with this method of writing, although perhaps in the first beginnings it is well to master the elementary facts of harmony unhampered by the addition of unfamiliar clefs.

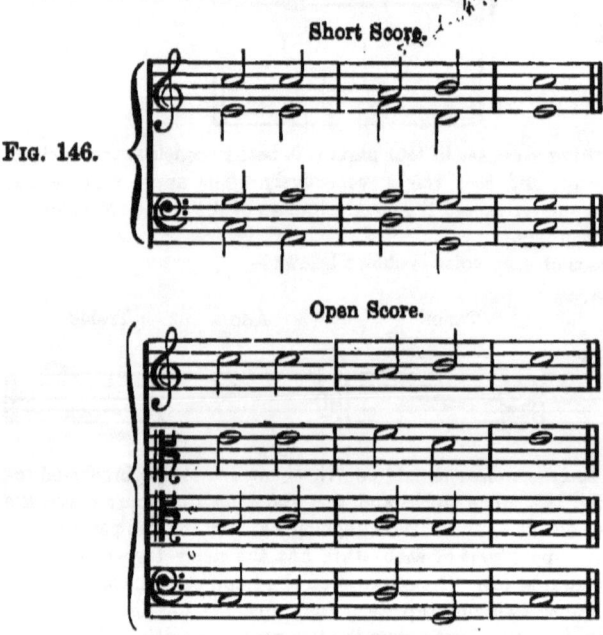

FIG. 146.

303. When an exercise is written it should be examined carefully to see if it is free from error, thus:

(a) Examine the *leading-note* each time it occurs to see if it proceeds properly.

(b) See if there are any *consecutive fifths* or *octaves*. In doing this it is best, at first, to examine separately each pair of parts, viz. treble and alto; treble and tenor; treble and bass; then alto and tenor; alto and bass; and, finally, tenor and bass.

(c) See if any note is incorrectly doubled.

When the exercise appears to be satisfactory, play it over on the pianoforte to test what you have written.

304. *** It is very important that the student should be able *to hear mentally* what he is writing. With most people this is a very slowly acquired power, but the student should not rest until by constant practice he is able *mentally to hear* the sound of the chords and successions of chords he is writing.

EXERCISES.

1. Write on two staves common chords in four parts and in various positions, on the *tonic, dominant, subdominant, supertonic* and *submediant* of the scale of C major [each chord to be independent of its neighbours]. Do the same in G major and in F major.

2. Add two inner parts to each of the following, using only common chords.

Remember §§ 289-96 and 298.

EXERCISES

* Omit the 5th.

8. What is a *perfect cadence*? Write a perfect cadence in four parts in each of the following major keys, using proper key-signature: E♭, A, G, A♭, E, and B♭.

CHAPTER XXV.

COMMON CHORDS IN SUCCESSION—*continued.*

805. When two successive chords have no note in common there is greater danger of *consecutive fifths* and *octaves*. To avoid this, let the two parts which in the first chord form a perfect fifth or perfect octave proceed by **contrary motion**, whenever possible.

We shall see this best by examining some examples.

806. I. At (a) fig. 147 the common chord on the *dominant* is followed by the common chord on the *submediant*. At (b) the common chord on the *submediant* is followed by the common chord on the dominant. In neither case have the successive chords notes in common.

Fig. 147. (a)   (b)

(a) In the first chord *bass and tenor* (G, D) form a *perfect fifth*; they proceed by contrary motion.
Similarly *bass* and *alto* (G, G) form a *perfect octave* and proceed by contrary motion.
(b) *Bass* and *alto* form a *perfect fifth*; *bass* and *treble* are a *perfect octave*. Both move by contrary motion.

807. II. The *dominant* common chord is rarely followed by that on the *subdominant*, but the succession *subdominant, dominant* is very common.

Fig. 148.
(a)   (b)   (c) Bad.   (d) Bad.

(a) Common chord on *subdominant* followed by common chord on *dominant*; the parts of the first chord forming *perfect fifth* and *octave* move in contrary motion.

(b) The same succession of chords, but now the first chord has the *fifth* doubled.

808. N.B.—Notice that when, as at (b), the subdominant common chord with doubled fifth is followed by the dominant common chord, the *latter has the root three times and no fifth*. For the *tenor* (C) cannot go to B, as that would be doubling the leading-note and would give consecutive octaves with the treble, as at (c), § 298 (a), and to take it to D would produce *consecutive fifths* (d).

MELODIC PROGRESSION

309. We have already seen that chords should move to and from each other with as little *leaping* as possible. Each *part* or *voice* should be considered as a *melody*, and should follow the rules which regulate the construction of melody.

The chief points to be here remarked are:

310. I. No part should move by an **augmented interval**.[1]

For example, in proceeding from the common chord on the *subdominant* to that on the *dominant*, it would be bad to write as at (a) fig. 149, because the alto (F) moves upwards to B from the fourth to the seventh degree of a major scale, which is an *augmented* interval.

This would be corrected by writing as at (b) where the interval F to B *downwards* is a *diminished interval*.

Fig. 149.

311. II. If any part moves by a *diminished* interval the part should return at once to some note within that diminished interval.

The reason for this is that every *diminished* interval is dissonant and requires resolving (§ 271).

Fig. 150.

(a) F to B *downwards* is a diminished fifth proceeding to C, which lies between F and B.

(b) F to G♯ *downwards* is a diminished seventh proceeding to B.

---

[1] Some exceptions to this rule will be explained later (§ 430).

EXERCISES.

In the following exercises *carefully avoid* consecutive fifths and doubled leading-note.

Add two inner parts to the following, using only common chords. Remember § 288.

CHAPTER XXVI.

COMMON CHORDS IN MAJOR KEYS.

812. A **common chord** may be written upon every note of a major scale except the leading-note.

The chord on the leading-note has a diminished fifth and is called a *diminished triad* (p. 102, n. 2).

FIG. 151.   Common chords.   Diminished Triad.

Of these common chords three are *major*, and three *minor* (marked *). The common chord on the *mediant* is not much used (v. also § 643).

So far we have only required the student to add two inner parts. We shall now give exercises in which the melody has to be supplied as well as the inner parts. Before doing this we must explain some additional laws of progression which refer specially to the outer parts.

813. The two **outer** parts (*i.e.* the *treble* and *bass* in four-part harmony) are called the **extreme parts.** The middle parts (*i.e.* alto and tenor) are called the **inner parts.**

814. Hidden consecutives. The *extreme parts* may not proceed by *similar* motion to a **perfect fifth, perfect octave,** or **unison.**

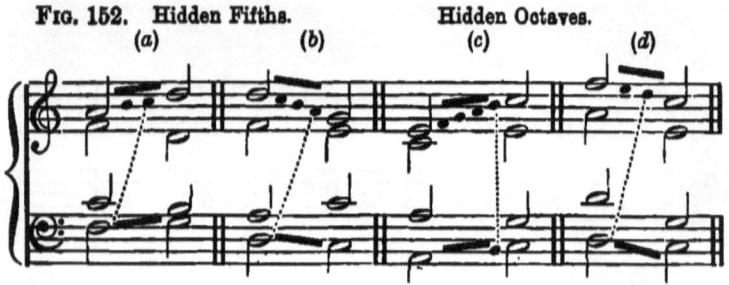

FIG. 152.   Hidden Fifths.   Hidden Octaves.
(a)   (b)   (c)   (d)

At (a) the treble goes to D, the bass to G by *similar motion*. The effect of this is almost as bad as if we filled in the small notes, thus making fifths between treble C, D, and bass F, G.

At (b) we have another example of the same thing.

At (c) and (d) we have octaves approached in the same way.

These faults are called **hidden consecutive fifths** or **octaves** because the absence of the intervening notes (shown above in small notes) *hides* the fifth from the eye although their ill effect is heard.

815. Hidden consecutives are bad *only* between the extreme parts.

816. There are several exceptions to the rule against *hidden consecutives*. For the present, the most important of these are the following:

There is no objection to *hidden consecutives* between the extreme parts when the chord on the **tonic** moves to the chord on the **dominant** or *vice versâ*, or when the **tonic** chord moves to the **subdominant** and *vice versâ, provided the upper part moves only by the step of a second.*

Fig. 153.

Allowable Hidden Consecutives.

Ton. Dom.　Dom. Ton.　Ton. Subdom.　Subdom. Ton.

Exercises.

In working the following, the student must avoid consecutive fifths, &c., between *any* parts, and in writing the treble see that the rules on *hidden consecutives* are followed.

Note.—The final chord usually has the root (tonic) in the treble, but it may have either *root*, *third*, or *fifth*.

Take special care with the distribution of the first chord in a F. B. exercise. If one distribution does not work well begin again, trying another. Try to make the treble part as melodious as possible.

Add three upper parts to the following basses, using common chords:

(1)

INVERSION OF COMMON CHORDS 119

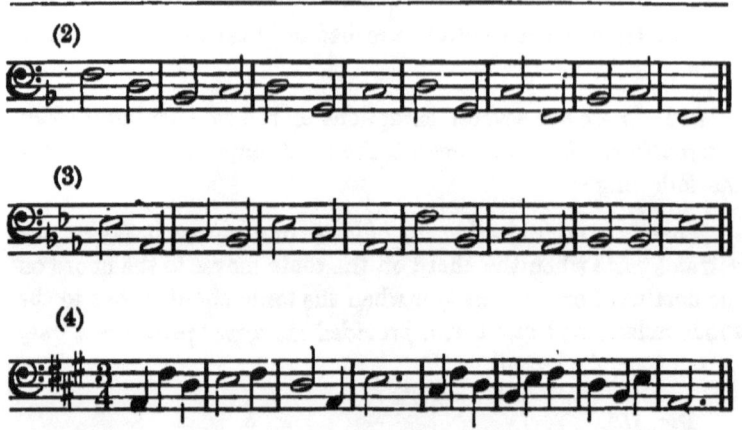

₊ *Before passing to the next chapter it would be well to study §§ 669-87 on harmonising melodies, and to do the exercises set in Section I.*

CHAPTER XXVII.

FIRST INVERSIONS IN MAJOR KEYS.

317. The note from which a chord is built up by adding *thirds* is called the root of the chord.

So long as the *root* is in the bass, the other notes of a chord may be altered in position without altering the nature of the chord. Thus (*a*), (*b*), (*c*) in fig. 154 have each a different distribution of the parts, but they are all the same chord because the *root* remains in the bass.

FIG. 154.

318. When a chord has in the bass any other note than its root the chord is said to be **inverted**.

FIG. 155.

(a) is the common chord with the *root* in the bass.

(b) is the same chord, but now the root is in the upper part, and the *third* of the original chord is in the *bass*. This is called the **first inversion** of (a).

(c) is the same chord again, but now the *fifth* of the original chord is in the *bass*. This is called the **second inversion** of (a).

319. The **first inversion** of a common chord has the *third* of the original chord in the bass ; the *root*, being inverted, is now the sixth note from the bass, and the *fifth* is a third from the bass. A first inversion, therefore, consists of a bass-note with the **third** and **sixth** above it.

FIG. 156.

320. Carefully distinguish between *root* and *bass*. The root is the note from which a chord is built up by adding thirds ; the bass-note is the note which happens to be lowest, *e.g.* in (b) fig. 156, E is the bass-note, but it is *not* the root.

N.B.—In dealing with inversions of chords it is best to *think of each note in relation to the chord from which the inversion came*, *e.g.* fig. 156 (b) C is the root ; G is the fifth, E is the third.

321. **Figured Bass.** In writing exercises on basses it is necessary to indicate what chords are to be used. This is done by figures placed (usually) under the bass, and a bass with such figures is called a **Figured Bass**.

The figures indicate the *interval* of each note of a chord *from the bass-note*.

322. Since the notes of a *common chord* are the root with its third and fifth, the figuring[1] for a common chord is $\frac{5}{3}$; but, as a rule, no figures are used with common chords, it being understood that a bass-note without figures has a common chord (§ 363).

---

[1] It is not usual to indicate the doubled note of a chord in the figuring, though this is sometimes done for some special reason ; the figuring for a common chord with the root doubled is then $\frac{8}{5}$.

823. The figuring for a *first inversion* is $^6_3$ or 6, for very frequently the 3 is omitted from the figuring, and thus the figure 6 implies a third as well. On this account a first inversion is often called a **chord of the sixth.**

824. Sometimes a first inversion is followed by a common chord on the same bass-note. The figuring for the common chord cannot then be omitted, the figuring for the two chords being 6 5.

FIG. 157.

825. In figured bass the figures are almost always arranged with the highest uppermost. But it must be distinctly understood that the figures do not (as a rule) indicate the *arrangement* of the chord, but merely its constituent notes. Thus the following are all figured 6.

FIG. 158.

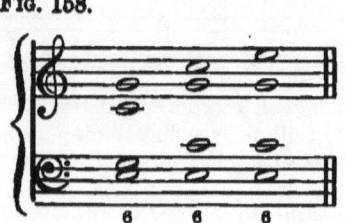

826. All the common chords of the major key and the diminished triad on the leading-note (§ 812) can be used in their *first inversion*. There is, therefore, a **chord of the sixth** on every degree of the *major scale*.

FIG. 159.

The chord marked * is the diminished triad.

827. Doubling. The rules for doubling in a *common chord* apply equally to a *first inversion*. The best note to double is the *root* (*a*); the next best is the *fifth* (*i.e.* the third of the first inversion) (*b*).

When the bass-note is the *minor* third from the root it is often advisable to double it (*c*).

828. When the *bass* of a *first inversion* is the **major third** from the root it **must not be doubled** unless the two parts having the doubled note move to it and from it by the step of a second and in *contrary* or *oblique* motion (*d*).

Fig. 160.

When there is a succession of *chords of the sixth* on a bass moving *stepwise* special care must be taken to avoid consecutives.

829. The first point to be attended to is the position of the *fifth* (*i.e.* the third from the bass). If the *fifth* is placed in the highest part it will be a fifth above the inverted root, and if we have a succession of chords similarly arranged it is clear that we shall get a series of *consecutive fifths* (*a*).

830. This can be avoided by keeping the *root* in the *upper* part (*b*). For then the interval from fifth to root is a fourth, and there is no objection to *consecutive fourths* if they occur between *upper* parts (§ 442).

Fig. 161.

331. In actual composition such a series of first inversions on basses moving stepwise is usually written in three parts. If they are written in four parts another precaution is necessary which may be expressed as follows:—

332. When a succession of *first inversions* on a bass moving stepwise is written in *four* parts, the **same note of the chord must not be doubled in two successive chords.**

The best plan is to double the *root* and *third* alternately, though sometimes the *fifth* must be doubled. Of course the *leading-note* must *not* be doubled.

Fig. 162.

333. **Note on Hidden Consecutives (§ 314).** When a chord moves from a first inversion to the root position of the same chord, there is no ill effect of hidden consecutives.

Exercises.

1. Add two inner parts.

(1)

2. Add three upper parts to the following:

CHAPTER XXVIII.

SECOND INVERSIONS OF COMMON CHORDS IN MAJOR KEYS.

334. The **second inversion** of a common chord has the *fifth* in the bass; the *root* is then a *fourth* above the bass, and the *third* is a *sixth* above the bass. The chord is therefore **figured** $_4^6$, and it is often called the *chord of the six-four*, or the *six-four*.

335. The student should play this chord, the $_4^6$, on the piano, when he will notice that it has an unfinished effect, as if it required to be followed by some other chord. This is because the root is now a fourth above the bass, and the *interval of a fourth from the bass always has a dissonant effect* (v. § 442).

SECOND INVERSIONS IN MAJOR KEYS

FIG. 163.

336. Doubling. In a 6-4 chord the fifth (i.e. *bass-note*) is by far the best note to double, though either of the others *may* be doubled.

337. The *only*[1] common chords which can be used in the *second inversion* are those on the *tonic*, *dominant*, and *subdominant*.

FIG. 164.

338. Second inversions, then, can only occur on (*a*) the dominant, (*b*) on the supertonic, (*c*) on the tonic.

339. The *second inversion* most used is that on the *dominant*. It[2] often occurs before a *perfect cadence*, as in the following example:

FIG. 165.

---

[1] Examples will be found in the great composers of second inversions of all the common chords, but second inversions require such delicate handling that the student is strongly urged to confine his attention to those mentioned in the text.

[2] This is often called a *cadential six-four*.

340. In the same way the *second inversion* on the *tonic* is often used before the common chord on the tonic.

FIG. 166.

341. Owing to the dissonant nature of the root in a six-four chord it is subject to very stringent rules as regards the way in which the bass moves to it and from it. Although the student will not require these rules until he has to harmonise melodies, it will be well to give them here to complete the subject.

342. I. Rules for approaching a 6-4 chord.

(1) A six-four chord may be preceded by a chord on the same bass-note (fig. 166), or by a chord on some other bass-note (fig. 165).

(2) When the chord before the six-four is a *first inversion* the bass-note must proceed by step, *i.e.* must *not* leap.

(3) When the chord before a 6-4 is in its *root* position the bass may either leap or proceed by step.

FIG. 167.
(a) Bad. (b) Good. (c) Good. (d) Good.

At (a) the chord before the 6-4 is a *first inversion* and therefore the bass must not leap.

At (b) we again have a first inversion, but the bass proceeds by step.

At (c) the bass leaps, but it is from a chord in its root position.

343. This rule, of course, does not apply to a six-four preceded by a first inversion of the same chord.

FIG. 168. Good.

344. II. **Rule for leaving a 6-4 chord.**

A 6-4 chord must be followed by a chord—either (*a*) on the *same* bass-note, or (*b*) on the *next* bass-note above or below it.

FIG. 169.

345. III. **Rules for the 6-4 with regard to accent.**

(1) When a 6-4 chord is *followed* by a chord on the *same* bass-note, the 6-4 must occur on the accented part of the bar, unless it is also *preceded* by a chord on the same bass-note as in fig. 166.

FIG. 170.

When a 6-4 is followed by a common chord on the *same* bass-note it is necessary to add figures after the 6-4 to indicate the common chord, as in the second bar above. This also shows the sequence of the parts; the sixth goes to the fifth, the fourth goes to the third, the other parts remaining stationary.

(2) If a 6-4 is followed by a chord on another bass-note, the 6-4 may occur either on the accented or unaccented beat.

FIG. 171.

346. In one case, and in one case only, can there be two six-fours in succession, viz. the six-fours on the supertonic and tonic.

In using these another law of part-writing is necessary: No part may move in consecutive fourths[1] with the bass. Consecutive fourths *between upper parts* are unobjectionable.

FIG. 172.

347. Sometimes the bass of a common chord moves in *arpeggio* (§ 658), while the upper parts remain stationary. In these cases chords of the sixth and the six-four are produced. These may be figured in the ordinary way (*a*), or a long line may be drawn under the arpeggio bass (*b*); the line indicating that while the bass moves the upper parts remain, and the chord continues the same.

FIG. 173.

---

[1] There is *one* exception to this rule, v. § 442.

SECOND INVERSIONS IN MAJOR KEYS

EXERCISES.

Add two inner parts to the following:

(1)

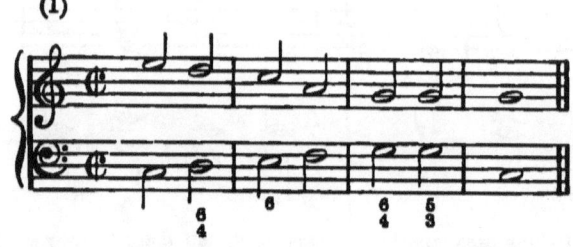

(2)

Add three upper parts to the following:

(3)

(4)

(5)

₊ *For melodies v. p. 258.*

CHAPTER XXIX.

COMMON CHORDS IN MINOR KEYS.

∗ *A not unwelcome variety may be brought into the work by taking chapters xxxi., xxxii. before the present chapter. The exercises of those chapters are arranged to allow of this.*

348. The chief forms of the minor[1] scale are the *Diatonic* or *Melodic*, and the *Harmonic*.

349. In the diatonic minor scale the intervals from the *tonic* to the *sixth* and *seventh* notes are *major* in ascending; *minor* in descending.

FIG. 174.

Diatonic Minor Scale.

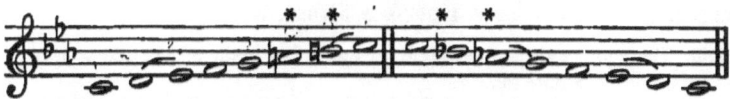

350. In the Harmonic minor scale the interval from the *tonic* to the *sixth* is *minor*; from the *tonic* to the *seventh* is *major*, both ascending and descending.

FIG. 175.

Harmonic Minor Scale.

351. In fig. 151 we have seen that the chords in the major key are built up out of the notes of the major scale.

352. The chords in a minor key are made up out of the notes of the harmonic minor scale.

For the present, then, the student must dismiss from consideration the *diatonic minor*, and keep in mind that the notes he is to use in minor keys are those of the *harmonic minor*.

---

[1] For fuller details see Pt. I., Chapter XI.

353. The *major sixth* can never[1] be used as part of a chord, and the *minor seventh* only in one case, to be explained in § 369. How these notes are used in music—not as parts of chords—will be explained later (§ 532).

354. Let us build **triads** out of the *harmonic minor scale*.

Fig. 176.

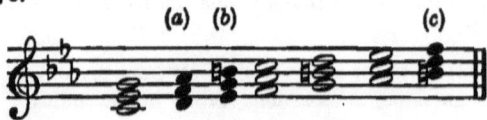

355. We see that the second, third, and seventh of these triads are *not common chords*, because it will be remembered that a common chord must have a perfect fifth (§ 278).

356. The chord on the supertonic (*a*) has a diminished fifth, and so has that on the leading-note (*c*).

The chord on the mediant (*b*) has an *augmented fifth* (§ 642).

357. There are, then (fig. 176), **only four common chords** in each minor key, viz. on the **tonic, subdominant, dominant, and submediant.**

358. Notice specially that in *minor keys* the dominant common chord is always major.

359. In using common chords in minor keys the rules observed in the case of common chords in the major must be followed, but two of these are so important that it will be best to repeat.

360. **No part may move by an augmented interval.**

Thus in going from the common chord on the submediant to that on the dominant, the parts must not be arranged as at (*a*) because A♭-B♮ is an augmented second. They must be rearranged as at (*b*), for C-B♮ is minor second.

Fig. 177.

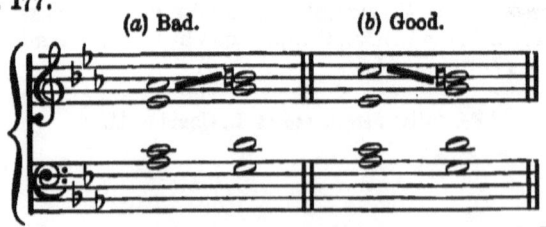

[1] This statement requires a slight qualification, but the beginner may rest satisfied with it for the present (§ 596).

361. In passing from the common chord of the *dominant* to the common chord of the *submediant*, or *vice versâ*, the dominant chord must be complete, and the **submediant chord must have its third doubled.**

Fig. 178.

362. Doubling. As in § 281, the notes to be doubled (in order of advisability) are:—root, fifth, minor third; the leading-note, of course, must never be doubled.

363. Figuring. We have seen that the common chord is not usually figured, but the third of the dominant common chord in the minor always has an accidental, and *accidentals must always be shown in the figuring*. This is done by placing the necessary accidental underneath the bass-note, and it must be remembered that an *accidental standing alone (without a figure) under a bass-note always refers to the* third *of the chord*.

Fig. 179.

364. Formerly there was among musicians a great aversion to ending a composition with a *minor chord*. To avoid this the *third* of the last chord of a piece in a minor key was sometimes omitted altogether, the chord consisting of the *root* and *fifth*, an example of which can be seen in the last

COMMON CHORDS IN MINOR KEYS

movement of Mozart's 'Requiem.' But more frequently the *third* of the last chord was made major, as in the following example from the prelude to Bach's Fugue in D *minor*.

Fig. 180.

365. When the third of the final chord in a minor key is made major, it is called the **Tierce de Picardie** or *Picardy Third*. It is frequently used in modern music, especially in church music, *e.g.* in the 'Inflammatus' of Dvořák's 'Stabat Mater' (pub. 1881).

366. It is interesting to note that all the preludes (12) and fugues (12), in minor keys in Vol. I. of Bach's 'Wohltemperites Klavier' (written in 1722), with one exception end with the Tierce de Picardie.

EXERCISES.

1. Write out the *harmonic minor* scale of A, D, E, F, and F♯.

2. Write *triads* on all the degrees of the scale of G minor, and indicate which of these are *common chords*.

3. Write in four parts all the *common chords* in F♯ minor and C♯ minor.

NOTE.—These chords are to be independent of each other and separated by double bars.

4. Write in four parts the *dominant* common chord correctly followed by the *submediant* common chord in E minor, D minor, and F♯ minor.

5. Write in four parts the *submediant* common chord correctly followed by the *dominant* common chord in A minor, F minor, and G minor.

6. Add two inner parts to the following:

Add three upper parts to the following :—

CHAPTER XXX.

INVERSIONS OF TRIADS IN MINOR KEYS.

867. First inversions. The four common chords in minor keys can be used in their first inversion. It was pointed out (§ 826) that a diminished triad can be used in its first inversion, so that we shall have first inversions of the triads on the second and seventh degrees of the minor scale.

For the inversion of the triad on the mediant *v.* § 642.

868. The following table will show the first inversions above described. The stave below shows the chords from which each first inversion is derived.

Fig. 181.

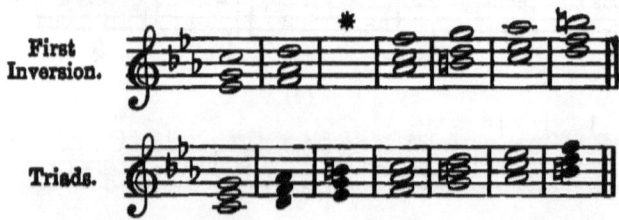

869. When the bass of a minor movement descends stepwise from the tonic to the minor sixth (as in the descending form of the diatonic minor scale), the seventh is made minor, and in this case, *and in this case only*, the minor seventh of the scale may be used as the bass of a first inversion, *v.* § 858.

Fig. 182.

870. **Second Inversions.** As in the major key, the only common chords to be used in the second inversion are those on the *tonic, dominant,* and *subdominant,* giving chords of the 6-4 on the dominant, supertonic, and tonic.

Fig. 183.

136   HARMONY

The rules for the treatment of second inversions in §§ 336-45 apply equally here, and the student will do well to recapitulate them.

371. **Figuring.** In the 6-4 (and the 6-3) on the supertonic in a minor key the sixth is the leading-note, and as this is always major (*i.e.* raised from its condition according to the signature) the figuring must always show an accidental. Sometimes instead of this accidental a stroke is drawn through the figure. Thus ♮ means the raised sixth, *i.e.* either ♮6 (if by the signature it is flat) or ♯6 (if by the signature it is natural).

FIG. 184.

371*a*. **The origin of the minor scale.** In the construction of the melodies of the Mediæval Church eight different scales—commonly called *modes* or Gregorian modes—were used. These *modes* or scales began on different degrees but they *only used the natural notes* without inflection, so that the semitones did not occur in the same place in each mode as they do in the modern scales.

Of these modes, the *Æolian* beginning on A, the *Dorian* beginning on D, and the *Phrygian* beginning on E bore a certain resemblance to our minor scale, because they had each a minor third; but they had no leading-note. As music developed, it began to be necessary to raise the seventh note of these modes to make a leading-note, and by degrees the three modes merged into the minor scale as we know it.

We have already explained (Pt. I., §§ 122-5) why the sixth note of the minor scale is sometimes raised in ascending and restored in descending.

EXERCISES.

Add two inner parts.

(1)

INVERSIONS OF TRIADS IN MINOR KEYS

Add three parts to the following:

. *For melodies v. p. 254.*

CHAPTER XXXI.

THE DOMINANT SEVENTH IN MAJOR KEYS.

372. By adding a *third* above any triad we get a *chord of the seventh.*

FIG. 185.

Of all the chords of the seventh, that on the *dominant* is the most important, and for the present we shall confine our attention to it.

373. The **dominant seventh is obtained by adding a third above the dominant triad. It consists of the dominant (the root) with the major third, perfect fifth, and minor seventh above it.**

NOTE that the major third is the *leading-note.*

FIG. 186.

Dominant 7th.

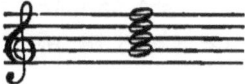

374. The dominant seventh introduces us to a series of chords differing very much from triads. All the notes of the triads yet dealt with are concordant (§ 271) to each other. But some of the notes forming the dominant seventh are dissonant to the others. Thus, from the root to the seventh is a dissonant interval. Again, from the third to the seventh is a *diminished fifth,* which also is dissonant.

A chord containing any dissonant interval is called a discord, and as explained in § 271, the notes forming the dissonance require resolution.

375. In the dominant seventh, the *seventh* and the *third* are dissonant, and in passing from a dominant seventh to a following chord the **seventh must fall a second**; the third (*i.e.* the leading-note) must **rise a second.**

FIG. 187.

876. Figuring. The full figuring for a dominant seventh would be $\frac{7}{5}$, but the figures 5 and 8 are usually omitted unless they are altered by an accidental. The usual figuring therefore is 7, and the figure 7 under a bass-note implies the third and fifth as well as the seventh.

877. Doubling. As the dominant seventh consists of four notes it can be used in four-part harmony without *doubling*.[1] Sometimes, however, the *fifth* is omitted, and then the *root* must be doubled. As *no dissonant note can be doubled* [2] the third and seventh must never be doubled.

878. Omission of notes from the dominant seventh. The third and seventh are the distinctive notes of the chord and cannot therefore be omitted; and the root, of course, cannot be dispensed with. The fifth, then, is the only note which can be omitted.

Before dealing specially with the resolutions of the dominant seventh we shall state an important rule which applies to the resolution of *all* discords.

879. In resolving a discord **no note may proceed by similar motion to the note** (*or its octave*) **on which the dissonant note resolves.**

Fig. 188.
Bad.

The dissonant note F resolves on E, and the bass moves by *similar motion* to the octave E. This has the worst possible effect of hidden consecutives (§ 814).

880. Resolution [3] **of the dominant seventh.** The dominant seventh may be followed by any chord which allows the dissonant notes—the seventh and third—to resolve properly.

---

[1] When the dominant seventh is used in harmony of more than four parts, either root or fifth may be doubled.

[2] Since a dissonance must always resolve, if a dissonant note is doubled both notes would have to be resolved alike, and we should get consecutive unisons, or octaves (§ 296).

[3] These resolutions should be played over on the piano and learnt, so that the student may be able to hear them *mentally* when seen on paper.

881. The commonest resolution of the dominant seventh is on the tonic triad. The *seventh* must fall a second; the *leading-note* must rise a second. The *root* rises a fourth (or falls a fifth), and the *fifth* may go to the root or third of the next chord.

FIG. 189.

382. When, as in this case, the dominant seventh is resolved on the tonic triad, one of the chords, if in four parts, *must* be incomplete.[1] If the dominant seventh is complete the tonic triad will omit the fifth. If the triad is complete the seventh must omit the fifth and double the root.

FIG. 190.
(a) Dom. 7th complete.   (b) Dom. 7th incomplete.

383. The tonic triad on which the dominant seventh resolves is often in the second inversion, in which case it is better to have the seventh incomplete (compare § 336).

FIG. 191.

---

[1] In harmony of five parts both chords can be complete.

THE DOMINANT SEVENTH IN MAJOR KEYS 141

884. Another common resolution of the dominant seventh is on the triad of the submediant.

As before, the seventh must fall, the leading-note must rise.

Fig. 192.

885. In this resolution care must be taken with the fifth of the dominant seventh. If it rises a second we get consec. fifths with the bass, and it must therefore fall to the third of the next chord.

If as at (c) the dom. seventh has the root doubled a greater danger is present—that of taking (as at d) the doubled root to the octave of the note on which the seventh resolves (§ 379).

886. We may, therefore, give the following rule:—**When the dominant seventh is followed by the triad on the** *submediant*, **the second chord must have its third doubled,** and it is best to have the dom. seventh complete, as at (a) and (b), rather than as at (c).

887. **Ornamental Resolution.** Before resolving, the seventh may proceed to another note (either root or fifth) of the chord, provided that it eventually proceeds to its proper resolution (a).

Or the seventh may be transferred to another part, where it must be resolved (b).

Fig. 193.

⁎ *Other resolutions of the dom. seventh will be found in §§ 485-7.*

L

142 HARMONY

888. The *dominant seventh* is of great importance in harmony, from the fact that it definitely determines the key, though not the mode. The chord (*a*) in fig. 194 may be in C or G or F major; but the chord (*b*) can only be in C major or minor (*v.* § 408).

FIG. 194.

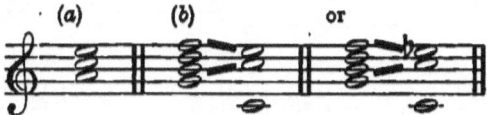

889. If we examine the *Harmonic Series* explained in Part I., § 155, we find that, besides the octaves of the root or generator, the earliest intervals formed by the harmonics are the *major third, perfect fifth, minor seventh.* Thus if we write out the first seven harmonics of G (*a*) and then use the last four of these we get the dominant seventh on G (*b*).

FIG. 195.

390. When a discord is formed by notes which are among the harmonics of the root of that discord, it is called a *fundamental discord* because it is founded on the harmonic series.

The *dominant seventh* is therefore a *fundamental discord*.

EXERCISES.

1. Write the dominant seventh in the following major keys, using correct key-signature :—G, D, A, F, B♭, E♭.

2. Correctly resolve each of the following dominant sevenths on the tonic triad :—

THE DOMINANT SEVENTH IN MAJOR KEYS

3. Resolve the dominant sevenths in (*a*) on the second inversion of the tonic triad; resolve those in (*b*) on the triad of the submediant.

4. Write the dominant seventh in E, D, A, A♭, D♭, and B major; and resolve each in three ways.

5. Write the dominant seventh *in* F major; write the dominant seventh *on* F.

6. Add three upper parts to the following :—

* This figuring means that the first chord of the bar (a minim) is a com. ch. with the root doubled; on the third beat this doubled root descends to the seventh, which with the third and fifth remaining forms a dom. seventh.

CHAPTER XXXII.

INVERSIONS OF THE DOMINANT SEVENTH.

891. As there are four notes in the dominant seventh, there will be three inversions.

FIG. 196.

(a) Dom. 7th in G major. (b) 1st inversion. (c) 2nd inversion. (d) 3rd inversion.

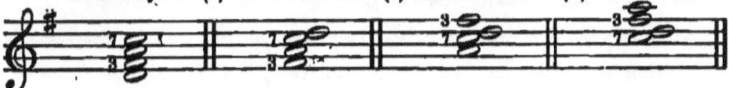

892. In dealing with these inversions it is necessary to bear in mind which were the dissonant notes (*i.e.* seventh and third) of the original chord, for they are treated in the inversions exactly as they were treated in the original chord, *i.e.* the seventh falls a second; the third rises a second. Thus in fig. 196 we have the dominant seventh in the key of G. The seventh is C; the third is F♯, and in all the inversions C the seventh must fall, and F♯ the third must rise.

893. **The first inversion has the leading-note in the bass.** The root being inverted is now a sixth from the bass, and the chord consists of the bass-note, with the *third, fifth,* and *sixth* above it (fig. 196 (b)).

394. The **Figuring**[1] in full would be $^6_5_3$, but the 3 is usually omitted from the figuring unless it requires an accidental.

895. **Resolution.** The 1st inversion or $^6_5$ usually resolves on the tonic triad. The *bass* (*i.e.* the leading-note) *must rise*; the *fifth* from the bass (*i.e.* the seventh of the original chord) *must fall* (fig. 197 (a) (b)).

FIG. 197.

(a)   (b)   (c)

$^6_5$ $^6_5$ $^6_5$ 6

396. If the $^6_5$ is followed by the submediant triad this latter chord must

---

[1] Remember that the figuring indicates the interval between each note of the chord and the *bass-note*.

INVERSIONS OF THE DOMINANT SEVENTH 145

be in its first inversion, for, as the bass of the $\frac{6}{5}$ is the leading-note, it must rise (c). This resolution of a $\frac{6}{5}$ is not very often used.

397. **The second inversion** of the dominant seventh has the supertonic in the bass. Both the root and the third are now inverted, and become respectively the fourth and sixth from the bass (fig. 196 (c)).

398. **Figuring.** It is figured $\overset{6}{\underset{3}{4}}$ or $\frac{4}{3}$.

Evidently the 3 cannot be omitted from the figuring, for then there would be nothing to distinguish this chord from the $\frac{6}{4}$ (§ 334). But the 6 is often omitted, and $\frac{4}{3}$ under a note means that the sixth as well as the fourth and third are to be added.

399. **Resolution.** The $\frac{4}{3}$ is usually resolved on the tonic triad in its root position. As in the original chord and in the $\frac{6}{5}$, the *seventh falls* a second, the *third rises* a second.

FIG. 198.

400. Sometimes the $\frac{4}{3}$ resolves on the first inversion of the tonic triad. In this case the bass rises to the third of the next chord, and the *seventh* may either *fall* as usual, or (to avoid doubling the major third of the next chord) it *may rise*.

This is the only case in which the seventh is allowed to rise.

FIG. 199.

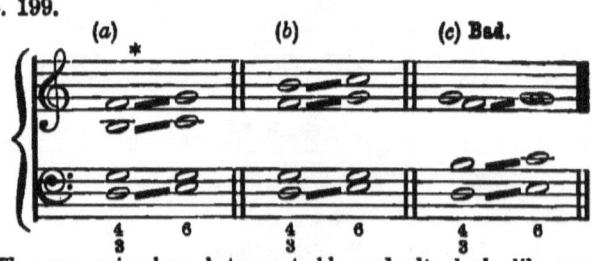

* The progression here between treble and alto looks like consecutive fifths, but this is allowable because one of these fifths is diminished, *v.* § 436.

401. In using the resolution described in § 400 the student must avoid a progression like that between alto and treble at (c). No two parts may go from a second to a unison.

FIG. 200.   Bad.

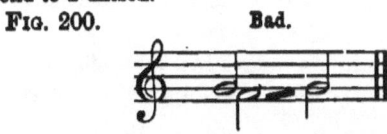

To avoid this, see that the *seventh* is above the root as at (a) and (b) (fig. 199).

402. The **third inversion** of the dominant seventh has the sub-dominant in the bass. The *root*, *third*, and *fifth* are now inverted, and become respectively the second, fourth, and sixth.

403. **Figuring.** This chord is figured $^6_4$ or $^4_2$.

404. **Resolution.** The $^4_2$ usually resolves on the first inversion of the tonic triad. The seventh (the bass-note) falls a second; the leading-note rises a second.

FIG. 201.

405. As in the case of the original chord (§ 387), the dissonant notes in the inversions of the dominant seventh may be resolved ornamentally (a).

Or the different inversions may follow each other, provided that the dissonant notes are finally resolved (b). But the last inversion must not be followed by the root position of the original chord, as the effect of the seventh rising is bad (c).

FIG. 202.

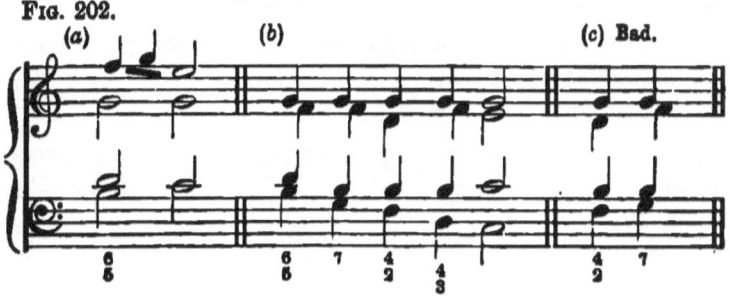

INVERSIONS OF THE DOMINANT SEVENTH

406. A horizontal line ──── placed under two or more bass-notes means that the chord belonging to the first bass-note is to be continued though the bass moves, and as a rule[1] the three upper parts remain stationary as at (*a*), (*b*), (*c*).

When as at (*c*) this line stands under a bass descending from *dominant* to *subdominant*, the **third inversion of a dominant seventh** is produced, and care must be taken to resolve this discord.

Horizontal lines used as at (*d*) mean that the notes indicated by the figures with lines are to be continued while the other part moves.

Fig. 202 *bis*.

Exercises.

1. Write the dominant seventh in the key of D major, and resolve it on the tonic triad; write each of the inversions of this chord, and resolve on the tonic triad, or on one of its inversions. Figure each chord.

2. Do the same in the following keys: D major, A major, A♭ major, E♭ major.

3. Write and correctly resolve the second inversion of the dominant seventh in E major and in F major.

4. Write on each of the following bass-notes the inversion of the dominant seventh which can occur on that note. Correctly resolve, and figure the bass (*v.* §§ 393–402).

---
[1] *See*, however, § 546.

5. Add three upper parts to the following:—

₊ *For melodies v. p. 255.*

CHAPTER XXXIII.

THE DOMINANT SEVENTH IN MINOR KEYS.

407. The **dominant seventh in minor keys**, just as in major keys, is formed by adding a third above the dominant common chord.

408. As the dominant common chord in minor keys always has the leading-note (*i.e.* the raised seventh) for its third, it is clear that the dominant seventh is exactly the same chord whether the key be major or minor.

FIG. 203.

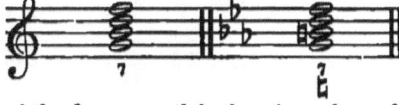

409. The 3rd of the dom. seventh in the minor always has an accidental, and this must be indicated in the figuring by placing the required accidental under the figure 7 (§ 363).

THE DOMINANT SEVENTH IN MINOR KEYS

410. The dominant seventh in minor keys is exactly like that in major keys, and it is subject to the same rules for doubling and resolving explained in §§ 375–84.

In resolving, the leading-note (the third) must rise a second; the seventh must fall a second.[1]

The two most usual resolutions are shown below :—

FIG. 204.

(a) Resolved on tonic com. chd. (b) Resolved on submediant com. chd.

411. The **inversions of the dominant seventh** in the minor are exactly like those in the major. They are shown below, with their figuring and resolutions.

412. Notice that, except when the leading-note is in the bass, the figuring will have an accidental. In the second inversion the leading-note is a sixth from the bass, and so the 6 must have the accidental, and of course it cannot then be omitted from the figuring. In the last inversion the leading-note is a fourth from the bass, and in the figuring the 4 has the accidental.

FIG. 205.

Dom. 7th.   1st inversion.   2nd inversion.   3rd inversion.

---

[1] In the *major* the seventh falls a semitone ; in the *minor* it falls a tone, in each case going to the third of the scale.

EXERCISES.

1. Write in four parts the dominant seventh and all its inversions with proper figuring in A, E, D, and G minor.

2. Write with proper figuring the dominant seventh or inversion which can occur on each of the following bass-notes, the key being *minor*:—

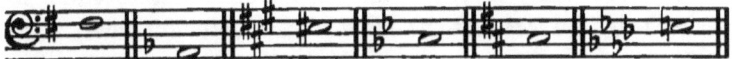

3. Figure the following chords and name the root (§ 276) of each :—

4. Add three upper parts to the following basses :—

* The 8 merely means that the bass is doubled. In proceeding to the next chord 8 goes to 7 ; 6 to 5, and 4 to 3.

CHAPTER XXXIV.

SECONDARY OR NON-DOMINANT SEVENTHS.

413. A *third* added above a triad gives us a chord of the seventh. All such chords except that on the *dominant* are called secondary (or *non-dominant*) sevenths.[1]

414. Secondary sevenths differ from dominant sevenths in their use by the fact that the *seventh* (the dissonant note) must be prepared.

415. Preparation of a dissonant note means the sounding of that note as a *consonant* note in the preceding chord. Preparation must occur in the same part or voice as the dissonance (*v.* § 492).

Fig. 206.

* Here C is the *dissonant* note, being the seventh from the root. It is prepared by being sounded (by the same voice) in the preceding chord as a *consonant* note.

416. Resolution.—Secondary sevenths are resolved on a chord the root of which is a *fourth* above the root of the seventh. The *seventh* falls a second; the *bass* rises a fourth.

417. As the *third* of a secondary seventh is not the leading-note it is free to rise or fall.

Fig. 207.

[1] Called also *diatonic sevenths* and *essential discords*. See explanation in § 547.

418. Any secondary seventh may be used provided there is no objection to the triad from which it is formed, and provided that the chord on which it would resolve is allowable.

The chords of the seventh on the *subdominant* and the *leading-note* are not used except in *sequences* (§ 464) on account of the nature of the triads, on the *leading-note* and *mediant* respectively, on which they would resolve (§ 312).

419. The secondary sevenths commonly used are :—

In major keys, those on the *tonic, supertonic, mediant*, and *submediant*. In minor keys, those on the *supertonic* and *mediant*.

The secondary seventh most used is that on the **supertonic**. It very often precedes a *perfect cadence*, as in fig. 207.

420. **Inversions of secondary sevenths.**—Like the dominant seventh, secondary sevenths have three inversions, but only the first and third are used.

421. The **first inversion** has the third in the bass. The seventh now becomes the fifth from the bass, and it must resolve as in the original chord, by descending a second. The *bass* (being the third of the original chord) now rises a second to the root of the resolution. It is figured $^6_5$.

FIG. 208.

422. The **third inversion** has the seventh in the bass. It resolves on the first inversion of a common chord, the bass (the seventh of the original chord) falling a second. It is figured $^4_2$ or $^6_4_2$.

SECONDARY OR NON-DOMINANT SEVENTHS

423. As this third inversion resolves on the first inversion of a com. ch. it can occur on any note of the scale which will allow of this resolution, viz. in the major on every note; in the minor on the *tonic, supertonic, mediant,* and *dominant.*

Fig. 209.

424. A **sequence** (§ 464) of chords of the seventh on roots rising a fourth or falling a fifth is of common occurrence.

When such a sequence is in four parts the chords will be alternately complete and incomplete to avoid consecutive fifths (compare § 382). In five parts all the chords will be complete.

Fig. 210.

Notes.—1. The third of each chord remains (*i.e.* is *prepared*) to be the seventh of the following chord.

2. At * the dominant seventh is prepared. This is not necessary, but it is always allowable.

Fig. 211 shows a sequence consisting of sevenths in the first inversion, followed by common chords.

Fig. 211.

425. Secondary sevenths may, like dominant sevenths, be resolved ornamentally (§ 387).

426. Secondary sevenths should be carefully distinguished from dominant sevenths. We pointed out that the dominant seventh consists of *root, major third, perfect fifth, and minor seventh*. This is never so in secondary sevenths; either *both third and seventh are minor*, as in the supertonic seventh; or *both are major*, as in the tonic seventh. Secondary sevenths do not decide the key, while dominant sevenths do (§ 388). Thus the following seventh may be either in the key of C (supertonic seventh), in F (submediant seventh), or in B♭ (mediant seventh).

FIG. 212.

427. NOTE.—In early attempts at writing, musicians confined themselves to concords. In time discords were introduced, but at first these were either passing-notes (§ 527) or prepared discords. In those days even the dominant seventh was always prepared. In the beginning of the seventeenth century an Italian musician, Claudio Monteverde, was bold enough to use the dominant seventh *without preparation* for the first time, and, though this was strongly opposed by conservative musicians, men's ears by degrees got accustomed to the unprepared discord in the case of the dominant seventh. In time the secondary sevenths came to be used without preparation, and now musicians do not hesitate to use any essential discord without preparation. But the student must remember that only he who knows how to prepare a discord is fit to use it unprepared, and therefore we strongly urge beginners to prepare all secondary sevenths until they are sufficiently advanced to exercise their own judgment. The same applies to resolutions. Many other forms of resolution than those in § 416 are used by the great masters, but this is much too wide a subject to be entered upon here.

EXERCISES.

1. Complete the following:—

SECONDARY OR NON-DOMINANT SEVENTHS

2. Add three upper parts.

(1)

(2)

(3) Hymn Tune.

(4)

(5) (§ 365)

* These chords are formed by adding a third above the mediant triad which in the minor has an *augmented fifth*. This interval is dissonant and must be prepared (as well as the seventh), and resolved by rising a second. This augmented triad on the mediant of minor keys (without the seventh) can be used in its root position and first inversion if the dissonant fifth is prepared and the chord resolved on the submediant common chord. Another way of looking at this chord is shown on p. 238 n.

CHAPTER XXXV.

RECAPITULATION OF THE LAWS OF PART-WRITING.

428. Melodic Progression. — Each part should proceed smoothly, with as little *leaping* as possible.

It is always best to move by step (*i.e.* in *conjunct movement*). When this is not possible it is better for the parts to leap by the smaller intervals (third and fourth). There is no objection to the leap of an eighth, but as a rule this is only possible in the bass or treble. The leap of a major seventh and intervals beyond the octave are absolutely forbidden (*v.* also § 711).

429. No part should proceed by an *augmented interval*.

Fig. 213.

430. Exceptions to this are allowed (*a*) when the notes forming the augmented interval form part of the same harmony (§ 553); (*b*) in a *sequence* (§ 464); (*c*) in the notes of the harmonic minor scale used as passing notes (§ 528).

431. If any part proceeds by a *diminished interval* the part should return at once to some note within that diminished interval.

Fig. 214.

432. The parts must not overlap or cross.

Fig. 215.

RECAPITULATION OF THE LAWS OF PART-WRITING 157

433. The **leading-note** must never be doubled (but see § 469). When it occurs in a perfect cadence it *must* rise to the tonic (*a*). When it is followed by a tonic chord (but not in a perfect cadence) it must rise, but not necessarily to the tonic (*b*). In all other cases it may rise or fall, but it should rise whenever possible (*c*).

FIG. 216.

HARMONIC PROGRESSION.

434. Consecutive fifths.—No two parts may *move* in *perfect fifths* with each other.

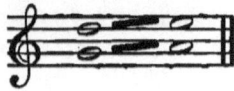

FIG. 217.

435. *Perfect fifths* in consecutive chords are not forbidden when they do not occur between the same parts (*a*); nor are the fifths objectionable between the same parts if both parts are stationary (*b*).

FIG. 218.

436. When one fifth is *diminished*, consecutive fifths are allowed between the inner parts, or between the upper and one of the inner parts. This is always most satisfactory when the perfect fifth comes first. Between the extreme parts consecutive fifths had better be avoided, even when one is diminished.

FIG. 219.

437. No two parts may move in octaves or in unison with each other (§ 296).

438. This rule does not apply when all the parts are singing or playing a whole passage in unison or in octaves. In the following example from Handel's *Hallelujah* chorus (twelfth bar) the whole band and chorus are singing and playing the same melody, and there is no harmony.

FIG. 220.

439. Nor does it apply when the same melody is played in two or more parts, as in the following example from Beethoven (P.F. Sonata IV.) where the melody is in octaves, the music being only in three parts.

FIG. 221.

RECAPITULATION OF THE LAWS OF PART-WRITING

440. Hidden consecutives.—The *extreme* parts may not proceed *by similar motion* to a **perfect fifth, perfect octave, or unison** (§ 814).

441. **Except** (*a*) when the *tonic* chord moves to the *dominant* chord or *vice versa*; or when the *tonic* chord moves to the *subdominant* chord or *vice versa*, provided in both cases that the upper part moves only by the step of a second (§ 316).

(*b*) When a chord moves from a first inversion to the root position of the same chord (§ 333).

442. No part may proceed in *fourths with the bass*, unless the second fourth is an augmented fourth. Consecutive perfect fourths between upper parts are unobjectionable (but see § 651).

Fig. 222.

443. No two parts may move in seconds or sevenths with each other.

Fig. 223.

444. No note may proceed by *similar motion* to the note (or its octave) on which a dissonant note resolves (§ 879).

Fig. 224. Bad.

445. False relation.—When a chord containing a *natural* note is followed by a chord containing the same note *sharpened* or *flattened* (or *vice versa*), the altered note must appear in the same part or voice. Non-observance of this rule produces *false relation* (fig. 225 a).

The bad effect is generally felt, even when the two chords in *false relation* are separated by an intervening chord (b).

446. When the altered note occurs in two parts (*i.e.* is doubled) in the first chord, it must be only altered in *one* part, or consecutive octaves will result.

Fig. 225.

(a) Bad.   Good.   (b) Bad.   (c) Good.

447. **Exceptions.** *False relation* is not produced when the third of the first chord is (a) the root or (b) the fifth of the second chord; (c) nor when the altered note forms part of a fundamental discord (§ 390).

Fig. 226.

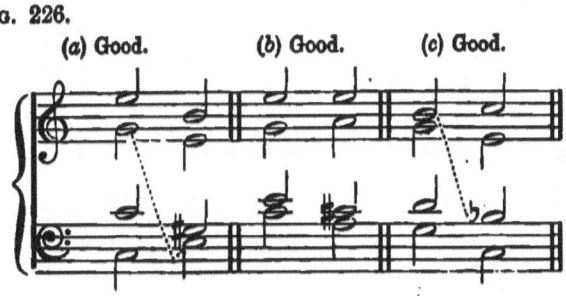

(a) Good.   (b) Good.   (c) Good.

448. Many examples of *false relation* which do not come under any of the above exceptions will be found in good composers. The question can only be decided by the good taste of the writer; but the student should strictly confine himself to the rules laid down above.

RECAPITULATION OF THE LAWS OF PART-WRITING

449. Passing notes and auxiliary notes (§ 527) do not produce false relation, and in this way the interval of a *diminished octave* is not infrequently used.

Fig. 227.

SCHUMANN, Eb Symphony.

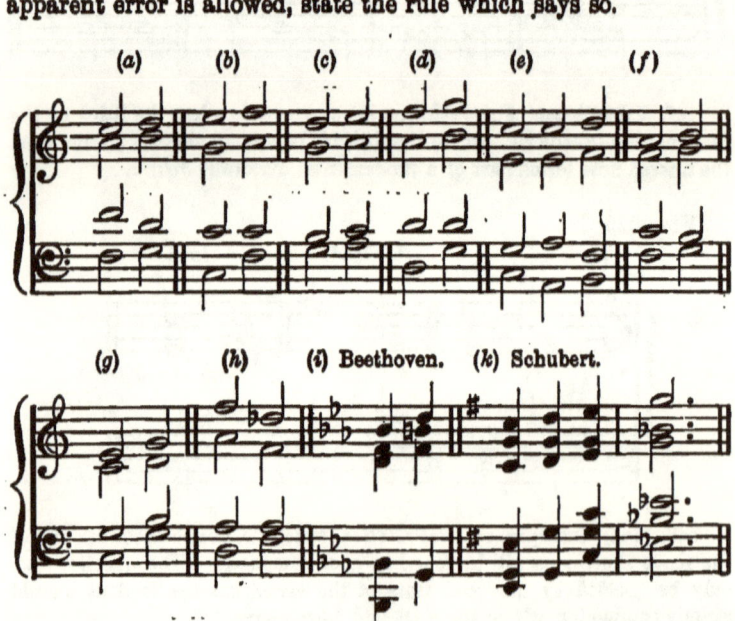

&c.

EXERCISES.

1. Point out the errors in the following. If in any case the apparent error is allowed, state the rule which says so.

(a) (b) (c) (d) (e) (f)

(g) (h) (i) Beethoven. (k) Schubert.

2. Point out the errors (if any) in the following, and correct them.

CHAPTER XXXVI.

CADENCES.

450. All good melodies are constructed on some definite plan. For example, the following consists of two exactly similar halves, each half being four bars in length.

Fig. 228.

451. We might call the whole eight bars a musical sentence and each part a phrase. Thus the melody in fig. 228 consists of two *phrases* of four bars each. It must not be imagined that all melodies consist of two phrases or that all phrases are four bars long. What we wish to point out is that melodies can be divided into phrases which are related to each other. This division of music into phrases &c. constitutes *rhythm*, and as that will be fully dealt with in Part III. it may be left for the present.

452. Each phrase into which a melody is divided ends with an appropriate cadence, and we may now proceed to the study of cadences.

CADENCES

453. A **cadence** or *close* means the ending of a melody or musical phrase. The chief cadences are **Perfect, Plagal, Imperfect,** and **Interrupted.**

454. A **perfect cadence** or **full close** consists of the *dominant common chord*[1] followed by the *tonic common chord*, both chords being in their root position.

FIG. 229.

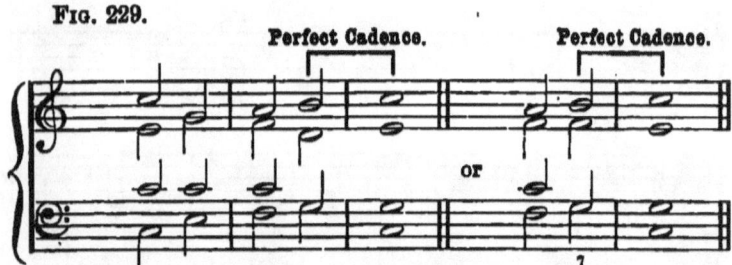

455. The perfect cadence is used at the end of a composition, or at the end of an important section. In most cases it is arranged (as in fig. 229) so that the *tonic chord* occurs on the first beat of the bar, the *dominant* chord being on the last beat of the previous bar. There are, however, many exceptions to this.

456. The **plagal cadence** consists of the *tonic common chord* preceded by the *subdominant common chord*.

457. In modern music the *plagal cadence* is only (as a rule) used at the end of a composition and *after* a perfect cadence. A very good example is seen at the end of the *Hallelujah* chorus in Handel's 'Messiah.' It has a restful and even solemn effect, and on this account it is much used in church music. The *Amen* at the end of hymn tunes is usually this cadence.

FIG. 230.

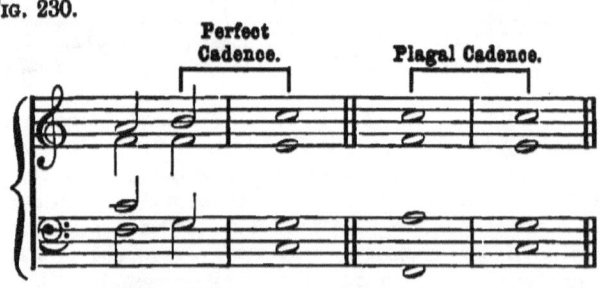

---

[1] Instead of the dominant common chord we often have the dominant seventh.

458. The term *perfect cadence* is applied both to the perfect and plagal cadences. To distinguish between the two, the perfect cadence consisting of *dominant* and *tonic* chords is called **authentic**; the cadence consisting of *subdominant* and *tonic* is called **plagal**.

459. The **imperfect cadence** or *half-close* ends on the *dominant common chord*. The chord before the dominant may be any suitable chord, but most frequently it is the *tonic common chord*.

FIG. 231.

460. When the *dominant chord* in a cadence is followed, *not* by the tonic chord, but by some other chord, we have an **interrupted cadence**.

The commonest *interrupted cadence* is the *dominant chord*, followed by the *submediant common chord* in its root position.

FIG. 232.

461. The *imperfect* and *interrupted* cadences cannot be used at the end of a composition or even at the end of an important section, for if we play figs. 231-2, we shall see that these cadences do not suggest the end of a complete musical idea. They rather indicate a sort of short pause before the completion of the idea. We saw in § 451 that a melody can be divided into *phrases*, each phrase having its own cadence. The *perfect cadence* is used for the end of a melody, *i.e.* for the last cadence; the *imperfect* and *interrupted* cadences are used for the cadences in the middle of a melody (*v.* § 694).

Fig. 233.

Example of middle cadence (*imperfect*).

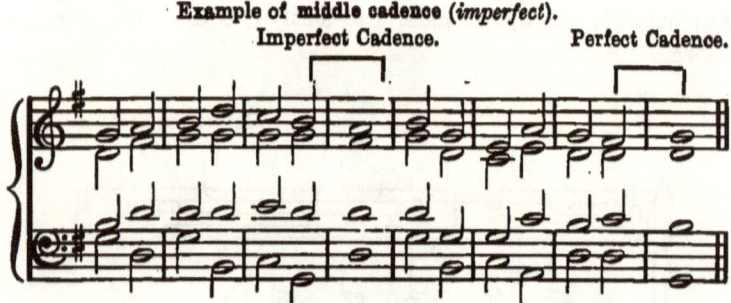

Fig. 234.

Example of middle cadence (*interrupted*).

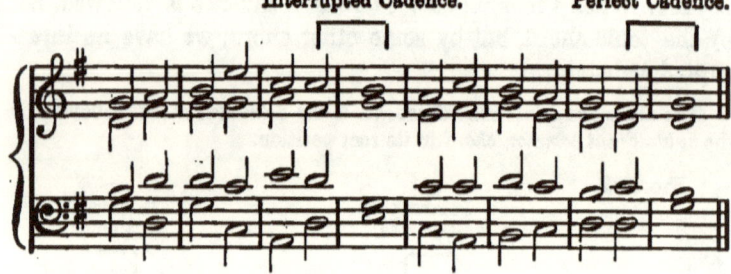

462. From the way in which cadences are used to mark off the divisions of a melody or musical sentence, they are sometimes compared to the punctuation marks used in writing. Thus the *perfect* cadence is compared to a full-stop; the *interrupted* and *imperfect* cadences resemble in their use the comma and the semicolon.

463. If either of the chords used in a perfect cadence is in its inverted form, the cadence is called an *inverted cadence*. An inverted cadence can only occur as a middle cadence.

CHAPTER XXXVII.

SEQUENCES.

464. A sequence is the repetition of a progression of melody or harmony on other notes of the scale. In every repetition each part moves by the same degree as in the original pattern progression, and the repeated *groups* follow each other at regular intervals of pitch.

Fig. 235.

&c.

In fig. 235 we have a *sequence* consisting of two chords repeated three times. In each repetition the *treble* descends a second; the *alto* repeats a note; the *tenor* descends a second; the *bass* descends a fourth. Further, each note in the second group is a third below the corresponding note in the first group, and so on for each succeeding group.

A *sequence* may consist of the repetition of two or more notes or chords. The repetitions may be either on higher or lower notes of the scale.

465. When all the notes in a sequence are according to the key in which it is written, it is called a **tonal sequence**,[1] as in fig. 235.

In a *tonal sequence* the intervals in each repetition are like the original in name but not always in *quality*. Thus (fig. 235) in the pattern both chords are *major*, but in the first repetition both are *minor*, while in the next both are major.

466. When every repetition is exactly like the original pattern in quality as well as in name, we have a **real sequence**. In a real sequence the key changes at each repetition.

---

[1] Sometimes called a *diatonic* sequence.

Fig. 236.

In fig. 236 every chord throughout is *major* as in the pattern. This is a *real sequence*.

A *real* sequence is much rarer than a *tonal*.

467. When a given *bass* or *melody* progresses sequentially the added parts should be also arranged in sequence.

468. Frequently the following out of a *sequence* will necessitate the breaking of some of the laws of progression. This is allowed, the interest of the sequence justifying what, taken by itself, would be objectionable.

It must be distinctly understood that these exceptions are only allowed in one of the repetitions of a sequence, and must on no account occur in the original progression.

469. The chief points *exceptionally* allowed in *sequences* are:
(1) The *leading-note* may be doubled (§ 433).
(2) The *leap* by an *augmented interval* in any part (§ 429).
(3) The use of the diminished triad and triad on the mediant (§ 312).

Fig. 237.

In fig. 237 at (a) the *leading-note* is *doubled*. In the last repetition the bass leaps an augmented fourth (F–B). The last chord is the *diminished triad*.

470. In sequences *second inversions* of common chords must never be used. The student will see the reason for this rule in § 888.

EXERCISES.

1. How should you describe the following passages? What irregularity is there at *, and what do you suppose is the probable reason of it?

2. Why are second inversions of common chords forbidden in sequences?

3. Complete the following:—

Add three upper parts to the following:—

SEQUENCES   169

CHAPTER XXXVIII.
MODULATION.

471. Few pieces of music, however short, remain in the same key throughout. The changing from one key to another is called **modulation**.[1]

Modulation is simplest when the key into which we modulate is related to the old one, and it will now be necessary to see what keys are related to each other.

472. Two keys are said to be **related** when they contain all, or nearly all, the same notes (§ 127).

Thus the scales of C and G major have all their notes alike except one, F♯. Similarly the scales of C and F have all their notes alike except B♭. We say then that C is related to G and to F.

Again, we have shown (§ 128) that every major scale has a *relative minor* which begins on a note a minor third below the old tonic. Then C *major* is related to A *minor*; G *major* to E *minor*; F *major* to D *minor*. And as C is related to G major and F major, C must be related through these to E minor and D minor. We may show this in a table thus:

C major is related to

F major		G major
D minor	A minor	E minor

473. The **related**[2] **keys to a major key**[3] are the *major keys* of the *dominant* and *subdominant*, and the *minor keys* of the *supertonic*, *mediant*, and *submediant*.

---

[1] Sometimes called *transition*, though some writers only apply this term to modulation to unrelated keys (§ 476).

[2] Called also *attendant* keys and *auxiliary* keys.

[3] If we write a triad on each note of a major scale except the leading-note, we have the *tonic chord* of all the keys related to that scale. Thus in C: D minor, E minor, F major, G major, A minor.

474. Proceeding as in § 472 we shall see that the **related keys to a minor key** are: the *relative major*, the *minor keys* of the *dominant* and *subdominant* with their *relative majors*. Thus:—

C minor is related to

F minor	E♭ major	G minor
A♭ major		B♭ major

475. It is worth remembering that related keys are those having the same key-signature or one sharp or flat more or less.

476. Modulation to a related key is called **natural modulation**.

Modulation to an unrelated key is called **extraneous modulation** (§ 666).

When the modulation is brought about by enharmonically changing one or more notes, it is called **enharmonic modulation** (§ 566).

NATURAL MODULATION.

477. Modulation to a related key is brought about by introducing a chord containing a note characteristic of the new key. This chord is usually a **dominant chord** (especially the dominant common chord and the dominant seventh **of the new key**). This new dominant should always be followed by other chords to establish the new key.

478. When the modulating chord is introduced immediately after a chord which is characteristic of the old key, the modulation is said to be **sudden**.

479. When the modulating chord is preceded by chords which belong equally to the old and new keys, the modulation is said to be **gradual**.

FIG. 238.

The modulating chord is marked *. At (a) the preceding chord could here only be in C, since the F is natural; at (b) the three chords preceding the modulating chord could be in C or G.

480. Such chords, which may be either in the key we are leaving or in that to which we are modulating, are called **ambiguous chords**.

481. Unless some special effect is intended, gradual modulation is always to be preferred.

482. The most frequent modulation for a piece beginning in a **major key** is to the *dominant*; for one beginning in a **minor key** to the *relative major*.

EXAMPLES OF MODULATION TO RELATED KEYS.

FIG. 239.

483. In modulating from a major key to the minor of the supertonic as in the last example, it is always best to introduce the minor sixth of the new key (in this case Bb) before the chord containing the leading-note.

484. We have noticed that the dominant seventh is exactly the same in tonic major and minor (§ 410). A modulation from *tonic major* to *tonic minor* by means of the dominant seventh is very common. An example will be found in Beethoven's P. F. Sonata, No. 16, beginning at bar 99.

485. As the **dominant seventh** is so much used in modulation it will be well to give some further examples of its resolution. In §§ 881-4 we have shown the usual resolutions, to which must be added the following:

486. The third resolves by *rising* a second,[1] *falling* a chromatic semitone, or *remaining* to be a note of the next chord.

487. The **seventh** may *fall* a second, *rise* a chromatic semitone, or *remain* to be a note of the next chord.

The other notes (*root* and *fifth*) of this chord are free in their progression (§ 380) provided they break no law of part-writing.

FIG. 240.

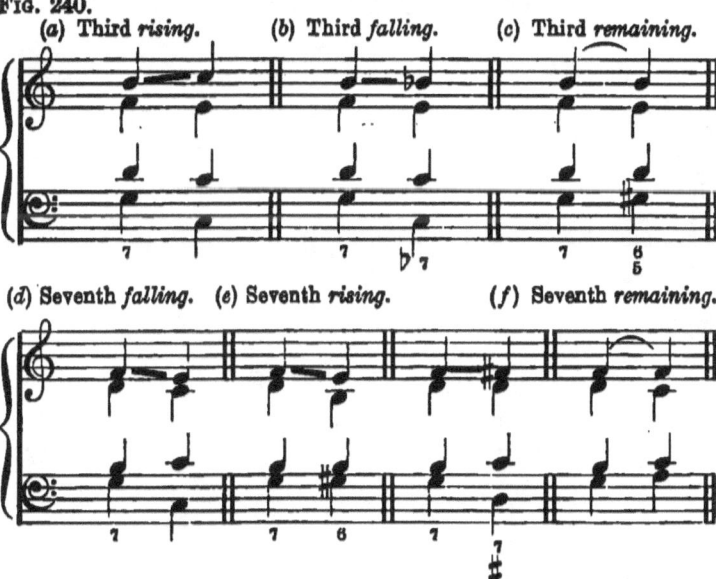

(a) Third *rising*. (b) Third *falling*. (c) Third *remaining*.

(d) Seventh *falling*. (e) Seventh *rising*. (f) Seventh *remaining*.

488. In each case where the dominant seventh is resolved exceptionally it leaves us on a chord the resolution of which will produce modulation, *e.g.* in fig. 240 (b) goes to F, (c) to A minor, &c.

---

[1] Examples of its rising a major second will be found in § 607.

MODULATION

EXERCISES.

NOTE.—The chord which produces the modulation *belongs to the new key*, and when this chord is a discord its constituent notes, in resolving, must be considered with reference to that new key.

I. Add two inner parts to the following:

(1)

Add three upper parts to the following:

(2) Hymn Tune.

CHAPTER XXXIX.
SUSPENSIONS.

489. If we compare (*a*) and (*b*), fig. 241, we see that they are exactly alike but for one thing: in (*a*) the treble D goes directly to C in the next chord; in (*b*) the treble D, instead of going at once to C when the chord changes, is held over, proceeding later to C. This note (D) is said to be **suspended**, and it is called a **suspension**.

FIG. 241.

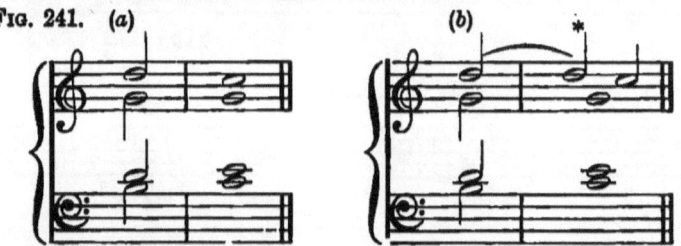

490. When a note of one chord is held over the next chord, of which it forms no part, it is called a **suspension**.

491. Since a suspended note is no part of the chord over which it is held, it is evidently *dissonant*. We have already had discords where the dissonant note is a part of the chord in which it occurs. Suspensions are called *unessential discords* because they are no part of the chord in which they occur.

492. A **suspension** must go through three processes:

    (*a*) It must be **prepared**, *i.e.* sounded as a part of a chord.

    (*b*) It must be **suspended**, *i.e.* held over another chord of which it is no part.

    (*c*) It must be **resolved** by proceeding to one of the notes of the chord over which it is suspended.

FIG. 242.

At (*a*) D is part of the chord; this is the *preparation*.
At (*b*) D is *not* part of the chord; it is simply *held over* or *suspended*.
At (*c*) the D proceeds to C, which is part of the chord; this is the *resolution*.

493. In resolving a suspension **the suspended note must move by step of a second** to a note of the chord on which it resolves.

Most suspensions resolve by *falling* a second, but in some cases they *rise* a second (§ 516).

494. As a matter of principle any note may be suspended provided that it can be resolved by moving a second, but the following are the chief suspensions used. The ninth; the fourth; the fifth on the third and seventh degrees of the major or minor scale, and the leading-note resolving on the octave with the tonic common chord.

SECTION I.—**The suspended ninth.**

495. In this case the note above the octave of the bass of a common chord is suspended, and then resolved on the octave.

Thus D is the note next above the octave of the root C (*i.e.* the ninth from that root), and it resolves on the eighth.

FIG. 243.

496. It is important to notice that after the suspended ninth is resolved we have an ordinary common chord. The suspended ninth, then, is merely a common chord with the note above the octave suspended and resolved, and this common chord, *together with the suspended note*, can be used in its inversions just like any other common chord.

The suspended ninth can be taken in the bass, and so we have three inversions which are shown in fig. 244.

THE SUSPENDED NINTH AND ITS INVERSIONS.
FIG. 244.

(*a*) Root position. (*b*) 1st inver. (*c*) 2nd inver. (*d*) 3rd inver.

SUSPENSIONS

497. It will readily be seen that in each of the above cases the bar containing the suspension has exactly the same common chord but in different inversions. In each case the same note (D) is suspended, and in each case it is resolved on the same note C, the root of the chord.

498. **Figuring.**—As in all other cases, we must count from the bass-note. The root position is figured 9 8.

In the **first inversion** the suspended note is now a seventh from the bass, and it resolves on the sixth; it is figured, therefore, 7 6, *i.e.* it is a chord of the sixth, with the sixth held over by a seventh.

In the **second inversion** the suspended note is a fifth from the bass, and it resolves on the fourth. It is figured $\begin{smallmatrix}6\\5\end{smallmatrix}\begin{smallmatrix}-\\4\end{smallmatrix}$, *i.e.* it is a $\begin{smallmatrix}6\\4\end{smallmatrix}$ with the fourth held over by a fifth.

In the **third inversion** the suspended note is in the bass, and as it resolves on the root the other notes of the common chord will be the second and fourth above the suspension. It is figured $\begin{smallmatrix}4\\2\end{smallmatrix}\begin{smallmatrix}-\\-\end{smallmatrix}$, or if the root is present in the upper part $\begin{smallmatrix}7\\4\\2\end{smallmatrix}\begin{smallmatrix}-\\-\\-\end{smallmatrix}$.

499. NOTE.—Where a suspension occurs in the bass it is sometimes indicated by an oblique line /. This sign means that the bass is to be accompanied by the notes of the chord belonging to the following note.

FIG. 245.

GENERAL RULES FOR SUSPENSIONS.

For examples see fig. 244.

500. (*a*) The suspension must be prepared in the same voice as that in which it is suspended.

(*b*) Suspensions must occur on the accented part of the bar.

(*c*) The note *preparing*[1] the suspension should not be shorter than the *suspended* note.

---
[1] This rule is often disregarded when the suspended note is sounded again instead of being tied.

(d) No part may move by *similar motion* to the note (or its octave) on which the suspension resolves (§ 879).

(e) No suspension is allowed in any progression which, if the suspension were absent, would produce forbidden consecutives.

FIG. 246.

It is clear then that suspended ninths cannot be prepared by eighths, nor sixths by fifths.

(f) The note (or its octave) on which a suspension resolves *must not be sounded at the same time as the suspended note*, except the ninth with the root in the bass (fig. 244 (a)).

Another exception is the ninth with the root in an upper part, *provided that the root is approached by step of a second*, and is at least an octave from the resolution of the suspension (fig. 247). This should, however, be used with great discrimination (see also § 513).

FIG. 247.

(g) It follows from (f) that a second cannot resolve on a unison.

501. The suspended ninth in major keys.

The **root position** can occur on any note that bears a common chord (§ 312).

The **first inversion** can occur on every note, because every note has a first inversion (§ 326).

The **second inversion** can only occur on those notes of the scale which have second inversions, viz. *dominant, tonic,* and *supertonic* (§ 338).

The **third inversion**, as it resolves on a common chord, can be taken on any note when the note below (*i.e.* that on which it resolves) bears a common chord.

SUSPENSIONS

502. The suspended ninth in minor keys.

There are fewer common chords in minor keys, and the augmented interval between the sixth and seventh notes interferes in some cases with resolution. The result is fewer suspensions can be used.

The **root position** can only occur on *tonic, dominant,* and *subdominant*.

The **first inversion** can occur on every note except the *tonic*.

The **second inversion** only on *dominant, tonic,* and *supertonic*.

The **third inversion** only on *supertonic, submediant,* and *dominant, i.e.* on the notes above those bearing common chords.

503. Caution.—There is a certain resemblance between the figuring of suspensions and of the chords of the seventh described in chapters xxxi.-xxxiv., but the student will easily avoid confounding these if he bears in mind the resolutions. Thus 7 6 shows that the seventh is resolved on the sixth of the same bass, and this is never the case with the sevenths referred to. Again, $^4_2$ $^-_-$ suggests the last inversion of chords of the seventh (§ 402), but that inversion resolves on a $^6_3$, and, therefore, it is plain that $^4_2$ $^-_-$ is a suspension.

504. In adding parts to a figured bass with suspensions, it must be remembered that when the suspension is resolved we have a common chord or one of its inversions. Thus the suspension must be accompanied by the notes belonging to the chord of resolution as shown by the second figure, thus 9 8 is accompanied by 5 and 3; 7 6 by 3 because the 6 means $^6_3$, &c. Remember, too, that while 7 alone means a chord of the seventh and implies $^7_5_3$, 7 6 means a $^6_3$ and *must not* be accompanied by the fifth.

505. Suspensions may occur in any voice, but in working exercises it is often most convenient to place them in the treble.

506. A suspension must resolve on the chord over which it is suspended, but when a 9 8 is resolved, the bass may at the same time move to the position of a first inversion as at (*a*) fig. 248. In any suspension *any* part may move to another note of the chord when the suspension resolves (*b*), or even to the note or the octave of the note on which it resolves, *provided in this latter case that it moves in contrary direction to the resolution* (*c*).

Fig. 248. (a)   (b)   (c)

EXERCISES ON THE SUSPENDED NINTH.

1. Fill in the following examples of suspensions according to the figuring:

(a)   (b)   (c)   (d)

2. Write before each of the following suspensions a chord which will suitably prepare the suspension:

(a)   (b)   (c)   (d) Minor

3. Write all the inversions of the following suspension, properly preparing the dissonant note in each case:

4. Write with suitable preparation the following suspensions in the key of D minor:—(*a*) the suspended ninth on the subdominant; (*b*) the first inversion[1] of the suspended ninth on the tonic; (*c*) the second inversion of the suspended ninth on the dominant; (*d*) the last inversion of the suspended ninth on the tonic.

5. Write three upper parts to the following F. B.:

* Suspension in the *alto*.

* The leading-note in suspension is allowed to descend.

Section II. The Suspended Fourth.

507. The **suspended fourth** resolves by falling to the third.

Fig. 249.

---
[1] The simplest way of doing these is to first write the *root position*, and then from that get the inversion required.

508. When the fourth falls to its resolution we have a common chord. The suspension is then merely a common chord with the *fourth* held over and then resolved.

As in the case of the suspended ninth, this common chord, together with the suspended note, can be inverted, as shown below.

THE SUSPENDED FOURTH AND ITS INVERSIONS.

FIG. 250.

(a) Root position. (b) 1st inversion. (c) 2nd inversion. (d) 3rd invers.

In each of these cases the suspended note (F) is the same, and the chords formed after resolution are simply the different inversions of the same common chord.

509. The **suspended fourth** in its root position is **figured** 4 3 or sometimes $^5_4$ $^-_3$, where the 5 merely means the fifth of the common chord.

510. The **first inversion** of the 4 3 has the third in the bass, and since the fourth resolves on the third the suspended note must be a ninth above the bass-note. As it is a *first inversion* its figuring would be 6, but the ninth is suspended and resolved on the eighth, and so the **figuring is** $^9_6$ $^8_-$ (fig. 250 (b)).

This suspension can be used with any first inversion except the first inversion of the dominant common chord, *i.e.* on the leading-note, because that would necessitate doubling the leading-note.

This inversion is another exception to the rule given in 500 (f), and in using it two points must be kept in mind:—

(a) The ninth cannot be approached by similar motion.

(b) The bass should be approached by step of a second.

SUSPENSIONS

511. The **second inversion** of the 4 3 has the fifth in the bass, and can only be used on those notes of the scale which can have second inversions. It is figured $^7_4\,^6_-$ and when the resolution is complete we get a $^6_4$ (fig. 250 (c)).

512. The **third inversion** of the 4 3 has the fourth in the bass, resolving on the third. The resulting chord is a chord of the sixth, and so this inversion can be used on the note above any note bearing a chord of the sixth. The figuring is $^6_2\,^-_-$ (fig. 250 (d)).

513. In the third inversion the third *can* be sounded in an upper part, but the student is advised not to avail himself of this exception to § 500 (f). If it is used care must be taken to follow the rules in § 500 (f) (g). This form with the figuring is shown below.

Fig. 251.

$^4_2$ $^7_6_2$ $^-_-$

In working exercises on the 4 3 all the rules of suspensions (§§ 492-500) must, of course, be followed.

514. The suspended fourth in major keys.

The root position occurs on any note bearing a common chord.
The first inversion on every note of the scale except the leading-note.
The second inversion on tonic, dominant, and supertonic.
The third inversion on every note.

515. The suspended fourth in minor keys.

The root position on tonic, dominant, and submediant.
The first inversion on the first, second, third, fourth, and fifth degrees.
The second inversion on the supertonic and dominant.
The third inversion on the first, second, third, fourth, and fifth degrees.

EXERCISES.

1. Fill up the examples of suspensions in the key of A minor.

2. Write out each of the following suspensions with suitable preparation; then write (properly prepared) all the inversions of (b) that are available.

3. Write out with suitable preparation the following suspensions in A major :—(a) The suspended fourth on the dominant. (b) First inversion of the suspended fourth on the supertonic. (c) The second inversion of the suspended fourth on the tonic. (d) Last inversion of suspended fourth on the supertonic.

4. Fill in the following :—

5. Show by an example why the suspension 4 3 cannot be taken on the fourth degree of the minor scale.

Section III. The 5 6, &c.

516. The *fifth* from the *third* and the *seventh* of major and minor keys may be suspended and resolved by *rising a second* to the *sixth* of the same bass-note.

In each case the chord resulting from the resolution is a first inversion, and the figuring is 5 6.

Fig. 252.

517. The **leading-note** may be suspended over the common chord of the tonic, resolving by *rising a second* to the octave of the root. The figuring is 7 8.

Fig. 253.

518. Suspensions which resolve by **rising** are called **retardations** by some authorities, but see § 545 in this connection.

519. Ornamental resolution. Like the dominant seventh (§ 387) any suspension may, before resolving, leap or go by step of a second to any note of the same chord, provided that it returns to its proper resolution before the chord changes.

Fig. 254.

520. *Passing notes* and *auxiliary notes* may be used in ornamental resolutions (§§ 528, 539).

Fig. 255.

521. Double and triple suspensions. The ninth and fourth may be suspended together, either in the root position of the chord or in any of the inversions.

In all *double* or *triple suspensions* the treatment of each suspended note is just the same as if each suspension occurred separately.

THE SUSPENDED NINTH AND FOURTH.

Fig. 256.
Root position. 1st inversion. 2nd inversion. Last inversion.
(a) (b)

522. Note. There are two forms of the last inversion, (a) when the ninth is in the bass, (b) when the fourth is in the bass.

523. The fifth on the mediant may be suspended together with the first inversion of a fourth and ninth of the tonic (a).

The fifth on the leading-note may be suspended together with the first inversion of a suspended ninth (b).

Fig. 257.

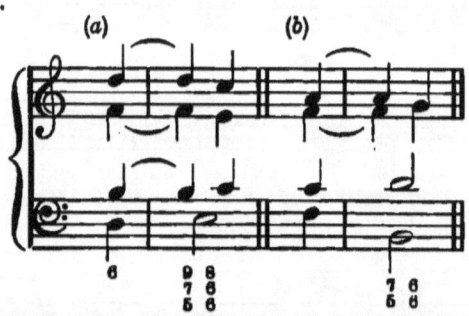

524. The suspension of chords.—The whole of a chord may be suspended over the following bass-note if the *root* of the second chord is a fourth above (or a fifth below) the *root* of the first. In resolving the suspended chord each dissonant note must move by step.

525. The figuring is shown by a line from the first to the second bass-note, and if the second chord is in its first inversion a 6 is added at the end of the line.

Fig. 258.

526. Suspensions with the dominant seventh.—The *third* of the dominant seventh is very frequently delayed by a suspended fourth (*a*); when the dominant seventh resolves on the tonic chord, the resolution of the seventh is frequently delayed as a suspended fourth.

Fig. 259.

EXERCISES.

1. Add three upper parts to the following:

At the places marked * modulations occur, and as long as the modulation lasts the notes must all be considered in relation to the new key.

2. Figure the following extracts from Mozart: (a) and (c) are in three parts. For the note * v. §§ 520, 541.

CHAPTER XL.

PASSING NOTES, AUXILIARY NOTES, ANTICIPATIONS, RETARDATIONS.

527. So far we have only used notes which are parts of chords or, as we may call them, *harmony notes*. For the sake of variety and embellishment notes which are not parts of chords are used, and we now proceed to explain them.

528. Passing notes[1] are notes used between harmony notes; they are used *to pass* from one harmony note to another.

Fig. 260 (*a*) shows a passage containing only *harmony notes*; (*b*) shows the same passage with *passing notes* added (printed in small type); (*c*) shows passing notes in several parts at the same time.

FIG. 260.

529. Rules for passing notes. Passing notes may be *diatonic* —in which case they will be according to the key in which the passage is written—or *chromatic*.

---

[1] Sometimes called *discords by transition*.

PASSING NOTES, AUXILIARY NOTES, ETC.

530. They may occur either on the unaccented or on the accented part of a beat, and, with the exception stated in § 548, they must always be quitted by step of a second.

In fig. 260 (b) are seen unaccented passing notes; fig. 261 shows accented passing notes.

FIG. 261.

531. When there are two passing notes in succession, the second may not return to the first, but must proceed in the same direction until a harmony note is reached.

FIG. 262.   Not

532. **Passing notes in minor keys.**—The melodic form of the minor scale (§ 849) is used to avoid the augmented interval between the sixth and seventh degrees of the harmonic minor.

Thus in passing from the *dominant* upwards to the *leading-note*, or *vice versa*, the major sixth is used; in passing from the *tonic* downwards to the *submediant* the minor seventh is used.

FIG. 263.
(a)   (b)

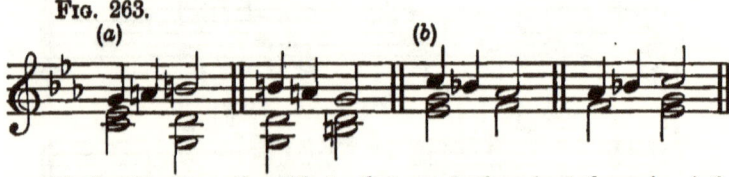

533. In *rising* from the fifth to the root in the minor, the major sixth and seventh are used; in *falling* from the root to the fifth, the minor sixth and seventh are used.

FIG. 264.   (a)   (b)

584. Chromatic passing notes may be used. When a chromatic passing note has been introduced, the passage must be continued in semitones until a harmony note is reached.

In writing chromatic passing notes the *arbitrary* form of the chromatic scale is usually employed (Part I. § 176).

FIG. 265.

535. Passing notes occurring in several parts at the same time must make satisfactory combinations or else must move by contrary motion, fig. 260 (c).

536. Passing notes do not justify an incorrect harmonic progression. Thus at (a) there are consecutive octaves just as much as at (b).

FIG. 266.

537. Care must be taken that the passing notes used do not produce consecutives. (a) *without* passing notes is correct, (b) *with* passing notes is incorrect.

FIG. 267.

538. It is better not to let passing notes proceed by oblique motion to the *unison*; oblique motion to the octave is unobjectionable.

FIG. 268.

PASSING NOTES, AUXILIARY NOTES, ETC. 193

539. Auxiliary[1] **notes** are notes a second above or below harmony notes. When the auxiliary note is *above* the harmony note, it will be either a tone or a semitone above, according to the diatonic scale of the music. When the auxiliary note is *below*, it must be a semitone below, except when the harmony note is the major third of a chord, in which case the auxiliary note may be either a tone or a semitone.

FIG. 269.

540. If, however, the fifth and third of a chord have auxiliary notes below at the same time, then the auxiliary note of the third *must* be a semitone below.

FIG. 270.

541. With the exceptions stated in § 548, auxiliary notes *must* be quitted by step of a second. They may be approached either by step (fig. 269) or by leap (fig. 271 (*a*)), and the leap may be by an augmented interval (§ 430). They may occur either on the accented or unaccented part of the beat (fig. 271 (*b*)).

FIG. 271.

---

[1] By some writers auxiliary notes and passing notes are classed together as passing notes. The difference between them is that passing notes *pass* from one harmony note to another, while auxiliary notes *return* again to the harmony note from which they started, as in fig. 269; or else merely stand before a harmony note, having no connection with the preceding harmony note, as in fig. 271.

542. The *shake, turn, appoggiatura,* and *acciaccatura* are examples of the use of auxiliary notes.

543. Changing notes. There is an important exception[1] to the rule that *passing notes* and *auxiliary notes* must be quitted by step. A passing note or an auxiliary note, instead of proceeding or returning to the harmony note, may *leap* a third to the note on the other side of such harmony note, provided that it returns at once to the harmony note.

Passing notes and auxiliary notes used in this way are called **changing notes** (marked *).

FIG. 272.
(a) Passing changing notes.   (b) Auxiliary changing notes.

544. Anticipations. One note of a chord may be sounded before the others, *i.e.* during a preceding chord to which it does not belong. Such a note is then *anticipated*, and it is called an **anticipation** (a).

Passing notes, as well as harmony notes, may be anticipated (b).

FIG. 273.

At (a) C is sounded during the dominant seventh on G. It clearly belongs to the next chord.

---

[1] There is another exception of common occurrence. When the harmony notes move by step of a second, the first harmony note may go to an auxiliary note in the opposite direction and then leap a third to the next harmony note. An example is seen on the fourth quaver of bar 2 in Exercise 1 (b), page 196.

545. Retardations. A note of a chord may be delayed by the holding on of a note from the preceding chord. Such delayed notes are called **retardations.** A *retardation* differs from a suspension by the fact that it may be quitted by leap.

Fig. 274.   Beethoven, Op. 13.
(*a*) Without *retardations.*   (*b*) With *retardations.*

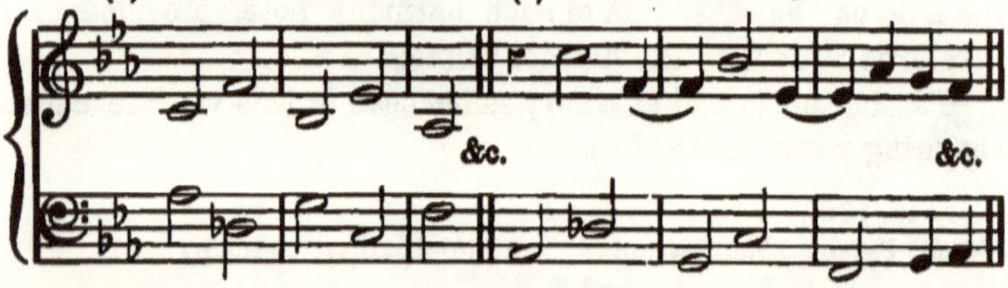

546. Figuring. *Passing notes,* &c., are not as a rule indicated in the figuring except in slow time. When passing notes, &c., occur in the bass, a straight line is drawn to indicate this, and in adding parts to such a bass the chord indicated at the beginning of the line is to be used and continued to the end of the line. Fig. 275 (*b*) (*c*).

Thus, in adding parts to a bass with changing notes, we sustain the chord indicated at the beginning of the line, fig. 275 (*a*), or we may add passing notes (*b*), or additional changing notes in some of the parts (*c*).

Fig. 275.

547. Recapitulation of the various kinds of discords:

(*a*) When the notes of a discord form part of the harmonic series of the root, the discord is called **fundamental** (§ 390).

(*b*) When the notes of a discord, not being fundamental, are made up out of the diatonic notes of the scale, it is called a **diatonic discord.** Such are non-dominant sevenths and ninths (§§ 414, 574). As the dissonant note in a diatonic discord is an *essential* part of the chord, diatonic discords are often called **essential discords** to distinguish them from the next kind (*c*).

(*c*) When the dissonant note is no part of the chord in which it occurs, but is foreign to it, it is called an **unessential discord.** Such discords are *suspensions, passing notes, auxiliary notes,* &c.

HARMONY

EXERCISES.

1. In the following examples explain all the notes which are not harmony notes and figure the bass.

(a) Mozart.

(b) Handel.

(c) Beethoven.

(d) Gounod (v. §§ 532–3).

2. In Question 1 (a) why are the first and second F's sharp, while the third is natural? (§§ 529, 589).

PASSING NOTES, AUXILIARY NOTES, ETC.

8. Point out any errors in the use of passing notes in the following:—

4. Add passing notes to the following:—

Passing notes in the *bass* in bars 3, 5, 6; *tenor*, bars 2 and 7; *alto*, bars 2, 4, 5; *treble* in all except bars 2 and 8.

5. Add three upper parts to the following, introducing passing and auxiliary notes in any parts where possible:—

CHAPTER XLI.

CHORDS OF THE NINTH.

SECTION I. The dominant ninth.

548. By adding another *third* above the notes of the dominant seventh we get the chord of the *dominant ninth*. The ninth may be either *major* or *minor*, and so we get two varieties of the chord: (a) the *dominant minor ninth*, and (b) the *dominant major ninth*.

FIG. 276.

549. The dominant ninth is a **fundamental discord** (§ 390), and the ninth is dissonant and requires resolution. Of the other notes of the chord, the seventh and third follow the rules already explained in treating of the dominant seventh.

550. In *major* keys both the *major* and *minor* dominant ninth can be used; in minor keys only that with the *minor* ninth is available.

551. As this chord consists of five notes, one of them must be omitted in four-part music. When the chord is in its root position **the fifth is omitted** (a).

In five-part music the fifth will be required. When the *fifth* is below the ninth it must rise when resolving, or consecutive fifths will result (b).

FIG. 277.

552. The **major ninth** must not be sounded *below* the *third* [1] because of the harsh effect. There is no objection to the *minor* ninth being below the third.

553. **Resolutions.** (*a*) The dominant ninth may resolve while the rest of the chord remains. In this case the ninth may proceed to the *root* or to the *third*.

It should be noted that the chord resulting from this resolution is a dominant seventh which still requires resolution.

Fig. 278.

(*a*) Dominant ninth resolving on root.   (*b*) Resolving on the third.

554. In these resolutions it must be remembered that (except the ninth with the root in the bass) **the note on which a dissonant note resolves may not be sounded at the same time with that dissonant note** (§ 500 (*f*)). When, therefore, the ninth resolves on the third, the third must not be present in the chord, and the fifth must take its place (fig. 278 (*b*)).

Note that at (*b*), fig. 278, A♭–B upwards is an augmented interval, but this progression is here allowable by § 430.

555. (*b*) The dominant ninth may resolve on the *tonic common chord*. The ninth falls a second, and the seventh and third follow the rules already explained.

---

[1] There is one important exception to this which the student may take note of, though we advise him to abstain from using it until considerable experience has cultivated his judgment. This is when the ninth descends at once to the root, the major third remaining.

At (c) an example is given in five parts to remind the student of the progression of the fifth (§ 551).

Fig. 279.

556. Figuring.—The dominant ninth is figured either 9 or $\frac{9}{7}$. When the minor ninth is used in major keys, a flat or a natural will be required in the figuring—*e.g.* $\flat\frac{9}{7}$ or $\natural\frac{9}{7}$.

Exercises on Section I.

1. Write in four parts the *dominant minor ninth* resolving on the third of the chord in the keys of A major, F major, E♭ major, G minor, D minor, and C♯ minor.

2. Write in four parts the *dominant major ninth* resolving on the tonic chord in A♭ major, D♭ major, and B major.

3. Add two inner parts to the following :—

4. Add three upper parts to the following :—
(1)

SECTION II. Inversions of the dominant ninth.

557. In the inversions of the dominant ninth the same notes are dissonant as in the original chord, and they are subject to the same rules of resolution. The root of a dominant ninth cannot be sounded in an upper part, and consequently *the root is omitted from all the inversions*,[1] but the *fifth* is always present.

558. Inversions of the dominant minor ninth. As there are four notes besides the root there are four inversions, all of which are available. They are shown in fig. 280 with their figuring.

FIG. 280.

(*a*) Root pos. (*b*) First inv. (*c*) Second inv. (*d*) Third inv. (*e*) Fourth inv.

559. Throughout these inversions the same note (A♭) is the original ninth, and throughout it will be resolved as in the original chord (§§ 553-5). Similarly in each case F is the seventh and B the third, and these notes are throughout subject to the rules of §§ 375. It will then be necessary only to show the resolution of one inversion, for the student will find no difficulty in understanding the others. The resolution on the third will not be shown for reasons stated below.[1]

FIG. 281.

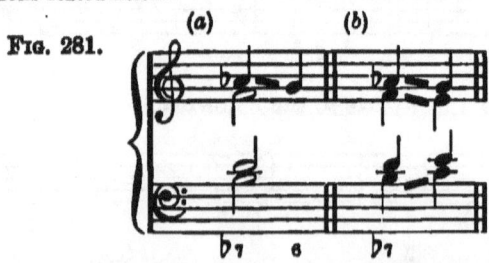

---

[1] There is an exception to this when the ninth resolves on the third. We have seen already that in that case the third cannot be used in the chord, and in this form the chord consists of root, fifth, seventh, and ninth, both in the root position and in all the inversions. These inversions, however, are rarely used.

560. The first inversion of the dominant minor ninth contains the interval of a diminished seventh (B♮-A♭). This chord is often called the chord of the diminished seventh, and it is so important in harmony that we shall devote Section III. of this chapter to the study of it, §§ 566-573.

561. **Inversions of the dominant major ninth.** We have already said that the major ninth must not be sounded below the third, and it is, therefore, clear that *the last inversion with the major ninth in the bass cannot be used.* The available inversions are shown in fig. 282, and after what has been said in § 559 it will not be necessary to show the resolutions.

FIG. 282.
(a) Root pos. (b) First inv. (c) Second inv. (d) Third inv.

Remember that in the case of the dominant major ninth the ninth *must* not be below the third (*v.* § 552).

562. The first inversion of the dominant major ninth is often called the chord of the leading seventh.

563. The figuring (fig. 282) of the inversions of the *dominant ninth* is identical with that of the *dominant seventh* and its inversions; but the student will not be likely to confuse the two if he keeps in mind the roots of the chords he is dealing with.

564. In finding the root of *fundamental discords* remember that the order in which the intervals occur, reckoning from the root, is **major third, perfect fifth, minor seventh, minor or major ninth** (§ 624).

565. **To find the root of a fundamental discord:** (a) arrange the chord so that the constituent notes stand a *third* above each other; (b) examine the intervals from the lowest note, and if the lowest interval is not a major third, then that lowest note is not the root; (c) add thirds below the lowest note until the order of intervals is major third, &c., as in § 564.

Thus in fig. 283, to find the root of chord (a), arrange in thirds as at (b). We now see that the lowest interval, G♯-B, is a *minor third*; G♯ is therefore not the root. Add a third *below* (*i.e.* E). The intervals now are

E–G$\sharp$, a *major third*; E–B, a *perfect fifth*; E–D, a *minor seventh*; E–F, a *minor ninth*. This is the order stated in § 564, and E is the root of the chord (a).

FIG. 283.

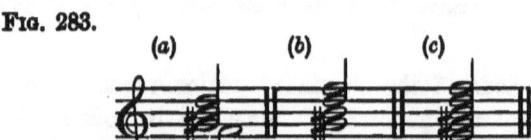

EXERCISES ON SECTION II.

1. Figure the following chords, and name their roots.

2. Write all the available inversions of the *dominant major ninth* in B♭ and E major, resolving each on the tonic common chord (or one of its inversions). Do the same for the *dominant minor ninth* in F and C$\sharp$ minor.

3. Add two inner parts to the following :—

4. Add three upper parts :—

SECTION III. **The diminished seventh; enharmonic modulation.**

566. The chord of the **diminished seventh** is the first inversion of the *dominant minor ninth*, and it occurs on the leading note of either major or minor keys. This chord is made up of three successive *minor thirds* ranged one above the other. This interval of a *minor third* is very convenient for enharmonic [1] changes; and as the diminished seventh consists of notes separated by this interval, we find this chord much used with enharmonic change.

---

[1] When two notes with different names have the same sound (*i.e.* are played by the same key on instruments like the piano), they are said to be enharmonic to each other. Thus C♯ and D♭ are enharmonic, because on a piano they both have the same sound. If C♯ occurs in a chord and D♭ in the following chord (*i.e.* D♭ written instead of C♯ a second time), it would be called an enharmonic change (*v.* Pt. I. §§ 163-173).

CHORDS OF THE NINTH

567. As an example we will take the diminished seventh on E♮ and make the enharmonic change in one note at a time, beginning with the highest note.

Fig. 284.

Roots.

I. The root of this chord is evidently C.

II. Here we change the highest note enharmonically by writing C♯ for D♭. The chord still sounds exactly as it did in I., but we have changed the harmonic origin; for if we rearrange this chord as explained in § 565, we shall find that its root is A.

III. is obtained from II. by enharmonically changing the second note from the top (A♯ for B♭). Following § 565 the root is now F♯.

IV. is obtained from III. by enharmonically changing the next (*i.e.* the third) from the top (F× for G♮). By § 565 the root is now D♯.

568. NOTE.—The chord IV. is most conveniently got by taking the original diminished seventh and enharmonically altering the *lowest* note (F♭ for E♮), when its root will be E♭. Notice that the two forms of IV. are identical in sound.

569. The following facts may assist the student in remembering the above changes:—

(*a*) The changes are made from the highest note downwards.

(*b*) The chords obtained by the changes are in the following order: 7; $\overset{6}{5}$; $\overset{6}{\underset{3}{4}}$; $\overset{6}{\underset{2}{4}}$; *i.e.* respectively the first, second, third, and fourth inversions of a dominant minor ninth.

(*c*) *When the changes are made in this order* the root of each chord is a minor third below the root of the previous chord (*e.g.* C, A, F♯, D♯).

570. We must now see to what use these changes are put. The chord I. evidently belongs to F major or minor, for it is derived from the dominant ninth (root C) of those keys. But the chord II. is derived from the root A, *i.e.* from the chord on the dominant of D major or minor. Now, suppose the chord I.

P

occurs in a piece in F major or minor, if it were regularly resolved we should continue in F. But by enharmonically altering the chord we can resolve in the key of D major or minor. Thus by means of the enharmonic change we can modulate from F major or minor to D major or minor. Similarly by using III. we go to B major or minor, and by IV. to G♯ (or A♭) major or minor.

571. When a modulation is brought about by enharmonic change it is called an **enharmonic modulation**.

572. NOTE. In using these chords the relation of each note to its root must be considered—*e.g.* in I. D♭ is the minor ninth and must *fall*; B♭ is the seventh and must *fall*; E is the leading-note and must *rise*. In II. C♯ is the leading-note and must *rise*; B♭ is the ninth and must *fall*, &c., thus:

FIG. 285.

573. To complete the subject we add examples of the use of the chords in fig. 284 modulating to minor keys. The student can easily make each modulation to the corresponding major key by remembering § 484. (See also § 665a).

FIG. 286.

CHORDS OF THE NINTH

Exercises on Section III.

1. Write the *diminished seventh* on C♯ and resolve it correctly; make enharmonic changes in three ways and give new resolutions. Add figuring and name the root of each chord. Do the same with the diminished sevenths on F♯, on D, on G♯.

2. Figure the following chords and give the roots:

3. Add three upper parts to the following:

4. Write a few bars modulating by means of the *diminished seventh* (a) from E♭ major to A minor; (b) from E♭ major to F♯ minor.

5. Figure the chords marked *, name their roots, and explain their resolution.

(a) Beethoven, Op. 90.

(b) Beethoven, Op. 10, No. 2.

(c) Schubert, Posthumous Sonata in B♭.

(d) Schubert, Posthumous Sonata in B♭.

Section IV. Secondary Ninths.

574. If we add a third above a secondary chord of the seventh we get a secondary chord of the ninth. Secondary ninths are resolved on a chord (concord or discord) whose root is a *fourth* above the root of the ninth.

575. The ninth must be prepared, and must resolve wherever it occurs by *falling* one degree. The ninth should be written above the *third*, and it is generally most convenient to place it in the highest part.

576. The seventh is treated exactly as in secondary sevenths, except in the first and second inversions, where, as the root is omitted, the seventh ceases to be dissonant and needs neither preparation nor resolution. In the third inversion, the seventh forms the interval of a fourth with the third of the original chord, and is therefore dissonant and requires both preparation and resolution.

The fifth of the chord being a fifth below the ninth requires care to avoid consecutive fifths (compare § 551).

577. Inversions. There are four inversions of secondary ninths, but the last inversion with the ninth in the bass cannot be used.

The root is omitted in all the inversions.

FIG. 287. Secondary ninths with resolutions.
Root position.   First inversion.   Second inversion.   Third inversion.

578. It will be seen that the figuring of the inversions of secondary ninths is identical with that of secondary sevenths and their inversions (chap. xxxiv.). These inversions, however they have been approached, may be left either as inversions of ninths or of sevenths, with the exception of the third inversion of the ninth, which is not available as a second inversion of a seventh. Whether these chords are ninths or sevenths will be recognised by the resolution.

FIG. 288.
Ninths.   First inversion.   Second inversion.   Third inversion.

FIG. 288 *continued.*
Sevenths. Root position.   First inversion.   Second inversion not available.

579. A secondary ninth may be used on any note, provided the dissonant notes can be properly prepared and resolved. Thus there is no ninth on the subdominant because its resolution would necessitate the leap of an augmented fourth in the bass, and because there is no common chord on the leading-note, the bass on which it would have to resolve.

580. In minor keys the small number of secondary ninths possible is due to the augmented interval in the harmonic minor scale, necessitating movement by an augmented interval which is forbidden except in sequences.

It would be an interesting exercise to write secondary ninths on each degree of the minor scale and explain which of these are not allowed. Secondary ninths are not so much used as secondary sevenths, and they are of comparatively little importance in actual composition.

EXERCISES ON SECTION IV.

1. Write the secondary ninth on the tonic of C minor, and show why this chord is not available. Write all the inversions and say which (if any) are available, giving reasons where an inversion is unavailable.

2. Add three parts to the following basses and name the root of every chord. In the case of the secondary ninth indicate as in fig. 287 the resolution of the ninth and (when necessary) the seventh.

(a)

CHAPTER XLII.

THE DOMINANT ELEVENTH.

581. By adding a *third* above the dominant ninth we get the chord of the dominant eleventh. The ninth may be *minor* or *major*[1] (§ 550).

582. The eleventh may resolve while the rest of the chord remains, in which case it proceeds: (*a*) to the *third*; (*b*) to the *fifth* of the chord.

Or the chord may resolve on a chord from another root, viz. the *tonic common chord* or a *supertonic discord*; in these cases the eleventh *remains* to be a note of the chord of resolution (*c*).

NOTE.—When the eleventh resolves on the fifth, the major ninth usually proceeds at the same time to the third as at (*b*).

Figuring.—In fig. 289 the eleventh is figured 11 to show more clearly its origin. In actual practice the eleventh appears as a *fourth, i.e.* the simple interval from the root instead of the compound (§ 252).

FIG. 289.

---

[1] Of course it cannot be *major* in a *minor* key.

583. The following points should be noticed in the chords shown in fig. 289.

(1) The third and fifth are usually omitted from the chord.

(2) The third *must* be omitted from the chord when the eleventh resolves on the 3rd (*a*). The fifth must be omitted whenever the eleventh resolves on the fifth (*b*).

584. **Inversions.**—The root is omitted from all the inversions, except when the eleventh and ninth resolve respectively on fifth and third, as at * fig. 290. The seventh and ninth are subject to the rules of the dominant seventh and ninth. When, however, those notes of the chord with which the seventh or ninth is dissonant are not present, the seventh and ninth are free in their progression. There are five inversions, but the first is very rarely used. In fig. 290 will be found the more important forms of the inversions with their common resolutions. The fourth inversion can only be used with the *minor* 9th.

Fig. 290.

585. **The added sixth.**—The most familiar inversion of the dominant eleventh is the third. It occurs on the seventh from

the root of the chord, *i.e.* on the fourth of the scale. This chord is often called the **added sixth**, because it looks like the subdominant triad with a sixth added. It is very much used immediately before the dominant chord in perfect cadences.

FIG. 291.

586. It will have been noticed that many of these forms of the inversions of the dominant eleventh are identical with the secondary seventh on the supertonic, and that while the student was advised to prepare the secondary sevenths he may use the dominant eleventh like all *fundamental discords*, without preparation. This is merely another way of regarding the same chord, and bears out what we said in § 427, viz. that at first this secondary seventh was only used as a prepared discord, but that when by degrees men's ears recognised it as part of a dominant chord it ceased to require preparation, and also became freer in its resolution.

EXERCISES.

1. Write out the dominant eleventh (in four parts) in the key of F minor with several resolutions. Write inversions of the chord as in fig. 290, with figuring and resolutions.

2. Write with resolution the chord of the added sixth in G, A♭, and B major; in F, C♯, and B minor.

3. Add three upper parts to the following :—

(1)

214   HARMONY

CHAPTER XLIII.

THE DOMINANT THIRTEENTH.

587. The **dominant thirteenth** is obtained by adding a third above the dominant eleventh. This third may be *major* or *minor*, and we therefore get the following varieties of this chord:

FIG. 292.

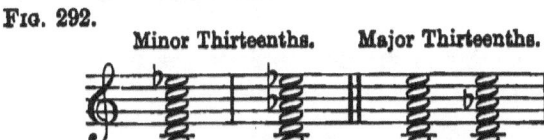
Minor Thirteenths.   Major Thirteenths.

588. **Resolution.**—The thirteenth may resolve while the rest of the chord remains : (*a*) on the fifth, or (*b*) the seventh of the

same chord; or it may resolve on the tonic common chord. In this case the thirteenth may remain (*c*), fall a third (*d*), or rise a semitone (*e*).

FIG. 293.

589. NOTES.—1. The form of the chord shown at (*e*) is very frequently written enharmonically for convenience, as at (*f*). Such a way of writing a note is often called convenient notation.

2. The form of the chord at (*e*) and (*f*) can only occur in *major* keys.

3. In figuring the thirteenth is usually given as a sixth, the simple interval instead of the compound, but in writing out exercises *the thirteenth should not be sounded* below the seventh except in the last inversion, when it is in the bass.

590. The chord of the thirteenth very rarely occurs in its complete form. In using the chord the principle explained in § 554 must be observed, *e.g.* when the thirteenth resolves on the fifth, that note must not be present in the chord, &c.

The treatment of the notes of the chord up to the eleventh is exactly what has been already explained in Chapter XLII., with, of course, the proviso of § 584.

There are six inversions, but of these the fifth, having the eleventh in the bass, is very rarely used.

591. The usual forms of the chord are—

(*a*) The thirteenth with the root and third.

(*b*) The thirteenth with the root, third, and fifth. This is chiefly used in its last inversion.

(c) The thirteenth with the root, third, and seventh; when the thirteenth must be sounded above the seventh.

(d) The thirteenth with the root, third, seventh, and ninth (*major* or *minor*).

The *minor* thirteenth is given, but the student can easily rewrite these examples, using the *major* thirteenth with the additional rule that when the *major* thirteenth resolves on the tonic chord the thirteenth must leap to the tonic (compare fig. 293 (d)).

FIG. 294.

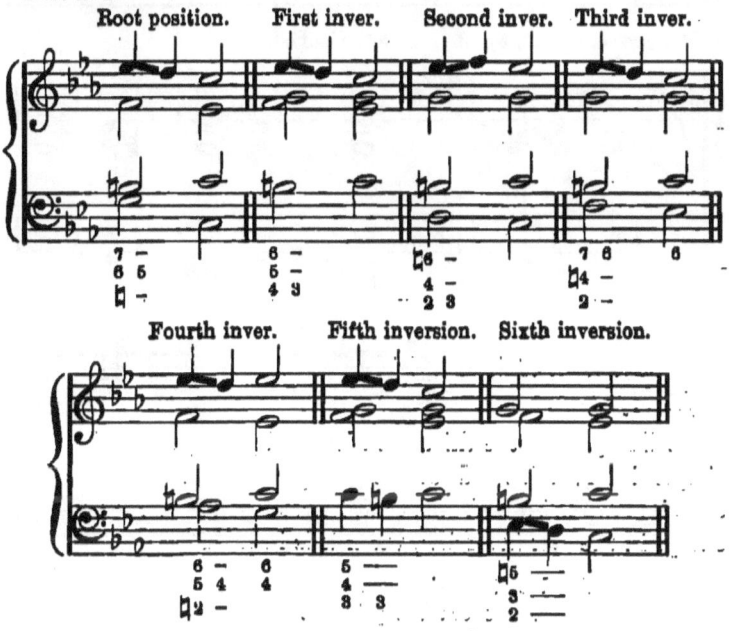

EXERCISES.

1. Figure the chords marked * and name their roots, and describe the method of resolution.

(a) Grieg.   (b) Sir J. Stainer.

THE DOMINANT THIRTEENTH 217

2. Add three upper parts.

[1] The key, as would be seen if the context were given, is D major, although the signature is three sharps. There is a violin part above this extract, but it in no way alters the constitution of the chords.

CHAPTER XLIV.

CHROMATIC CONCORDS.

592. In fig. 295 the chord (*a*) is used to modulate to the key of G; at (*b*) the same chord is used but in this case no modulation is produced.

FIG. 295.

593. Any chord must belong either to the key of the passage preceding it or to the key of the passage following it. (*a*) above is clearly the dominant common chord in the key of G, for it is used to produce a modulation. But in the case of (*b*) the passage before and the passage after are both in the key of C, and the chord (*b*) therefore belongs to the key of C and it is called a chromatic chord.

594. A chromatic chord is one which contains one or more notes foreign to the signature[1] **of the key in which it occurs, but which does not cause a modulation.**

Note.—*Chromatic chords* do not of necessity contain a chromatic interval.

595. Chromatic chords which may be used in both major and minor keys are the major common chord on the supertonic; the major common chord on the minor second.

596. The major common chord on the supertonic has in the major its third, and in the minor its third and fifth, chromatically altered.

The *third* of this chord (which is the augmented fourth of the key) may *never be doubled*, and in moving to the following chord it must either rise or fall a semitone.

---

[1] The accidental used with the leading-note of minor keys is not considered chromatic, because, although not indicated in the signature, it belongs to the key.

In order that this chord may not produce modulation, it must be followed by some chord containing the unaltered diatonic fourth of the scale, or by some form of the tonic common chord.

The chord may be used in its first inversion, subject to the same rules.

Fig. 296.

597. The major common chord on the minor second may double its third, and there is no restriction as to what chord shall follow it.

Fig. 297.

598. The *first inversion* of the major common chord on the minor second occurs on the fourth of the scale. It is of very common occurrence, and is called the **Neapolitan sixth**.

Fig. 298.

(a) major. (b) minor.

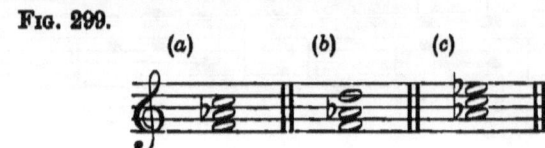

599. In addition to the chromatic chords described above, all the common chords peculiar to the minor key, with the exception of the minor common chord on the tonic, may be taken chromatically together with their available inversions in the major key. These are (a) a minor common chord on the *subdominant*, with its first and second inversions. (b) A first inversion with a minor third on the *subdominant*. (c) A major common chord on the *minor sixth* of the key with its first inversion.

Fig. 299.

(a)   (b)   (c)

Exercises.

Add three upper parts to the following :—

(1)   Hymn Tune.

CHAPTER XLV.

CHROMATIC FUNDAMENTAL DISCORDS.

SECTION I.—**Supertonic and Tonic Sevenths.**

600. Chromatic chords of the seventh are used on the *supertonic* and on the *tonic* of major and minor keys. These chords consist of exactly the same intervals as the dominant seventh, and they are therefore *fundamental discords*.

601. The **supertonic seventh** is obtained by adding a *minor third* above the chromatic common chord on the supertonic (§ 596).

602. The *supertonic seventh* must be followed by some chord containing the diatonic fourth of the key, or by some form of the tonic common chord, as in § 596.

The third of this chord can never be doubled, and in resolving it must either *rise* or *fall* a semitone.

The **seventh** must *fall* a second, or *remain* to be a note of the following chord. In the latter case, the seventh may be doubled, when one of the doubled sevenths may leap while the other remains.

FIG. 300.

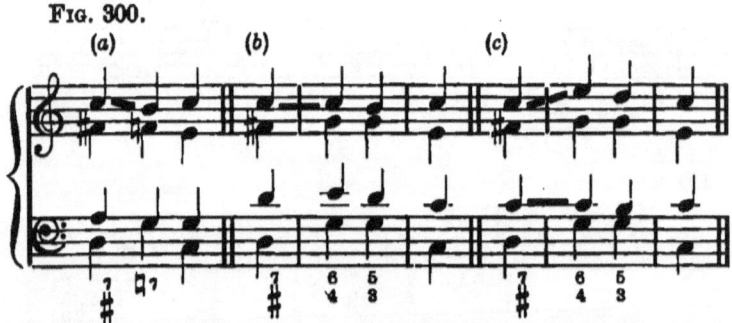

603. The *supertonic seventh* is used in all its three inversions, subject to the same rules as in the original position. In the second inversion the root may be omitted and the seventh doubled, thus giving a chromatic chord of the sixth (with a major sixth) on the submediant.

604. The **tonic seventh** consists of the major common chord on the tonic, to which is added a minor seventh.

In major keys the seventh and in minor keys the third is chromatic.

FIG. 301.

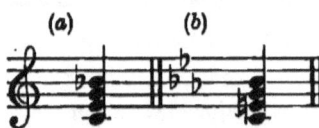

605. The *tonic seventh* must be followed [1] by a dominant discord, or by a supertonic discord.

---

[1] It may also be followed by the *subdominant* chord, provided that the chords which immediately follow such resolution are distinctive of the key (*v.* Ex. (*d*) p. 282).

606. The **third** of this chord must never be doubled; it must either (a) *rise* a minor second, or (b) *rise* a major second, or (c) *fall* a chromatic semitone.

607. The **seventh** of this chord must either (a) *rise* a chromatic semitone, or (b) *fall* a second.

FIG. 302.

* This chord is the third inversion of a chromatic supertonic ninth, described in § 609.

FIG. 303.

608. The tonic seventh may be used in all its three inversions subject to the same rules as in the original position. In the second inversion the root may be omitted, but the seventh may not be doubled. This gives a chromatic chord of the sixth (with a minor third) on the dominant.

EXERCISES ON CHROMATIC SEVENTHS.

Add three parts to the following basses:—

CHROMATIC FUNDAMENTAL DISCORDS

SECTION II.—Supertonic and Tonic Ninths.

609. Chromatic chords of the ninth are formed by adding a third, *major* or *minor*, above the chromatic chords of the seventh on the *supertonic* and *tonic*.

FIG. 304.

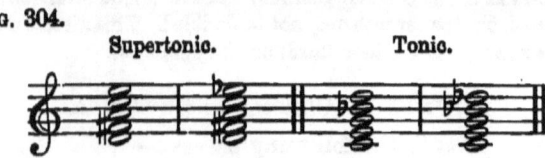

610. In minor keys the minor form alone is available; in major keys both forms are used.

611. The **supertonic ninth** may be resolved on the root, or third, of the chord, while the rest of the chord remains. It then follows all the rules of the dominant ninth (§§ 553-4).

612. The *supertonic ninth* may also be resolved on a *dominant discord*, or on an inversion of the chord of the tonic (cf. § 602). The ninth must then (*a*) *fall* a second, (*b*) *remain* to be a note of the next chord, or (*c*) if minor, *rise* a chromatic second.

226 HARMONY

The other constituents of this chord, up to the seventh, are subject to the rules already explained in treating of the *supertonic seventh* (§ 602).

FIG. 305.

613. The minor ninth resolving upwards as at (c) is frequently (especially in the *inversions*) written as at (d)—a chromatic semitone above the root.

614. The rules for the omission of the root and for the position of the third and the major ninth, and for the available inversions, are the same as for the dominant ninth (chap. xli.).

Below are shown the inversions of the **supertonic minor ninth**, with figuring.

FIG. 306.

CHROMATIC FUNDAMENTAL DISCORDS

615. The **tonic ninth** may be resolved like the *dominant and supertonic ninths* while the rest of the chord remains (§ 611).

If resolved on a chord on another root it must be followed by a *dominant discord* or by a *supertonic discord.* The *ninth* then resolves (*a*) by *rising* (when it is the *minor* ninth) a chromatic semitone, (*b*) *remaining* (if the *major* ninth), or (*c*) by *falling* a second.

The notes of this chord up to the seventh are subject to the rules of the tonic seventh (§ 605).

FIG. 307.

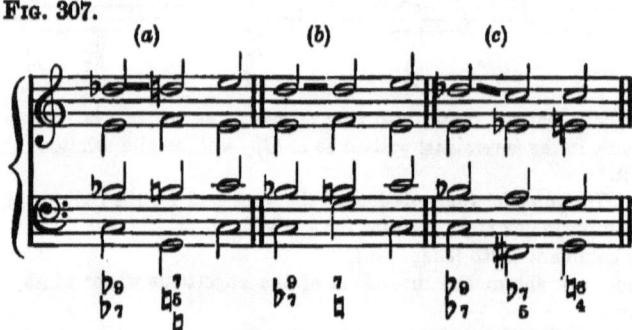

Inversions of the tonic minor ninth with figuring are shown below.

FIG. 308.

Exercises on Chromatic Ninths.

(a) Hymn Tune.

(b) Hymn Tune.

Section III.—Chromatic Elevenths and Thirteenths.

616. Chords of the eleventh may be formed by adding a third above the ninths on the *supertonic* and *tonic*. These elevenths (especially that on the supertonic) are so little used that the mere mention of them will suffice here.

617. By adding the thirteenth (minor or major) from the root to the *supertonic* and *tonic* ninth we get the **supertonic thirteenth and tonic thirteenth.** In a minor key only the minor form can be used; both minor and major are available in major keys.

618. The thirteenth may *fall* a second, *remain* to be a note of the next chord, or (when it is *minor*) *rise* a chromatic second.

Fig. 309.
Supertonic thirteenths.

Fig. 310.
Tonic thirteenths.

Exercise on Supertonic and Tonic Thirteenths.

It will be useful to remember that the *leading-note* is the thirteenth of the supertonic; the *submediant* is the thirteenth of the tonic.

Hymn Tune.

Section IV.

Fundamental Discords AND THE Chromatic Scale.

619. All fundamental discords are derived from one of three roots—the **tonic**, the **supertonic**, the **dominant**. The order in which the intervals are added in the harmonic series (§ 389) is *major third, perfect fifth, minor seventh, minor or major ninth, perfect eleventh, minor or major thirteenth.*

620. We have already shown how to find the root of fundamental discords. We give one further example, following the method of § 565. (*a*) is the discord; (*b*) the same arranged in thirds; in (*c*) thirds are added below until the order of interval corresponds to that of a fundamental discord. The lowest note (*c*) is therefore the root.

Fig. 311.

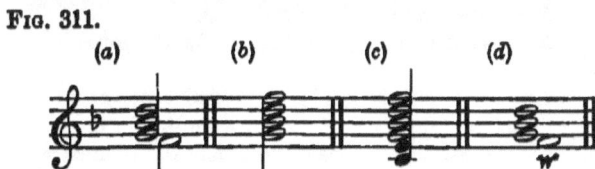

621. This method only tells us the *root*. The resolution of the chord, and the key in which it occurs, will show whether that root is dominant, tonic, or supertonic.

622. The sign ⋌, called a direct, is sometimes used, as in fig. 311 (*d*), to indicate the root of a chord.

623. The chromatic scale. In Part I., § 175, it was shown that the *harmonic* [1] *chromatic scale* is obtained by lowering the upper of each pair of tones (*e.g.* the note between C and D is called Db) except that between the fourth and fifth, which is always the raised fourth (F♯ in C). It will be useful to show the appropriateness of this name by explaining how the notes of this form of the scale are derived.

624. If we carried on the harmonic series described in § 389 we should see that, leaving out the octaves of the *generator*, the intervals reckoning from the generator are *perfect fifth, major third* (or tenth), *minor seventh*, and *minor ninth.*

625. Starting from C, and writing these intervals in close order, we get the notes shown in fig. 312 (*a*).

If we begin again, this time taking as generator the first new note in the series from C, *i.e.* G, we get the notes shown at (*b*).

---

[1] The *arbitrary* form is shown in § 176.

Beginning again with the first new note (*i.e.* omitting octaves of the generator) of G we get the notes shown at (*c*).

Fig. 312.

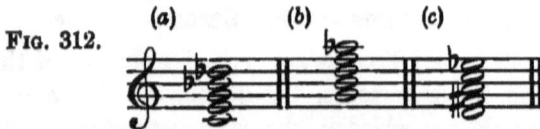

626. The three generators, *tonic*, *dominant*, and *supertonic* with the harmonics shown above supply all the notes of the *harmonic chromatic scale*.

Fig. 313.

627. The three *roots* are printed as semibreves.
From the **tonic** are derived: E♮ the third; B♭ the seventh; D♭ the ninth.
From the **supertonic**: F♯ the third; A♮ the fifth; E♭ the ninth.
From the **dominant**: B♮ the third; F the seventh; A♭ the ninth.

628. Since the supertonic is thus derived from (*i.e.* is an harmonic of) the dominant, and the dominant from the tonic, it is clear that the whole scale is derived from the tonic. We can now give a more complete definition of key.

A key means a collection of notes, the first of which is called the key-note or tonic, to which key-note the other notes of the series have a certain relation.

Exercise.

Give the roots of chords marked * and figure them.

Note.—(†) This is the dominant chord of D minor; Mendelssohn's part-writing is very free and abounds in infractions of rules the student should not imitate.

(*a*) Mendelssohn's 'Elijah.'

(b) Beethoven, Op. 81.

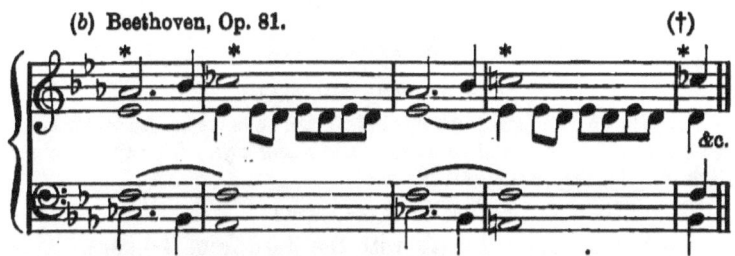

(†) The remainder of the passage not quoted shows that it is in E♭ major.

(c) Gounod, 'Mirella.'

(d) Schumann, Op. 97.

(e) Beethoven, Op. 92.

CHAPTER XLVI.
THE AUGMENTED SIXTH.

629. The chord of the **augmented sixth** can be taken on the *minor sixth* and on the *minor second* of both major and minor keys. That on the minor sixth is by far the most frequently used.

630. The chord occurs in three forms:

(*a*) The augmented sixth with the third from the bass. This is called the **Italian sixth**.

(*b*) The augmented sixth with the third and fourth from the bass; this is called the **French sixth**.

(*c*) The augmented sixth with the third and perfect fifth from the bass; this is called the **German sixth**.

FIG. 314.
(*a*) Italian sixth. (*b*) French sixth. (*c*) German sixth.

631. There are different opinions among musicians as to the **harmonic derivation** of these chords, but the following is a commonly accepted view. The bass-note (A♭) is considered as the *minor ninth* of the *dominant* (the above examples are in C); the other notes of the chord are derived from the supertonic.[1] The sixth from the bass (F♯, the sharpened fourth of the scale) is the *major third* of the *supertonic*; the *third* (C) is the *minor seventh* of the *supertonic*, while the fourth (D) and fifth (E♭) are respectively the *root* and *minor ninth* of the *supertonic*. Thus the chord is said to be derived from two roots, and it is spoken of as a chord with a **double root**.

632. Doubling.—The notes forming the interval of the augmented sixth can never be doubled. The only form in which it is necessary to double a note is the Italian sixth. Here the third is to be doubled.

633. Resolution. The augmented sixth on the minor sixth of the scale resolves:

(*a*) On the tonic common chord or one of its inversions.

(*b*) On the dominant common chord or its first inversion.

---

[1] As the supertonic is among the notes derived from the dominant (§ 625), some musicians regard this chord as derived from the dominant only.

(c) On an inversion of the dominant minor ninth.
(d) On a supertonic discord.
The resolutions (a) and (b) are the commonest.

634. In resolving, the two notes forming the augmented sixth should not move in *similar* [1] motion with each other. The other notes of the chord proceed as they do when used in the supertonic discords (§§ 602, 612).

FIG. 315.
Italian sixth.

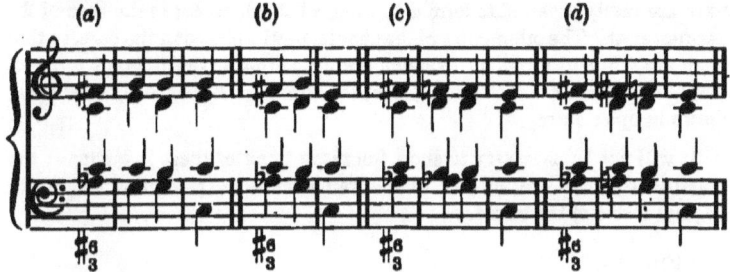

FIG. 316.
French sixth.

FIG. 317.
German sixth.

685. NOTE.—The German sixth resolving directly on the dominant common chord would produce consecutive fifths. This can be avoided by resolving the fifth (*i.e.* the minor ninth of the supertonic) while the rest of the chord remains as at (*b*) above. In practice this chord usually resolves on the second inversion of the tonic common chord.

636. Inversions. The two notes which form the interval of the augmented sixth are rarely inverted to form a diminished third, except in the case of the German sixth. The other notes of the chords may be placed in the bass, so that there are different forms of inversion corresponding to the different forms of the chord. These are shown in fig. 318, the forms most frequently used being shown in open notes.

It will not be necessary to show the resolutions of these inversions; the constituent notes are subject to the same rules of resolution as in the original forms of the chord.

FIG. 318.

Inversions of the augmented sixth.
(*a*) Italian sixth.   (*b*) French sixth.   (*c*) German sixth.

637. The **augmented sixth** on the *minor second* is not so frequently used as that on the minor sixth. It occurs in the same three forms.

It consists of the minor ninth of the *tonic*, with the third and seventh of the *dominant*. To these are added, in the French and German sixths, the root and minor ninth of the dominant respectively. Thus the two roots of these chords are tonic and dominant.

638. With the one exception, that in minor keys this chord may not resolve on the common chord of the tonic, each of the notes of this augmented sixth proceeds in resolving just like the corresponding notes of the augmented sixth on the minor sixth. It will therefore not be necessary to show all possible resolutions.

FIG. 319.

639. The chord of the *augmented sixth* is sometimes written inaccurately, one of its notes being written enharmonically for convenience in reading (§ 566). In the example below E♮ is written for F♭ (the minor ninth of the supertonic in D♭ major).

FIG. 320.

Beethoven, Op. 57.
(a)   (b) correct form.

EXERCISES.

Add three upper parts to the following:

CHAPTER XLVII.

THE DISSONANT TRIADS.

640. If we omit the root from the first inversion of a dominant seventh we get the diminished triad on the leading-note (fig. 151). This is occasionally (though not very often) used. An example will be seen in Beethoven's P.F. Sonata, Op. 78, in the thirty-fifth bar after the double bar.

If this chord is used its origin should be remembered. The only note that can be doubled is the third, the other notes being dissonant.

641. In the first inversion of this triad, *i.e.* the $^6_3$ on the *supertonic*, the third (*i.e.* the original seventh) may be doubled, because the relation of this note to the bass is not now dissonant. If this third is doubled it is best to let the upper of the two thirds fall and the lower rise.

FIG. 321.

642. The triad[1] on the mediant of a minor key has an augmented fifth, and it is therefore dissonant. It may be used in its root position and first inversion. The dissonant note must be prepared and resolved by rising a second. This dissonant triad resolves on a common chord, the root of which is a fourth above the root of the triad (fig. 322 (*a*)).

643. According to some authorities the triad[1] on the *mediant* of major keys is dissonant. It is subject to the same rules of preparation, resolution, and inversion as that on the mediant of minor keys (fig. 322 (*b*)).

FIG. 322.

(*a*) Minor.   (*b*) Major.

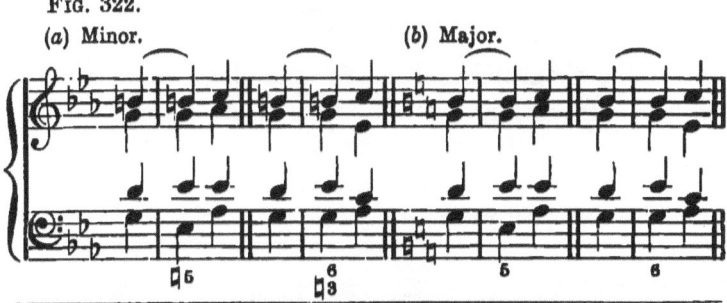

---

[1] The origin of these chords is the dominant thirteenth (ch. xliii.), and this accounts for the fact that these dissonant triads are not infrequently found in a second inversion. Thus in the triad on the mediant of the minor, the root of the triad (E♭, fig. 322) is the thirteenth of the dominant; the third (G) is the root; the fifth (B♮) is the leading-note.

THE DISSONANT TRIADS

644. The **augmented triad** on the mediant of minor keys, subject to the rules of § 642, may be used in the relative major keys; thus the *augmented triad* of C minor in E♭ major; that of A minor in C major.

In this case the dissonant note is best approached by step of a semitone.

645. Thus there is an augmented triad [1] on the tonic of major keys.

FIG. 323.

646. An augmented triad, subject to § 642, is also found on other notes of the scale, especially on the *dominant* and on the *subdominant*. Schumann is exceedingly fond of using that on the subdominant.

647. All these augmented triads are occasionally used in the second inversion, as in the following example:—

FIG. 324.

Schumann, Op. 68, No. 30.

EXERCISES.

Add three upper parts:—

(1)

---

[1] This is chromatic in major keys (*v.* p. 219 n.).

240   HARMONY

CHAPTER XLVIII.

PEDAL NOTES, ARPEGGIOS, GROUND BASS.

648. A **pedal** is a note sustained through a succession of chords of which the pedal may or may not form a part.

The pedal-note occurs most frequently, though not always, in the bass, and this is probably the origin of the term, the pedal-note being often played by the pedals of the organ. The French and German name for pedal-note is *organ-point*.

649. The only notes which can be used as pedal-notes are **Tonic** and **Dominant**, and of these the latter is by far the more usual.

FIG. 325.

(a) Example of **Tonic pedal**.   Handel.

PEDAL NOTES, ARPEGGIOS, GROUND BASS 241

(b) Example of **Dominant pedal.**

Mendelssohn, Scherzo e Capriccio.

650. A *pedal* passage usually begins with a chord, of which the pedal-note is a part (fig. 325), but it may begin with a chord of which the pedal-note is not a part.

The pedal passage should end [1] with a chord of which the pedal-note forms a part (fig. 325).

651. When the pedal-note does not form part of the chords above it, the next note above the pedal must be considered as the bass, and must follow all rules which relate to the movement of the bass.

Thus at (a), fig. 326, the pedal-note is no part of the chord, therefore the note D is the bass of a second inversion which may not leap (§ 844). This is corrected at (b).

FIG. 326.

652. **Modulation in a pedal passage.**—The chords used during a pedal passage should only be those—diatonic or chromatic—belonging to the key [2] of the passage.

The only [1] chords foreign to the key which are allowed on a pedal are the major common chord and fundamental discords on the sixth of the major key. These are allowed on a dominant pedal, provided they are followed by a chord containing the seventh of the dominant.

---

[1] There are exceptions to this rule in modern music.
[2] A passage on a dominant pedal may modulate to the key of the dominant, when the pedal becomes the tonic. A passage on a tonic pedal may modulate to the subdominant key, when the pedal becomes the dominant of the new key.

242   HARMONY

653. In **Figuring** the chords above a pedal the intervals may be reckoned either from the pedal-note or from the part next above the pedal-note.

654. Inverted Pedal.—The pedal-note may be sustained in an upper part; it is then called an inverted pedal.

FIG. 327.

(a) Pedal in the highest part.   Beethoven, Op. 31, No. 2.

(b) Pedal in middle part.[1]   Beethoven, Op. 12, No. 3.

655. Double Pedal.—Sometimes both dominant and tonic are sustained together, in which case the tonic must be below the dominant.

---
[1] To this extract there is a violin part (not given).

FIG. 328.

Mendelssohn, S.w.W. 35.

656. Brahms (*Deutsches Requiem*) has a whole movement constructed on a tonic pedal. Haydn (*Trio* in *Clock Symphony*) repeats the tonic common chord exactly in the way of a pedal, while a solo implying chords of which the sustained notes form no part is given out by the flute.

657. A pedal-note is sometimes ornamented by being alternated with an auxiliary note. There is an example of this in Beethoven's P.F. Sonata vii., beginning at the eighteenth bar from the end of the first movement.

658. When the notes of a chord are played in succession instead of being struck all at once, the chord is called an **arpeggio** (§ 223).

Arpeggios in succession are not allowable unless the succession of chords from which they are derived is allowable.

(*a*) is incorrect, because the chords which the arpeggios represent have consecutive fifths (*b*).

FIG. 329.

659. Auxiliary notes may be used with the essential notes of an arpeggio.

The arpeggios at (*a*) are derived from the chords at (*b*). The notes are auxiliary.

FIG. 330.

660. Ground Bass.—Sometimes a bass part is repeated several times, having at each repetition different harmonies or the same harmonies varied by suspensions or passing notes &c. A bass so repeated is called a *Ground Bass*.

Many whole movements, especially of the time of Bach and Handel, were constructed on a ground bass. An example will be seen in the chorus *To Song and Dance*, No. 66, Handel's *Samson*, where a phrase of two bars is repeated twenty-one times.

EXERCISE.

Add three parts to the following :—

CHAPTER XLIX.

MODULATION—*continued*.

661. We have already drawn attention to the use made of the *diminished seventh* in enharmonic modulation. This is by no means the only chord so used. Another chord specially adapted for enharmonic modulation is that form of the augmented sixth called the **German sixth**, which can be enharmonically changed into a dominant seventh.

FIG. 331.

662. It will readily be seen that this chord may be approached in one key, as an augmented sixth (*e.g.* in C), and left as a dominant seventh (*e.g.* in D♭), and thus we get an extraneous modulation from C to D♭.

FIG. 332.

663. This same chord (fig. 332) might be the augmented sixth on the minor second of G, and then we should get a modulation from G major to D♭ major. Again, the augmented sixth is the same in minor and major keys, and so is the dominant seventh. The above examples, then, might be from C major or minor to D♭ major or minor, &c.

664. Any of the chromatic concords §§ 595-599 may be approached as chromatic in one key, and left as diatonic chords in a new key, *e.g.* the Neapolitan sixth in C (major or minor) may be left in the key of A♭ major, &c.

FIG. 333.

665. Any *major common chord* in a key may be considered as the chromatic common chord on either the *minor second* or *minor sixth* (§§ 597, 599), and left accordingly.

FIG. 334.

At (*a*) the dominant of C is left as the chromatic common chord on the minor second of F♯. At (*b*) the same chord is left as the chromatic common chord on the minor sixth of B.

665*a*. By enharmonic change (§ 570) any *chord of the diminished seventh* may be resolved as if derived from four different roots, producing modulation into four major and four minor keys. Each of these four roots may be regarded as the **dominant, supertonic, or tonic** (§§ 611-15) of a key. Therefore each of the chords shown in fig. 284 may be resolved in three major and three minor keys. Thus from any *diminished seventh* we can modulate into any of the twelve major or twelve minor keys.

666. The methods described in §§ 662-5 all produce *extraneous modulation*. Another very common method is to take one of the notes of a

MODULATION   247

common chord in a key and leave it as one of the intervals of either the
tonic common chord or the dominant seventh of the new key. See below,
fig. 335.

667. Sometimes an extraneous modulation is produced by passing
through a series of keys, each key being related to that immediately preceding, *e.g.* C, G major, G minor, B♭ major, B♭ minor, D♭ major. Thus
eventually we modulate from C major to D♭ major, an extraneous modulation.
Such a modulation is sometimes called a **compound modulation** (fig. 336).

668. The methods of modulation are innumerable, and the best way
of studying them is to go to the works of the best composers. We conclude
with two examples of extraneous modulation.

FIG. 335.

Beethoven, Op. 7.

At * the leading-note of C minor (the extract opens in E♭ major) is
treated as the root of the dominant seventh in E major.

Fig. 336.

Schubert, Post. P.F. Sonata in B♭.

We have here a modulation from D♭ through G♭ minor (here enharmonically shown as F♯ minor) to A major.

Exercises.

1. By means of the German sixth treated enharmonically modulate (*a*) from G minor to A♭ major, (*b*) from F major to G♭ minor.

2. By § 664 modulate (*a*) from B♭ major to G♭ major, (*b*) A major to F major.

3. By §§ 665-6 modulate from D major (*a*) to F♯ major, (*b*) to C♯ major (*c*) to E♭ major.

CHAPTER L.

HOW TO HARMONISE A MELODY.

Section I.

669. In harmonising melodies the process followed in filling up a figured bass is reversed. We have now to find a suitable chord as the accompaniment of a given note, and a suitable series of chords which can follow each other.

670. It will be convenient to begin our exercises in this subject by confining ourselves to the use of **common chords**.

671. We saw in § 351 that the common chords of a key are made up out of the notes of that key. Therefore every note of a diatonic scale may be harmonised as a part of some common chord.

672. But each note can occur in more than one common chord, *e.g.* C may be (*a*) the root (or octave) of the *tonic*; (*b*) the third of the *submediant*; (*c*) the fifth of the *subdominant*.

Fig. 337.

673. Each note, then, can be harmonised in three different ways, and we must now learn how to find out which to use.

674. Of the common chords and triads in major keys all are of common occurrence except the *mediant common chord*, and the *leading-note triad*. In harmonising melodies the student will do well to avoid these altogether, at any rate at the beginning. We propose, then, to use only the common chords on the first, second, fourth, fifth, and sixth degrees of the scale. This relieves us of some of the greatest difficulties, *e.g.* the leading-note is not to be harmonised as the fifth of the mediant, nor as the root of the triad on the leading-note, for we do not intend to use those chords. Therefore, for the present, the **leading-note must be treated as the third of the dominant triad**.

675. The other common chords can be used in any order, but the common chord on the supertonic followed by that on the tonic, and the common chord on the dominant followed by that on the subdominant, should be avoided.

676. **The beginning of a melody.**—Many melodies begin with the *tonic common chord*, and usually the tonic (*i.e.* C in the key of C) is the first note, although the first note may be the third (*i.e.* E) or even the fifth (*i.e.* G) of the chord. Some melodies begin with the *dominant chord*, and then the first note may be the root (*i.e.* G), or the third (*i.e.* B), or the fifth (*i.e.* D) of that chord.

A melody may begin on any note of the scale, but the beginnings described above are the most usual, and those which a student is most likely to meet with at first.

677. The end of a melody.—All melodies *must* end with the *tonic common chord*, and the last bass-note must be the **tonic**. The last note of the treble may be the *tonic*, or the third, or (very rarely) the fifth.

Practically all melodies end with the **perfect cadence**, and consequently the last chord but one will be a *dominant chord* (§ 454).

We will now apply these principles to the following melody:—

Fig. 338.

678. As most melodies begin with a tonic chord, E is evidently the third of a chord on C. We therefore use a tonic chord, taking care to arrange the parts carefully. It is usually best to double the root, so we will begin with the following, which has the merit of an even distribution:—

Fig. 339.

679. The next note of the melody is D. D may be the root of a chord on D, the third of a chord on B (best avoided), or the fifth in a chord on G. Which shall we choose of the two that are equally good? It is rarely good to use a common chord on the tonic and then immediately one on the supertonic, so we select the dominant chord. In writing the next chord, which will consist of G, B, D, we must remember that B is the leading-note, and must on no account be doubled. Also that, as G belongs to chords 1 and 2, it will be best to keep it in the same part. Thus:—

Fig. 340.

With the exception of the bass, each part moves without leaping.

680. Note, No. 3, C, may be the root of C, third of A, or fifth of F. It *cannot be the fifth of F* here, because, as G was the last bass-note, this would give us consecutive fifths between treble and bass as at (*a*); and to make it a part of the chord on C would be simply repeating No. 1, which would be monotonous. Let us treat it then as the third of a chord on A.

In moving to the next chord several points must be looked to; the bass goes to A. Clearly, then, the alto G can*not* go to A, or we shall get consecutive octaves. The alto goes to E, and the leading-note, which *ought to rise*, goes to C.

Fig. 341.

(*a*) Bad.

(*b*) Good.

681. No. 4 may be the root of a chord on A; the third of one on F or the fifth of one on D. We reject the first because we have used that chord in No. 3. We reject the last because the bass would naturally fall, and we should have hidden fifths as at (*a*). We therefore use the chord on F (*b*).

Fig. 342.

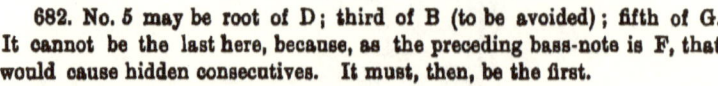
(*a*) Bad.　　　(*b*) Good.

682. No. 5 may be root of D; third of B (to be avoided); fifth of G. It cannot be the last here, because, as the preceding bass-note is F, that would cause hidden consecutives. It must, then, be the first.

No. 6 and 7 we know, from § 677, belong to dominant and tonic respectively, because they are in the cadence.

The whole melody then stands as below:—
FIG. 343.

683. Note that chord No. 5 has no fifth. The reason is clear: the treble A cannot remain, for the melody goes to D; F cannot be omitted because it is the third of the chord, and the tenor C cannot go to A because that would cause consecutive fifths with the bass.

684. Note. In harmonising melodies, of course, all the rules of part-writing and doubling must be followed, and advantage should be taken, when possible, of a note common to two chords, as between 1 and 2; 3 and 4 (fig. 343).

685. As far as possible, variety should be sought. If the same chord is used twice, variety may then be secured by letting some of the parts move as in fig. 136.

686. The student who means to succeed in harmonising melodies must acquire the difficult art of mentally hearing what he writes. With this in view the student is advised to play over many of the good hymn tunes which he will find in almost any hymnal. He will thus get accustomed to *good successions of chords*, and gradually acquire that power of hearing we have spoken of.

687. When harmonising a melody it is a good plan to write the bass first, for it is comparatively easy to mentally hear a melody and its bass at the same time. When a good bass is obtained it will rarely be difficult to fill in the parts. In distributing the notes of the chords used, the *treble* and *alto* and the *alto* and *tenor* should never be more than an octave apart.

EXERCISES.

Harmonise the melodies, using only common chords.

* Use the *tonic common chord* in both cases, and to avoid monotony let the bass leap an octave, and remember § 291.

* Read Chapter XXXVI. especially § 461; make G part of the tonic chord; F part of the dominant.

SECTION II.—Using Common Chords and Inversions.

688. In using **first inversions** remember that very often—though not always—the sixth is in the upper part. As a $^6_3$ can occur on every note of the major scale, every note of a melody *might* be the upper part of a $^6_3$. This would be too monotonous, and we must seek variety by mingling chords and inversions.

The first inversions most used are perhaps that on the third of the scale and that on the fourth.

689. Notice that the leading-note may now belong to the dominant common chord or to a first inversion on the supertonic (fig. 344 (*c*)).

690. When the same note occurs twice in the same bar it can often be harmonised with a common chord, and then a first inversion of the same chord, or *vice versa*. This is often the case, too, when the melody leaps a third up or down.

Learn by heart the following cadences, and transpose them into other keys :—

FIG. 344.

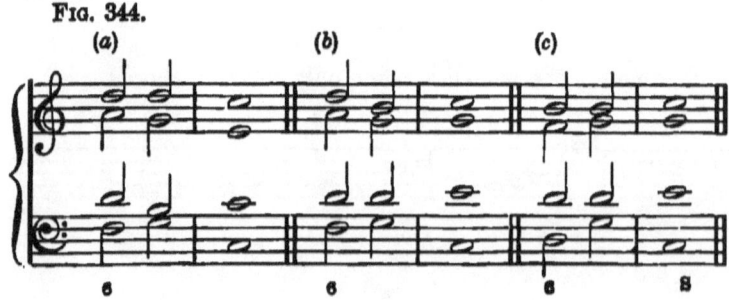

254   HARMONY

691. Second inversions afford such opportunities for error that the student is advised to use them at first only in cadences, or in cases like fig. 171, where the *bass proceeds by step*. Learn by heart the examples in figs. 165-171, and transpose to other keys.

Exercises.

Harmonise, using common chords and inversions; figure the bass.

⁎ *Before doing this exercise do those in Section I. again, now using first inversions as well as common chords, and then compare with the previous harmonising.*

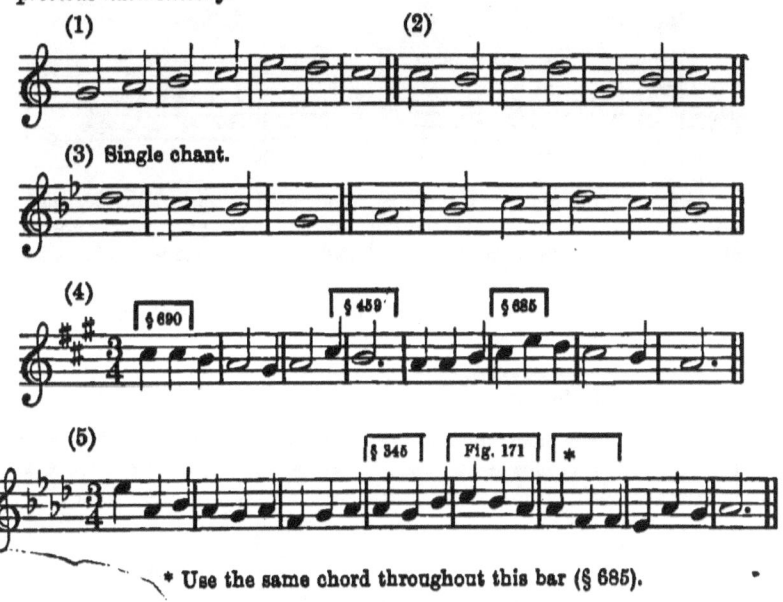

* Use the same chord throughout this bar (§ 685).

Section III.—Melodies in the Minor.

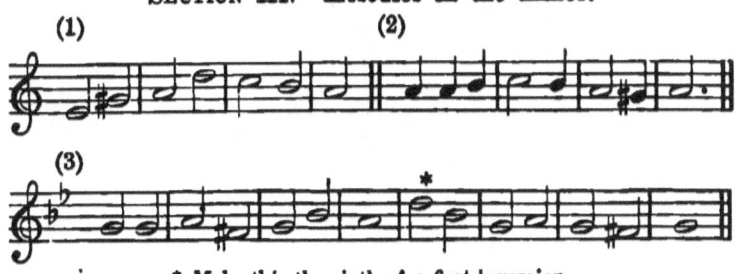

* Make this the sixth of a first inversion.

(4) (§ 369)

Section IV.—Using the Dominant Seventh.

692. Each of the notes forming the dominant seventh may be in the treble, and so treated provided the chord can resolve properly.

(a) Examples of the seventh of the dominant in the melody.

Fig. 345.

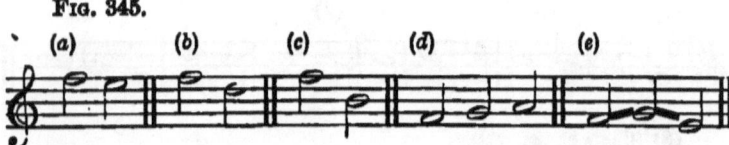

At (a), (b), (c), the note F could be harmonised as part of the dominant seventh, for at (a) it resolves regularly, and at (b) and (c) it merely goes to other notes of the same chord. In (b) and (c) both notes would have the same chord or an inversion.

At (d) F could *not* be part of a dominant seventh because it rises, and therefore does not resolve.

At (e) F may be part of the dominant seventh, because it eventually goes to E, and is therefore an example of ornamental resolution.

693. (β) If the dominant is in the melody it can be part of the dominant seventh when it is repeated or when it leaps to the tonic, but not when it falls to the third, for that would break the rule given in § 379. Thus:

Fig. 346.

It will scarcely be necessary to show examples of the third and fifth of the dominant in the melody.

EXERCISES.

Harmonise, using dominant sevenths or inversions as well as common chords and inversions.

** *Do Sections I. and II. again, now using the dominant seventh, and compare with former setting.*

(1)

Although the F resolves correctly, do not use a dominant seventh because the cadence in the next bar is clearly $^6_4$ $^7_3$, and that will necessitate the dominant in the bass for those chords. It is almost always bad to use on the last beat of a bar the same bass-note as that of the following bar.

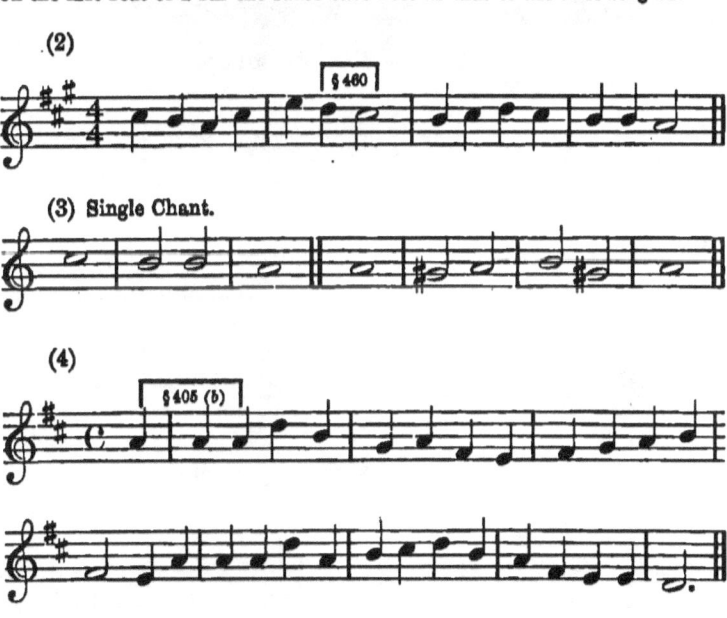

694. Middle cadences. We have shown in Chapter XXXVI. how cadences are used, and to complete the subject we must explain further the nature of middle cadences. Generally speaking, each phrase of a melody should end with a different cadence, and, of course, the perfect cadence must be reserved for the final one. But for a perfect cadence to have the complete effect of a full close (a) both the chords of the cadence must be in their root position; (b) the tonic chord should occur on the strong accent; (c) the tonic chord should have the root (*i.e.* the key-note) in the treble. When none of these conditions are satisfied, a perfect cadence may be used in the middle cadences.[1]

695. Further, most melodies of any length modulate (Chapter XXXVIII.), and when that is the case *a perfect cadence in the new key* is necessary to mark the modulation. With these exceptions middle cadences will usually be *imperfect* or *interrupted*.

696. The student should now analyse hymn tunes with regard to their cadences.

Thus the tune *Rockingham* in E♭ consists of four sections. Section I. ends on the tonic chord, but the treble has the dominant (B♭), and the preceding chord is not the dominant, thus it is not a perfect cadence. Section II. ends on the imperfect cadence. Section III. has a perfect cadence because it modulates to B♭, and, of course, Section IV. ends with a perfect cadence in E♭.

SECTION V.—With Modulation.
Read Chapter XXXVIII.

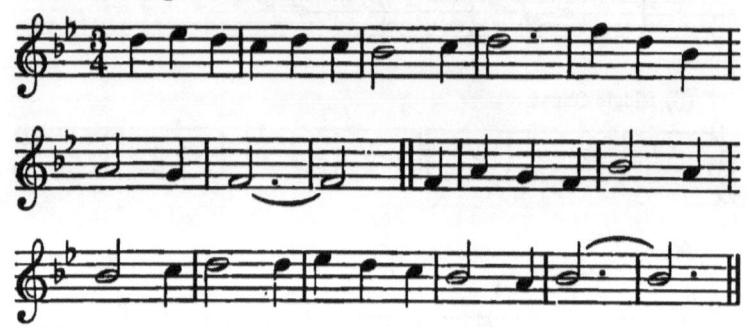

SECTION VI.—With Suspensions.

(1)

* Suspension in the treble. † Suspension in inner part.

---

[1] Not infrequently the first section of a hymn tune has a perfect cadence with all the conditions of § 694. The probable reason is the importance of establishing the original key in a short piece which modulates.

* Suspension in the bass. † Triple suspension.

SECTION VII.—With Passing Notes.

Passing notes to be introduced into any part.

* Accented passing note.

SECTION VIII.—Miscellaneous Examples selected from Examination Papers.

Any chords may be used, and opportunities should be sought for using the ninth, eleventh, thirteenth, and chromatic chords, with suspensions and passing notes.

COUNTERPOINT.

CHAPTER LI.

INTRODUCTORY.

697. **Counterpoint** has been defined as 'the art of combining melodies,' *i.e.* the art of adding one or more melodies above or below a given melody in such a way that the whole when heard together shall produce a satisfactory effect.

The word is derived from the Latin *punctum contra punctum*. In ancient music, notes, from their shape, were called 'points.' Thus, to write one note against another was to write *punctum contra punctum*.

698. The precise meaning of *Counterpoint* will be best seen by comparing it with *Harmony*. In harmony we are mainly concerned with the construction and relation of chords, troubling little about the individuality of each separate part. In counterpoint, on the contrary, while the harmonic basis must be clear and definite, it is imperative that each separate part or voice shall have a melodic interest in itself. Thus, in the following example, each of the five parts has a separate and well-defined melody, which is interesting in and for itself.

FIG. 347.

Mozart, Jupiter Symphony.

699. It is usual to practise counterpoint by writing melodies or parts *above* and *below* a given melody called the **subject** or the **canto fermo**.[1]

700. If a melody added to a subject only sounds satisfactory when heard in the position in which it is written, *i.e.* either above *or* below the subject, it is said to be in **simple counterpoint**. This is usually the case.

701. A melody, however, may be added to a subject in such a way that it sounds satisfactory both when heard above *and also* when heard below the subject, and such a melody is said to be in **double counterpoint**, fig. 348.

It will be seen that *double counterpoint* means *invertible* counterpoint.

Fig. 348.

702. When *three* (or *four*) parts are written so as to be invertible they are said to be in *triple* (or *quadruple*) counterpoint.

In fig. 347 we have an example of *quintuple counterpoint*, the five melodies there used being invertible.

703. Counterpoint was practised before Harmony. Indeed, when a certain advance in musical knowledge had been made in the study and practice of Counterpoint, Harmony stepped in and systematised that know-

---

[1] In the early attempts at writing music it was customary to select some well-known air or church hymn tune and to add parts to it, making it, as it were, the foundation of the music. This air was called the **Canto Fermo**, *i.e.* **fixed song** or **Plain Song**. This was sung or *held* (Latin, *teneo*) by the Tenor (*v.* § 246).

ledge from the point of view of the construction of chords, and Harmony has ever since continued and is still continuing to add fresh advances. The first attempts were very tentative, and writers of counterpoint limited themselves by very strict rules, especially as regards what combinations should be used.

704. When counterpoint is written according to the old rules and restrictions it is called **strict counterpoint**. When music, not bound by the rules of strict counterpoint, but written with all the resources of modern harmony, also gives an individuality to each separate part after the methods of counterpoint, it is said to be in **free counterpoint**.[1]

705. It is of the highest possible advantage for the student of music to practise counterpoint, and to practise it *bound down by the rules which regulated early counterpoint*.

The student is urged to accept this statement with the assurance that did space permit, it might be amply proved and made clear to him.

CHAPTER LII.

LAWS OF PROGRESSION.

706. Many of these laws are exactly like those given in harmony, but they are repeated here for the sake of completeness.

Melodic Progression.

707. When a part moves by *step* (either tone or semitone) it is said to move by **conjunct** movement; when a part proceeds by *leap* it moves by **disjunct** movement.

708. No part may proceed by an *augmented* interval except in one of the repetitions of a sequence.

709. When a part proceeds by a *diminished* interval it must at once return to some note within that interval (§ 431).

710. No part may leap a seventh or a ninth.

711. The interval of a seventh or a ninth may not occur in any part without at least two intervening notes (*a*).

Exceptions: a seventh with an eighth intervening (*b*); or a ninth with a tenth intervening (*c*).

Fig. 349.
(*a*) Bad.   Good.   (*b*) Good.   (*c*) Good.

[1] Music written in this way is often called *contrapuntal*.

712. *Before* a leap of an interval greater than a fifth it is best to proceed in a direction contrary to the leap (*a*). *After* a leap of an interval greater than a fifth, it is best to return to a note within the leap (*b*).

Fig. 350.
(*a*) Good.   (*b*) Good.

713. After moving by several successive seconds a part may not leap *in the same direction* to an accented note (*a*) ; but it may leap to an accented note *in the contrary direction* (*b*).

If the leap is to an unaccented note the part may leap either in the same or in contrary direction (*c*).

Fig. 351.
(*a*) Bad.   (*b*) Good.   (*c*) Good.

Harmonic Progression.

714. No parts may move in perfect fifths, octaves, or unisons, §§ 434-437.

715. No upper part may move in fourths with the bass (§ 442).

716. Hidden fifths, octaves, and unisons are forbidden between the extreme parts, except in moving to another position of the same harmony (§ 440).

717. Hidden fifths and octaves should be avoided when possible, even in the inner parts or between an inner and an extreme part. They are least objectionable when one of the parts moves by step.

718. No two parts may overlap or cross (§ 482).

719. In two-part writing a third may not be followed by a fifth when both parts move a second.

FIG. 352.

720. In two-part writing one major third may not follow another at the step of a major second.

FIG. 353.

721. The **leading-note** in counterpoint is not quite so restricted in its movement as in harmony. It may never be doubled except when it is a passing note, or in a sequence, or in an arpeggio while being held in another part (§ 757).

In a perfect cadence the leading-note must rise to the tonic. In other cases it is free to rise or fall.

722. The interval of the tritone (augmented fourth) may not occur between a note of the subject in one bar and a note of the counterpoint in another *when both parts proceed by step* (a) This is called **false relation of the tritone** [1] (*a*).

There is no false relation when one of the parts proceeds by leap (*b*), or when the movement by step is caused by a passing note (*c*).

FIG. 354.

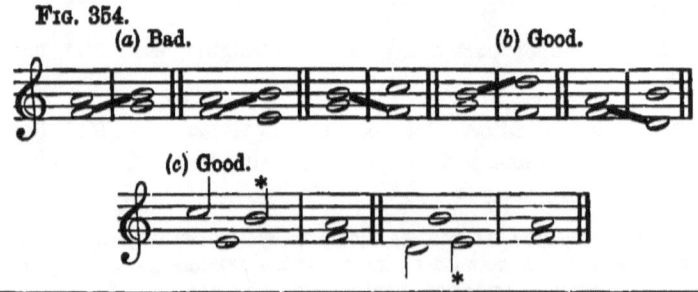

---

[1] Called also mi contra fa. According to the ancient rules, it was forbidden to have in successive chords the *mediant* (*i.e. mi*) of one key and the *subdominant* (*i.e. fa*) of the key a fourth above the first, *e.g.* the mediant of G, *i.e.* B, with the subdominant of C, *i e.* F.

723. **Harmonic combinations** which may be used in strict counterpoint are (*a*) **common chords** and **first inversions.**[1] (*b*) The only discords allowed are **passing notes** and **prepared discords**, *i.e. suspensions.*

724. In **major keys** the only available chords are: (*a*) the *common chords* on the first, second, fourth, fifth, and sixth degrees, together with their first inversions; (*b*) the *first inversions* of the triads on the third and seventh.

Fig. 355.

725. In **minor keys** the only available chords are: (*a*) the *common chords* on the first, fourth, fifth, and sixth degrees with their first inversions; (*b*) the first inversion of the triads on the second and seventh; (*c*) when the fifth of the minor scale is in the bass it may be accompanied by the interval of a sixth, and either the bass or sixth may be doubled, but no third may be added; (*d*) when in the minor the bass *descends* stepwise from the tonic to the minor sixth then the minor seventh may be the bass of a first inversion.

Fig. 356.

726. The chords mentioned in §§ 724-5 may follow each other in any order, except that the common chord on the second of the scale should not be followed by that on the tonic, except when both chords are in their first inversion.

---

[1] The second inversion is disallowed because it contains the interval of a perfect fourth from the bass, which even in modern harmony is dissonant (§ 335).

727. Rules for doubling. The *root* is the best note to double, the next best is the *fifth*. The *major third* should not be doubled unless the doubled note is approached and left in contrary motion and by step of a second. There is no objection to the *minor third* being doubled.

For doubling the leading-note see § 721.

728. Rule for omission of notes from a chord. The *fifth* should, as a rule, be omitted in preference to the *third*.

729. There are five species of counterpoint.

The *first species* has note against note, *i.e.* when there is one note in the counterpoint to each note of the subject.

The *second species* has two notes in the counterpoint to each note of the subject.

The *third species* has more than two notes in the counterpoint to each note of the subject.

The *fourth species* has two notes in the counterpoint to each note of the subject, but written in syncopation.

The *fifth species* or *florid counterpoint* is a mixture of the other species; it consists in the main of the fourth species, ornamented by combination with the second and third.

CHAPTER LIII.

FIRST SPECIES OF COUNTERPOINT.

730. Each species will be separately taken in two, three, and four parts. As we have remarked before, very strict rules are to be observed, and these rules apply to such points as the manner of beginning and ending an exercise.

SECTION I.—First Species in Two Parts.

731. Every exercise **must begin** with a *perfect* interval, either the unison, fifth, or octave when the subject is in the lower part; with the unison or octave when the subject is in the upper part.

Every exercise **must end** with a *perfect cadence*, *i.e.* the leading-note proceeding to the tonic, while another part proceeds from the supertonic or dominant to the tonic.

A perfect cadence must not occur in the course of an exercise, but only at the end.

Fig. 357.

732. Two-part counterpoint must not have the *unison* in any bar except the first and last.

733. The imperfect concords, thirds, and sixths, are preferred to the perfect concords, fifths, and octaves. The perfect fourth is entirely forbidden because of its dissonant effect (§ 835).

734. Contrary motion is preferable to similar motion.

735. To avoid monotony, do not use more than three *consecutive* thirds or sixths.

The same note should not be repeated in two or more consecutive bars.

The object of all these rules, it will be readily seen, is to avoid monotony and to make each separate part contrast well with the others and stand out independently.

EXAMPLES IN THE major.

(a) *Subject* in the alto ; *counterpoint* above.

(b) *Subject* in the treble ; *counterpoint* below.

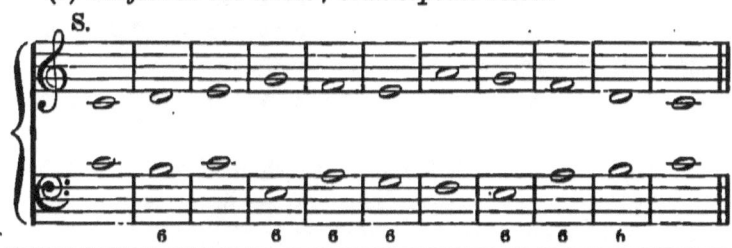

---

[1] The subject in counterpoint always ends with the progression supertonic to tonic. This is in order to allow a final cadence when the subject is placed in the bass.

EXAMPLES IN THE minor.

(a) *Subject* in the bass; *counterpoint* above.

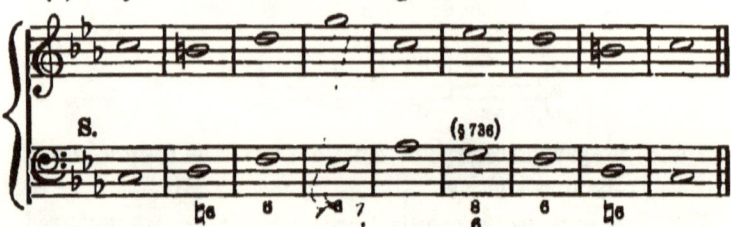

(b) *Subject* in the alto; *counterpoint* below.

736. Figuring. The student is advised to figure even two-part exercises. From §§ 723–5 he will have little difficulty in doing this. The only point to be specially noted is the interval of the sixth above the dominant in minor keys (§ 725 (c)). In order to distinguish this from a $\frac{6}{3}$ it is usually figured $\frac{8}{6}$, implying that either note may be doubled, but that no third may be added.

The student should now work exercises, using the *canti fermi* given on p. 287.

SECTION II.—First Species in Three and Four Parts.

737. With the increase of the number of parts the difficulty increases, and therefore in three and four parts some of the rules for two-part writing are relaxed. For example:

(a) Two parts may occasionally have a unison in the course of the exercise.

(b) The rule forbidding more than three successive thirds or sixths between any two parts is less strictly enforced, because variety is afforded by the third part.

(c) The repetition of a note is less objectionable than in two-part writing.

788. In other respects the rules to be followed remain the same. The general rules for the distribution of the notes of a chord (§§ 284-5) are to be followed; an even distribution is best; if that is not possible the widest interval should as a rule be between the two lowest parts.

789. In the **first bar** one of the parts must begin with a perfect concord; one of the other parts may have the third. In four parts begin with a complete chord.

740. As before, the exercises must end with the perfect cadence, in this case the tonic chord preceded by the dominant common chord with its root in the bass, or the first inversion on the supertonic.

Fig. 358.

Examples[1] in Three Parts.

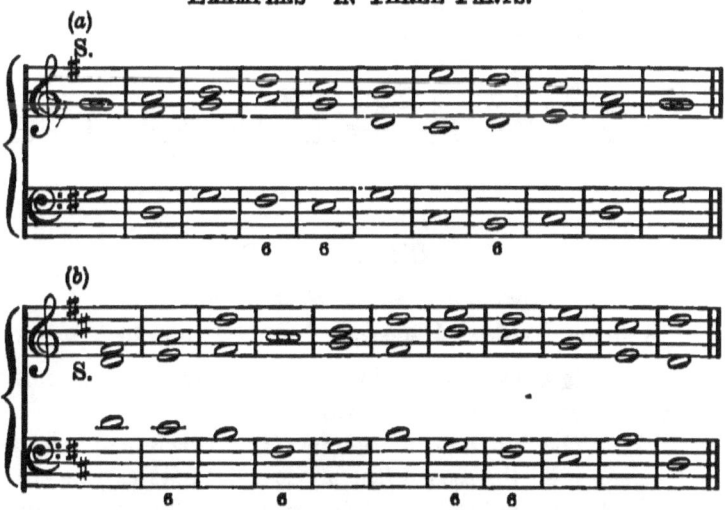

---

[1] These examples, to save space, are given in *short score*. The student, however, is advised to get accustomed to open score and the C clefs (§ 19) v. example § 802.

FIRST SPECIES OF COUNTERPOINT

EXAMPLES IN FOUR PARTS.

CHAPTER LIV.

SECOND SPECIES OF COUNTERPOINT.

SECTION I.—**Second species of counterpoint in two parts.**

741. In the second species the counterpoint has two notes to each of the notes of the subject.

742. The first note of each bar (*i.e.* the accented note) must be a concord; the second (the unaccented) note may be either a concord (*i.e.* another note of the same chord) or a passing note (or auxiliary note) approached and left by step. When possible a passing note is preferred (§ 528).

743. No bar except the first and last may have the unison at the accented beat. There is no objection to the unison at the unaccented beat.

744. Perfect fifths or octaves may not occur on the accented beat of two successive bars. Such fifths and octaves are best avoided even at successive unaccented beats.

FIG. 359.

745. To avoid monotony the same counterpoint should not be used twice in the same exercise even when the subject is different.

746. In each bar there must be only one chord.

An exception to this is when the counterpoint in the bass begins with a first inversion and there is no room for a passing note between that note and the bass in the next bar. In that case the bass may leap a fourth upwards or a fifth downwards.

FIG. 360.

747. Caution. When the counterpoint *leaps* in the bass care must be taken that it does not leap to a note which, by being in the bass, would produce a $\frac{6}{4}$ (§ 723-5), or a diminished fifth, or a fifth below the leading-note, such chords being disallowed.

FIG. 361.

748. Passing notes in minor keys. When the dominant and the leading-note are harmony notes the **major sixth** may be used between them, ascending or descending, fig. 268 (*a*).

When the submediant and the key-note are harmony notes, the **minor seventh** may be used between them, ascending or descending, fig. 268 (*b*).

If the leading-note begins two consecutive bars, the **major sixth** may be used as an auxiliary note; so also the **minor seventh** when the minor sixth begins two consecutive bars.

749. In the **first bar** the counterpoint must begin after a half-bar's rest. By entering after the subject, the counterpoint acquires greater point and individuality. The first note of the counterpoint must be a perfect interval.

750. **Cadences.** The principle underlying cadences in counterpoint is that there must be **only one chord in a bar.** This, in all species, must be the dominant common chord in its root position, or a first inversion on the supertonic (§ 740).

FIG. 362.

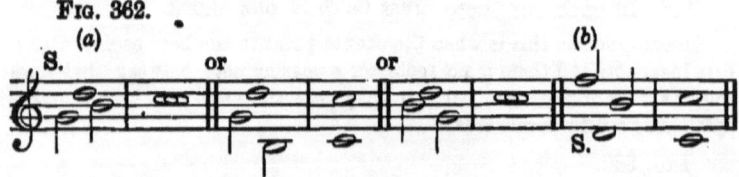

EXAMPLES IN TWO PARTS.

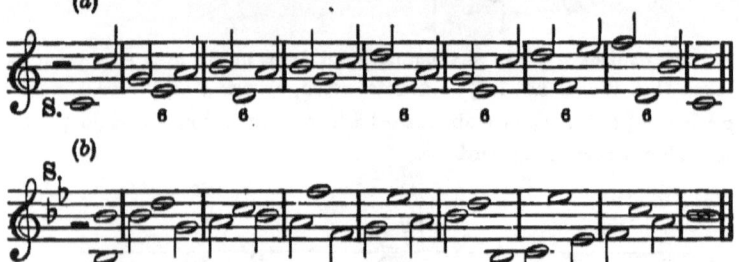

SECTION II.—**Second Species in Three and Four Parts.**

751. Only one of the parts will be in the second species, the others being in the first, following the rules of the first species.

752. As the part in the second species begins after a rest the

other parts must begin with a perfect interval. The moving part may begin with an imperfect interval.

Fig. 363.

758. **Cadences.**

Fig. 364.

* These moving notes may be used in the alto.

EXAMPLES IN THREE AND FOUR PARTS.

SECOND SPECIES OF COUNTERPOINT   275

CHAPTER LV.

THIRD SPECIES OF COUNTERPOINT.

754. The third species may have three, four, or six notes to one of the subject, four being the most usual.

755. The first note of each bar must be a concord; the others may be concords or discords, but all discords must be approached and quitted by step.

If the note to which a passing-note proceeds is also a passing-note, the passage must continue in the same direction in passing-notes until a harmony note is reached (fig. 262).

756. A second may not resolve on a unison, fig. 268.

757. When the counterpoint is in the bass the *fifth* of a chord may be used in arpeggio, provided that it is neither the *highest*, *lowest*, nor *last* note of the arpeggio. This also applies to doubling the leading-note.

FIG. 365.
(a) Good.   (b) Bad.

758. Changing-notes may be used in accordance with the rule stated in § 548.

759. Notes passing through the interval of a tritone are not allowed, except when they form part of a continuous passage beginning before and passing through this interval.

FIG. 366.
Bad.   Good.

760. The counterpoint begins after a rest equal in value to one note of the counterpoint.

761. Cadences, *v.* § 750, and notice the forms employed in the following exercises.

THIRD SPECIES OF COUNTERPOINT

Examples in Two Parts.

Examples in Three Parts.

EXAMPLE IN FOUR PARTS.

CHAPTER LVI.

FOURTH SPECIES OF COUNTERPOINT.

762. In the fourth species the counterpoint has two notes to each note of the subject, but the second note of each bar is tied to the first of the following bar in syncopation (§ 79).

FOURTH SPECIES OF COUNTERPOINT

763. The first note of each bar (except the last) must be either (a) a **suspension** prepared in the previous half bar, in which case it resolves by falling or rising a second; or (b) a concord, in which case it is free to rise or fall provided it leaps to another note of the chord.

The note on the second half of each bar must be a concord.

FIG. 367.

764. The rules for suspensions here are identical with those described in § 500, only it must be remembered that, *in strict counterpoint, second inversions cannot be used* (§§ 723–5), consequently the second inversions of chords with suspensions which are available in harmony are here excluded.

765. The suspensions available are: the *suspended ninth* with first and third inversions, according to §§ 501–2; the *suspended fourth* with first and third inversions, according to §§ 507–15; the *fifth* on the third and seventh of major and minor keys resolving by rising as in § 516.

766. No suspension is allowed in any progression which, if the suspension were absent, would have forbidden consecutives § 500 (e).

767. The note (or its octave) on which a suspension resolves must not be sounded at the same time as the suspended note, except the ninth and the fourth, according to the rules explained in § 500 (f). The note on which the suspended fifth resolves can *never* be sounded with that fifth.

768. The counterpoint must begin after a rest equal in value to one note of the counterpoint.

769. The chief cadences are shown in the following examples:

EXAMPLES IN TWO PARTS.

EXAMPLES IN THREE AND FOUR PARTS.

* When the fourth species is in the bass it is often necessary to break the syncopation to get a good cadence.

CHAPTER LVII.

FIFTH SPECIES OF COUNTERPOINT.

770. The fifth species has already been described as an ornamentation of the fourth species. This ornamentation is chiefly brought about by **ornamentally resolving** (§ 520) the suspensions, *i.e.* instead of proceeding immediately to its resolution, the suspended note may leap or go by step of a second to any other note of the chord provided that it then returns to the note of resolution, either (*a*) by leap, (*b*) by arpeggio, or (*c*) by passing-notes.

FIG. 368.

771. The even divisions of a bar of the third species may be subdivided into two quavers; four successive quavers should rarely be used except when the first is tied to a note held over from the preceding bar, as in fig. 368 (*c*).

FIG. 369.

772. A long note on the odd beat (*i.e.* first, third, &c.) of a bar may be followed by shorter notes on the next beat; but short notes on the odd beat may not be followed by longer notes on the even beats unless the long note is tied to a note in the following bar. There is an exception to this rule in cadences.

FIG. 370.

773. When a note is tied from one bar to the next, the part of the tied note before the bar-line must not be *shorter* than the part which follows.

774. A syncopation may be made either from a minim or a crotchet, but that from a minim is best.

775. Although the second and third species may be used, this should not be done for more than two consecutive bars.

776. It is best to begin the counterpoint after a crotchet rest.

777. For **cadences** see the following examples, remembering § 750:

Example in Four Parts.

CHAPTER LVIII.

COMBINED COUNTERPOINT.

778. The five species of counterpoint may be combined with each other, or two or more parts may at the same time have the same species of counterpoint.

In working these exercises the following additional rules are necessary.

779. No parts may move in seconds, sevenths, or ninths with each other.

780. The *lowest moving part*, even when not in the bass, must be considered as the bass, and must not move except in accordance with the rules for the bass (§§ 715, 728).

From this it follows that two upper parts may not move in fourths unless a lower part moves at the same time as the second fourth.

781. Each part must follow the rules of the species to which it belongs, with the additional rule that moving parts, although following the rules of their species, are not correct unless they move by consonant intervals with each other. An exception is allowed when a dissonant interval is approached and left by step of a second in contrary motion (c).

Fig. 371.

At (a) treble and alto are both correct according to their species, but the combination is incorrect because at * they make a fourth, which is not allowed because the alto is now the lowest moving part (§ 733).

At (b) this is corrected. The fourth between the treble and alto of bar two is allowed because the lower parts have moved, and therefore this fourth is between upper parts.

782. When the *fourth* species is used in two or more parts at the same time, or the *fourth* and *fifth* are combined, the rules for double and triple suspensions (§§ 521-3) must be followed.

783. No part may move by *similar* motion to the note (or its octave) on which a suspended note resolves, but any part may move in *contrary* motion to such note, §§ 879, 506.

784. When several parts are in the fifth species it is good to let the parts enter after each other. The parts should be contrasted as much as possible, one part moving while another has holding notes, &c. When possible, points of imitation should be introduced, as in Ex. (e) p. 287.

Examples of Combined Counterpoint.

(a)   Second and third species combined.

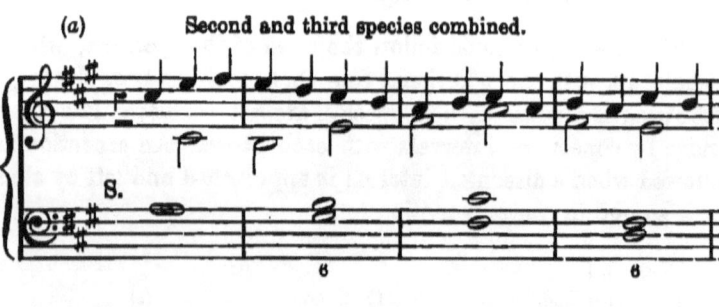

(b)   Second and fourth species combined.

(c) Second and fifth species combined.

(d) Second, third, and fourth species combined.

COMBINED COUNTERPOINT

(e)   Fifth species in three parts.

Canti Fermi FOR EXERCISES IN COUNTERPOINT.

These subjects should be used in every part, counterpoint being added above and below. They must be transposed when necessary to suit the compass of the part in which they are used. The same subject should be worked in all species.

Major.

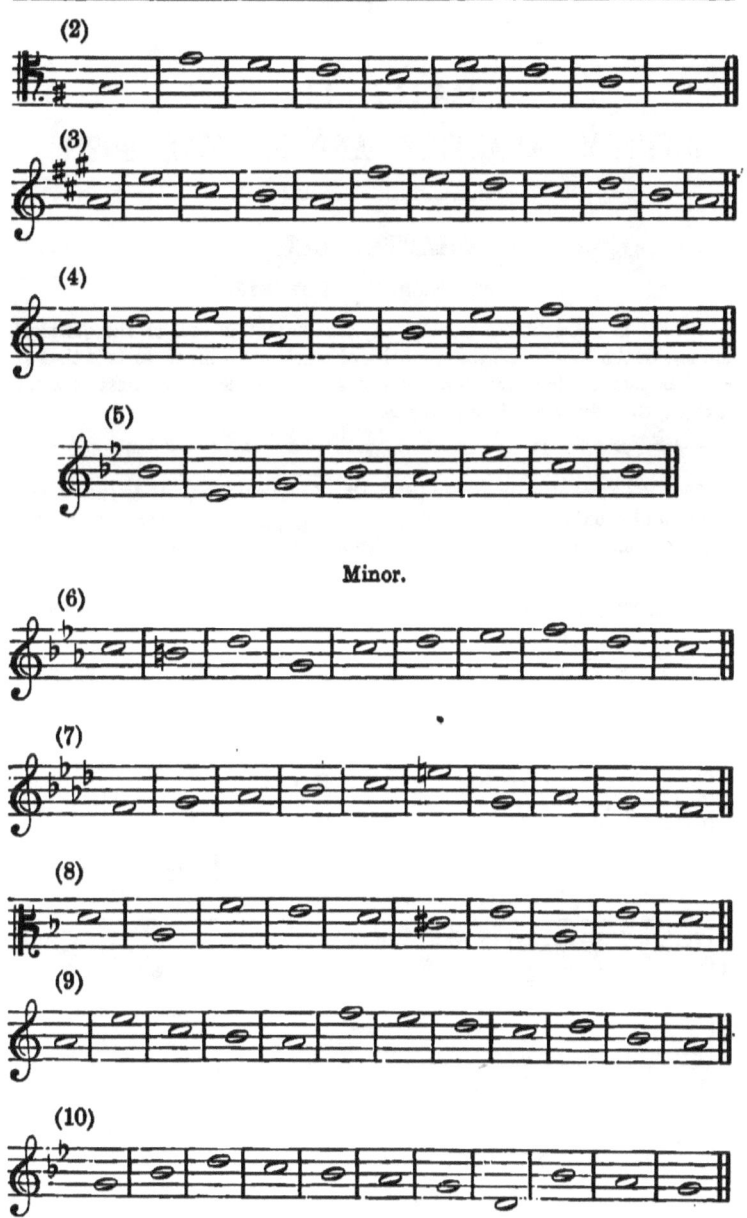

Minor.

MUSIC COURSE

PART III.
RHYTHM, ANALYSIS, AND MUSICAL FORM

CHAPTER LIX.
SENTENCES AND PHRASES.

785. It is scarcely too much to say that accent is one of the simplest and one of the most essential qualities of music. So much so is it that it would be impossible to sing a series of notes without laying a stress on some of them, thus *dividing them into sets*.

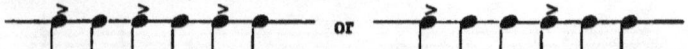

786. We have already shown (Pt. I. Ch. V.) how this accent divides music into sets of equal duration called bars or measures. But there is another way in which sounds are grouped with regard to duration. This will be seen from fig. 372.

FIG. 372. *Andante.*   MOZART, P.F. Concerto in E♭.

This is clearly a tune complete in itself; it is divided into bars, and further it is divided into two halves. The question arises, how are we to tell where divisions like this come? The answer is by the **cadences**. In this example an imperfect cadence comes in the fourth bar and this divides the tune into two halves, while a perfect cadence in the eighth bar finishes it.

All good music is constructed on some similar plan, *i.e.* it is divisible into parts which bear some relation to each other with regard to duration, and it is this relation in music which constitutes **Rhythm**. We may put it in another way.

787. Sounds are grouped—by *accent*—into sets called bars, and this is **Time**.

Tunes are grouped—by *cadence*—into sets of bars, and this is **Rhythm**.

Since cadences are used to divide music into rhythmical groups it becomes necessary to find out the true meaning of a cadence.

788. The word *cadence* properly means a *falling*, and in music it means a **close** or **ending**. It may be the ending of a complete musical idea, or merely the ending of a portion of an idea, as in the fourth bar of fig. 372.

A cadence in fact is a **point of repose**.

Since a cadence is a point of repose, *i.e.* a note or chord on which we can rest before proceeding further, it follows that the final chord of a cadence will be a **concord**.[1] A cadence therefore will usually consist of two chords, the first of which proceeds to the second, which is a concord.

789. The kinds of cadences have been already explained (§§ 453-63), but it will be well to recapitulate.

(*a*) A **perfect cadence** or **full close** consists of a dominant chord followed by the tonic chord.

(*b*) An **imperfect cadence** or **half close** ends on the dominant common chord preceded by any other chord.

(*c*) An **interrupted cadence** consists of a dominant chord followed by some chord other than the tonic, usually the submediant com. chd.

(*d*) A **plagal cadence** consists of the subdominant com. chd. followed by the tonic com. chd.

---

[1] See, however, § 796.

(e) If either of the chords of a perfect cadence is inverted the cadence is called an **inverted cadence**.

Besides the above there are many cadential endings which have no distinctive names.

Fig. 373.

790. The only cadence which can be used at the end of a melody or composition is the perfect cadence. The other cadences can only occur in the middle of a melody, and they are often classed together as **middle cadences**.

791. Now let us refer again to fig. 372. We only need to play it over to recognise that it sounds complete and finished, and further that it is plainly divided by the imperfect cadence in the fourth bar * into two halves of four bars each. We shall call the whole melody a **sentence** or **period** and each of the divisions a **phrase**. The vast majority of sentences used in music are, like that in fig. 372, eight bars in length and consist of two phrases, but we shall presently see that some sentences have three and others four phrases. We may, therefore, give the following definition:

A **sentence** is a passage which ends with a perfect cadence, and which consists of two or more parts called **phrases**.

792. The two phrases in fig. 372 are equal in length, but there is another relation between them. If we play to the end of the first phrase and then stop there is a feeling of incompleteness, something more is necessary to complete the idea. The second phrase has this completing effect. It is a sort of *reply* to the first, and it is often called the **responsive phrase**.

793. The cadence most used at the end of a first phrase is the *imperfect cadence*, but it is by no means the only one. The *interrupted cadence* is sometimes so used, though not very frequently.[1] There is one example in

---

[1] How this cadence is used will be seen later.

Pt. II. fig. 234, and another is seen in fig. 389, and another in the second movement of Schumann's P.F. Quintet, Op. 44.

794. The *plagal cadence* [1] is occasionally used at the end of a phrase. An example will be seen in the fourth bar of the well-known hymn tune *Rockingham*.

795. There are many cadential endings of phrases which have no definite names. In the next example the first phrase ends on the subdominant common chord.

Fig. 374.

Schumann, An den Sonnenschein.

To save space we only give the melody, but if the student will consult a copy of Schumann's songs he will see the subdominant common chord. Let it be said here that the only possible way of analysing music is by reference to the harmony, and that while we shall frequently only quote the melody, the student should not rest satisfied without referring to the original and noticing the harmony.

Fig. 375 shows a first phrase ending on the supertonic common chord.

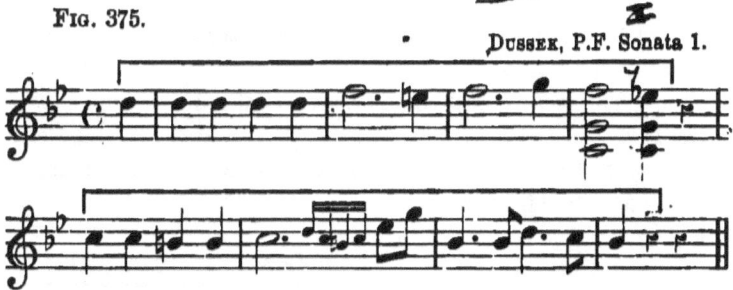

Fig. 375.

Dussek, P.F. Sonata 1.

796. In most cases the cadence ends on a common chord or an inversion, but sometimes a discord (especially the dominant 7th) is used with cadential effect.

---

[1] The use of this cadence is explained in Part II., § 457.

Fig. 376.

BEETHOVEN, Rondo a Capriccio.

797. We see in § 790 that the perfect cadence is usually reserved for the end of a melody. But for a perfect cadence to have the complete effect of a full close it must occur under the following conditions:

(a) Both chords of the cadence must be in the root position.

(b) The tonic chord should have the tonic (*i.e.* the key-note) in the treble.

(c) The tonic chord should occur on the strong accent of the bar.

When none of these conditions are satisfied a perfect cadence may occur as a middle cadence.

Fig. 377.

BEETHOVEN, P.F. Sonata XX.

Here the middle cadence is clearly perfect, but the first beat of the bar, *i.e.* the strong accent, has the third of the chord, and the tonic is not reached until the second beat, thus avoiding the feeling of finality.

FIG. 378.   MOZART, P.F. Sonata in C.

Here the tonic chord is delayed until the second beat of the bar, and the feeling of finality is further avoided by the tonic chord being in its first inversion.*

798. Further, many melodies modulate. When the first phrase modulates there is naturally a perfect cadence to establish the new key. When the second phrase modulates, the first frequently ends with a perfect cadence to better establish the original key.

FIG. 379.   SCHUBERT, P.F. Sonata in A minor.

The first phrase ends with a perfect cadence fulfilling all the conditions of § 797, for it will be seen that the upper G is merely an inverted pedal (§ 654). The second phrase modulates to the dominant.

In the next example the first phrase modulates to the dominant with a perfect cadence; the second phrase returning to the tonic.

Fig. 380.

BEETHOVEN, P.F. Sonata XVI.

799. Not infrequently the first phrase will have a perfect cadence even when the melody does not modulate. This is most frequently the case in short compositions (like hymn tunes) where the necessity for fixing the key is felt.

Fig. 381.

16th century.

Here both phrases are exactly alike, and both end with perfect cadences. The student must be warned against thinking that each phrase in such cases is a separate sentence. For, as was said in § 791, each sentence must consist of at least two phrases, *i.e.* a first phrase and a responsive phrase.

800. So far we have only dealt with sentences of **two phrases.** We now give examples of sentences of **three phrases** (twelve bars). Though not so usual as two-phrase sentences, they are far from uncommon, and an example will be seen in the first sentence of 'Rule, Britannia.' Here is another:

Fig. 382.

Mozart, Trio for P.F., Clarinet, and Viola.

The first phrase ends with a perfect cadence, but the tonic chord is delayed by a suspension until the third beat. The second phrase ends with a half-cadence; and the third phrase modulates to key of the dominant and ends with a full close. A similar example is seen in the *Menuetto* of Schubert's Octet, Op. 166.

801. Sentences of four phrases (sixteen bars) are quite common, and it will only be necessary to give one example.

Fig. 383. Schubert, P.F. Sonata in E♭, Op. 112.

Here are four phrases. The first ends on a dom. 7th (§ 796); the second ends with a half-cadence. The third phrase, like the first, ends on the dom. 7th, and the last with a perfect cadence. It should be noted that this sentence ends with the third of the chord in the melody. Notwithstanding § 797 this is not uncommon, and the student has only to play the above example to recognise that it has a proper feeling of finality.

It should be further noted that the first and third, the second and fourth phrases correspond in melody. This is very often, though by no means always, the case with sentences of four phrases.

802. It is very important to notice exactly **where a phrase ends**. When there are rests, as in fig. 372, this is simple enough, but in cases like figs. 374, 382 a certain difficulty arises, which the following considerations will do much to remove:—

(*a*) It cannot be too strongly urged that **it is impossible to divide melodies into phrases without referring to the harmony**, and that most phrases end on a common chord or an inversion. Thus in fig. 382 the first phrase ends on the third beat, because the minim C is merely a rising suspension resolving on D. Thus the common chord is not reached until the third beat.

(*b*) Many phrases end with a suspension, or with a progression like $^6_4\ ^5_3$ where the $^6_4$ has a dissonant effect (§ 335), which is only removed when the $^6_4$ proceeds to $^5_3$. Thus in fig. 382 the second phrase ends with $^6_4\ ^5_3$; and here the second beat is felt to be the end of the phrase. In fig. 374 the phrase ends on the third beat, for it is merely a suspension resolved by anticipation (§ 544). A comparison of the phrases will be of use. There is often a similarity of construction in the two phrases, which sets aside all doubt as to the end (see fig. 374).

(*c*) In very many cases the phrase ends on an accented beat (first or third), and it may be taken as a rule with very few exceptions that in the bar which contains the end of a phrase the note or notes on the unaccented beat belong to the following phrase unless they are *harmonically* connected with the preceding notes of the bar.

803. To make this clear we will analyse the following example:—

FIG. ~~344~~ 384.   BEETHOVEN, P.F. Sonata II.

298 RHYTHM, ANALYSIS, AND MUSICAL FORM

The division comes in the fifth bar, and we have marked the first phrase as ending on the second beat. We do this because the first chord is a discord which plainly resolves on the second chord (a first inversion of a common chord. Thus the common chord on the second beat is the *point of repose* which marks the end of the phrase. It should be noted, too, that with this division each phrase has a corresponding beginning.

In the above example we have added Beethoven's phrasing marks, in order to be able to warn the student against being led astray by the composer's slurs. In most cases, especially in older music, these are added without any reference to rhythmical divisions, being merely intended to indicate a *legato* style of playing.

804. Counting bars. In numbering the bars of a melody to be analysed it is best to number every separate bar division though it may not be a complete bar. Thus in fig. 384 the first division is numbered 1, though it is only one beat, and so with the last, which is only two beats. But although this example is numbered 1-9 solely for convenience of reference, the student must not forget that there are only eight whole bars, the first and the last together forming one bar. The same applies to the phrases; each phrase here is four bars in length, because the part of the first phrase in bar 1 added to the part of the first phrase in bar 5 makes up one complete bar.

Exercises.

1. Point out the *sentences* in the following hymn tunes (to be found in any hymnal), and divide them into *phrases*, stating what kind of cadence is used at the end of each phrase: 'Nicæa,' 'Benediction,' 'Rockingham,' 'Mendelssohn,' 'St. Agnes,' 'Easter Hymn,' 'St. Ann,' 'St. Peter.'

2. In the following movements show where the *first sentence* ends, and divide into phrases as in Q. 1.

Schumann, *Album for the Young*, Nos. 2, 4, 5, 6, 7, 15, 17, 20, 22, 24, 26, 37, 41.

SENTENCES AND PHRASES   299

Mendelssohn, *Christmas Pieces* (Op. 72), Nos. 1, 3, 5; *Songs without Words*, Nos. 14, 22*, 28*, 34*, 35*, 44, 45, 48.

* These have a short introduction, but it will be easy to see where the real melody begins.

Mozart P.F. Sonatas, the first movement of sonata in A (Novello, No. 11) and in F (Novello, No. 12).

Haydn, P.F. Sonatas, 1st movement in E♭ (No. 3, Peters).

Beethoven, P.F. Sonatas, I. 2nd movement; II. 2nd, 3rd, and 4th movements; IV. 2nd movement; VI. 1st movement; VII. 3rd movement; XI. 3rd and 4th movements; XII. 1st movement; XIV. 2nd movement; XV. 2nd movement; XIX. 2nd movement; XXVII. 2nd movement; XXXII. 2nd movement.

CHAPTER LX.

THE METHOD OF BARRING MUSIC.

805. So far all our sentences have consisted of eight, twelve, or sixteen bars and all our phrases of four bars. Look now at the following from Schumann's *Album for the Young*, Nos. 1 and 18:—

FIG. 385.

806. It is easy to see that each of these is a complete sentence, and yet the whole is in each case only four bars. Thus we apparently have sentences of four bars made up of phrases of two bars. The explanation is that sometimes pieces in common time (with four beats in a bar) ought to be written in $\frac{2}{4}$ time (with two beats in a bar). Thus (a) consists really of eight bars in $\frac{2}{4}$ time.

Similarly (though less frequently) there are pieces in $\frac{6}{8}$ time which should be in $\frac{3}{8}$. Thus (b) makes eight bars in $\frac{3}{8}$ time. So, too, not infrequently pieces in $\frac{12}{8}$ should be written with twice as many bars in $\frac{6}{8}$.

807. The number of bars in the sentence clearly depends on the method of barring, and proper **barring** does not depend on the number of notes but on the number of **accents**. A bar consists of a **strong accent** followed by one or two weaker **accents**. Now, in many cases in $\frac{4}{4}$ time there are two strong accents and two weak accents in each bar, and therefore each of these bars should be made into two with the signature $\frac{2}{4}$. Composers of the greatest eminence have not always been either careful or consistent (compare Schumann's *A. f. Y.*, Nos. 3 and 5) in the matter of barring, so long as the accents come in the right places.

808. There are even many pieces in $\frac{2}{4}$ time which have really four beats and two strong accents in a bar. In these cases it is possible to have a four-bar sentence which ought to be written as an eight-bar sentence in $\frac{2}{8}$ time.[1] Mendelssohn's *Songs without Words*, No. 44, is an example of this. Another even more convincing example is the slow movement of Beethoven's first *Rasoumoffsky Quartet* (Op. 59, No. 1).

809. We have shown that a real bar consists of one strong and one or two weak accents. Now, in $\frac{3}{4}$ time played rapidly[2] there is only one accent in a bar, and, as we cannot (as a rule) have two strong accents together, one bar in these cases has a strong accent and the next a weak one. Here, therefore, as a real bar must have the strong and the weak accent, it requires two written bars to make one rhythmic bar, and such pieces should be written in $\frac{6}{4}$ time, two bars being grouped into one. We give an example :—

Fig. 386.
Allegro assai.   Beethoven, Trio for P.F., Violin, and 'Cello, No. 1.

[1] Dvořák uses the signatures $\frac{4}{8}$ (in the Piano Quintet and *Stabat Mater*) and $\frac{2}{8}$ (in the Sextet). So also Franz, Op. 20, No. 2.

[2] In $\frac{3}{4}$ time played slowly there is in each bar a strong, a weak, and a

It is impossible to play this without accenting it as indicated, and it would be more correctly barred and certainly much easier to play if written as follows:—

Fig. 387.

Let the student halve the value of each note here and write it in $\frac{6}{8}$ time, he will see even more clearly that this view is correct. It may be asked why Beethoven did not write in $\frac{6}{4}$ or $\frac{6}{8}$ time if such is necessary for the proper performance. The reason is probably an historical one. This melody occurs in the scherzo of the trio. Now the scherzo (§ 966) was developed from the menuet, which was usually in $\frac{3}{4}$ time, and probably Beethoven wrote in $\frac{3}{4}$ time from a sort of habit, just as very many slow movements which ought to be in $\frac{4}{8}$ time are written in $\frac{2}{4}$.

810. In Part I., § 84, we drew attention to the displacing of the accent which may create the impression of a change of time. In many cases (e.g. Q. 7, p. 34) this is merely done for expression, the rhythmic relation of the bars remaining unaltered. In other cases, however, there is a genuine rhythmic change and in dividing such pieces into phrases this must be borne in mind. Thus in the example from Schumann's piano concerto quoted on p. 32 the whole sentence occupies sixteen bars, but it is shown in fig. 53 that the bars are really to be grouped in twos, thus making an eight-bar sentence of $\frac{3}{2}$ time.[1]

811. To sum up, though most sentences are of eight, twelve, or sixteen bars (i.e. two, three, or four phrases) there are sentences of nominally four half-strong accent usually on the last beat. When this last accent is prominent, it is possible to have a complete sentence of four bars, in $\frac{3}{4}$ time, as in Schumann's E♭ Symphony, second movement.

[1] There are occasional cases of this in $\frac{6}{8}$ time where sixteen bars must be grouped into eight bars of $\frac{12}{8}$ time. The episode in F in the Rondo of Beethoven's P.F. and V. Sonata, Op. 12, No. 1, is an example.

bars where each bar is really two. And similarly there are sentences of nominally sixteen bars where two bars must be grouped into one.[1]

EXERCISES.

1. Point out the sentences in the following hymn tunes, and divide into phrases; specify the kind of cadence: 'Winchester New,' 'St. Bride,' 'St. Mary,' 'Windsor,' 'Mannheim,' 'St. Stephen.'

2. Analyse as in question 1 the first sentence of the following movements; where possible rewrite the melody with a new time-signature:—Mendelssohn's *Songs without Words*, Nos. 4*, 9*, 16*, 44; Beethoven, P.F. Sonata XIII. (1st movement); III. (8rd movement); IV. 8rd movement (*minore*); VI. 2nd movement (the first section and the section in five flats); VII. 8rd movement; Schumann, *Album for Young People*, Op. 118, No. 2.

* These have an Introduction.

CHAPTER LXI.

SECTIONS AND MOTIVES. THE RELATION OF SECTIONS.

812. In most cases it is possible to subdivide *phrases* into smaller divisions. As a phrase contains four bars and four strong accents, it can be divided into two portions, which we shall call sections, each of which will consist of two bars and two strong accents. Thus:—

FIG. 388.   BEETHOVEN, P.F. Sonata XVI.

[1] Very occasionally a genuine change of time is produced by expression marks. There is an example of three bars of $\frac{4}{4}$ time grouped into four bars of $\frac{3}{4}$ in Mozart's *Idomeneo* ('Tutte nel cor vi sento').

SECTIONS AND MOTIVES. RELATION OF SECTIONS 303

813. Here the minims mark off each section so definitely as to leave no room for doubt. But in many cases this subdivision is not so easy, and we must find some method for all cases.

If we examine the harmony of the above passage we see that it is not merely the minims which mark off the ends of the sections, but that the end is really made by the *cadential effect* of the last two chords of the section. We have then only to remember what was said in § 788, viz. that a cadential effect is in most cases produced by proceeding from some chord to a second one which is *a concord*. If to this we add what is said in § 802 we shall have no difficulty in dividing phrases into sections.

814. In the next example the inverted cadence at (*a*) shows the end of the first section on D, the quaver C♯ clearly belonging to the next section. The second section is clear enough. The third section ends on a discord, but there is a cadential effect at (*b*).

FIG. 389.

BEETHOVEN, P.F. Concerto in G.

815. Except in suspensions and similar cases (§ 802) a section most frequently ends on the accented part of the bar, and *the*

following unaccented note or notes will belong to the following section.

816. In fig. 389 the sections are apparently of very different lengths. But it must be remembered that phrases are measured by accent. Here each section consists of two strong accents, and this is the equality which is felt.

Fig. 390.

817. In fig. 390 it is easy to see the end of each section, because a cadential effect is produced by suspension (a); the note on which the suspension resolves is clearly the end of the section.

It will be seen that the responsive phrase is not divided into sections. The reason is that (as sometimes happens) there is in this phrase no central point of repose which would warrant us in dividing into sections. In other words, the cadential feeling of the harmony at * is not strong enough to divide the phrase into two sections.

818. Here is a more complex case:—

Fig. 391.

SECTIONS AND MOTIVES. RELATION OF SECTIONS 305

The first section plainly ends at (*a*), for there is a strong feeling of cadence on the first beat, which is immediately upset by the following notes. The second section is perfectly clear. The third section is very instructive. The melody is merely an ornamented form of that used in section 1, but the harmony is now changed, and we do not end the section on the first beat of the bar as at (*a*), because here we have a suspension followed by a discord, and the *point of repose* is not reached until (*b*), where an interrupted cadence occurs.

819. A further subdivision is possible; a section may be divided into two portions, each of which is called a **motive**. As each section consists of two strong accents, each motive will consist of one strong accent, preceded by an unaccented note or notes. The motive ends on the accented note except where the notes immediately following are connected with it in harmony or in cases like suspensions. An example will make this clear.

FIG. 392.

It is easy to see why in so many of the motives in this example the accented beat is followed by an unaccented one. Thus at (a) we have a clear case of suspension. The D resolves on C, and we feel that the C belongs to and completes the motive. At (b), on the contrary, the motive clearly ends on the accented beat, for the following note has no harmonic connection whatever with the accented note.

820. We have seen that a musical sentence implies at least two parts, related to each other, a **phrase** and a **responsive phrase** (§ 792). As we advance we shall further see that this is the underlying principle in all music, and it applies not only in a movement, but also in the smallest subdivisions. A *motive* has an exactly similar construction, i.e. an unaccented [1] beat followed by a responsive accented beat.

We may now exhibit in tabular form the construction of an eight-bar sentence:

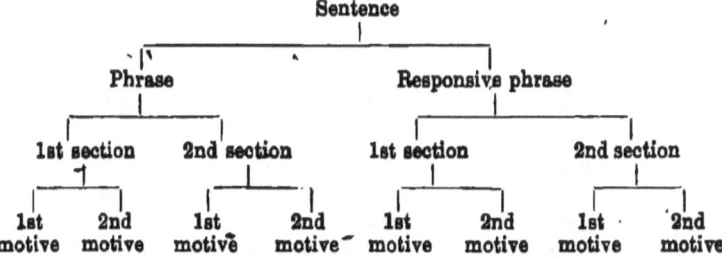

821. There is often a similarity in melodic outline between the various parts of a sentence. Thus in fig. 383 the first and third phrases are identical, and the second and fourth only differ in the last two notes. Here there is similarity of phrase. But as the majority of sentences are of two phrases,

---

[1] In fig. 389 and similar examples the first motive is without this unaccented beat. Prof. Prout (*Musical Form*, p. 27) terms such an example an 'incomplete motive.'

it will be better to institute a comparison between the *sections* of a melody. Thus in fig. 388, the first and third sections are identical; the second and fourth are almost identical, the little variation in the ending of Section IV. being necessary to bring it back to the original key. We will call Section I. A; Section II. B. As Section III. repeats I. we will call this A also, and to show that Section IV. is nearly identical with II., we will also call this B, but as there is a slight modification we will write this in italics. Thus our melody would stand in a sort of formula:

$$\overset{\frown}{A} + \overset{\frown}{B} + \overset{\frown}{A} + \overset{\frown}{B}.$$

This is by far the commonest arrangement of the sections of an eight-bar melody, but by no means the only one. Here is another:

Fig. 393.

BEETHOVEN, P.F. Sonata XXV.

This is clearly: $\overset{\frown}{A} + \overset{\frown}{B} + \overset{\frown}{B} + \overset{\frown}{C}.$

In fig. 394 we have $\overset{\frown}{A} + \overset{\frown}{A} + \overset{\frown}{A} + \overset{\frown}{B}.$

Fig. 394.

SCHUMANN, *Albumblätter.*

In fig. 372 each section is distinct, so we write $\overset{\frown}{A} + \overset{\frown}{B} + \overset{\frown}{C} + \overset{\frown}{D}.$

Other variations are possible, and it will be easy for the student to apply this method, if he remembers to use a letter for each section, and where two sections are melodically alike to employ the same letter.

822. There are other interesting ways of looking at the constituent parts of a melody. For example, in the following the second section imitates[1] the first, but in contrary motion (§ 822)—where Section I. rises, Section II. falls by a similar interval, and *vice versa.*

---

[1] These sections are played alternately by 'cello and viola.

FIG. 395.

SCHUMANN, P.F. Quintet.

823. The next example is very interesting.

FIG. 396.

BEETHOVEN, P.F. Trio, Op. 1, No. 1.

The phrase (I.) is repeated four times, and is then followed by the melody (II.), which is mainly made up of the fragment of I. marked (a) freely imitated. This is used twice, and then the next part (a*) of the melody is made from the figure (a) by halving the length of each note. The importance of this example lies in the fact that it shows how a whole melody may be developed out of one single little idea.

We shall have much to say about this aspect of music in the chapters which follow.

824. We have used the word **Figure**, and this is a convenient place to explain its meaning. A **Figure** is a group of notes which has a distinct and significant musical meaning, and which embodies a distinct idea. It is often, but not always, synonymous with motive.[1]

---

[1] *Motive* is used in more than one sense. It sometimes means the same as *sentence* or *period*. In § 819 it is used in its strict meaning in rhythm.

SECTIONS AND MOTIVES. RELATION OF SECTIONS 309

EXERCISES.

Divide the melodies mentioned on pp. 298-9 into sections and motives, and represent as in § 821 by means of letters, the relation of the various sections.

825. **Note to Chapter LXI.**—In Part I., Chapter V., we pointed out that there is a certain analogy between the use of accent in music and in poetry. This accent in poetry divides words and syllables into feet, and to a certain extent the *foot* in poetry corresponds to the *motive* in music. As the names used in Latin and Greek poetry[1] are sometimes, though not, however, very usefully applied to music, it will be well to define them.

A **foot** means an accented syllable combined with one or two other syllables which are generally short. The following are the names of some of the more frequently used feet:—

(*a*) Feet with **two** syllables.

A **Trochee** has an accented syllable followed by an unaccented one - ⌣ as con-*cert*.

An **Iambic** has an unaccented syllable followed by an accented one ⌣ ⊢ as in-firm.

(*b*) Feet with **three** syllables.

An **Amphibrach** has two unaccented syllables with an accented one between them ⌣ – ⌣ as in-con-*stant*.

An **Anapæst** has two unaccented syllables followed by an accented one ⌣⌣ – as co-lonn-ade.

A **Dactyl** has an accented syllable followed by two unaccented ones – ⌣⌣ as dif-fi-cult.

CHAPTER LXII.

HOW SENTENCES ARE LENGTHENED.

If all the sentences of a long composition were eight bars in length the greatest monotony would be the result, and we therefore find sentences both of more and of less than eight bars. We will first examine how sentences are lengthened.

826. In most cases **lengthening** is produced by repetition of some sort. Thus in the following we have a regular eight-bar sentence up to the sign *. But this is clearly not the end because

---

[1] It must be remembered that in classical poetry the foot was determined by *quantity* and not by accent.

there is an interrupted cadence, after which the seventh and eighth bars are repeated, thus making a sentence of ten bars, *i.e.* $4+\overparen{4+2}$.

Fig. 397.

827. This repetition is most frequently connected with the *cadence*, and we shall speak of it as *cadential repetition*. The part repeated may be simply the one cadence-bar, making nine bars, as in the Scherzo of Beethoven's P.F. Sonata XVIII.; or the final *section*, as in fig. 397, making ten bars ; or the whole of the *responsive phrase* may be repeated, making twelve bars, as in Mendelssohn's *S. w. W.*, No. 14.

The repeated portion is sometimes considerably modified, as in the following:

Fig. 398.

This example, like the last, is $4 + \overparen{4 + 2} = 10$. Finality is avoided in the eighth bar by using an inverted cadence at *.

828. Sometimes the cadence of the first phrase is repeated, making $\overparen{4 + 2} + 4 = 10$, and not infrequently such a repeated cadence will be in a new key, as in the following from Schubert's P.F. Sonata :—

Fig. 399.

It is easy to see that (*a**) is a repetition of (*a*) in the key of the dominant.

829. Another way of lengthening a sentence will be best understood by comparing the two following passages from Haydn's P.F. Sonata in E major.

Fig. 400.

This occurs as the first melody of a *minuet*; it is a regular eight-bar sentence[1] divided into two equal phrases at *. When the melody is repeated at the end of the minuet it takes the following form:—

Fig. 401.

[1] It is stated in § 791 that a sentence ends with a Perfect Cadence. There are, however, numerous cases where a passage ending with a half-cadence has all the feeling of a complete sentence in itself. The above is such a case. Compare the effect in the first eight bars of the minuet in Beethoven's P.F. Sonata XVIII.

The melody is now ten bars, the lengthening being produced by repeating (in free sequence) the two bars marked (a) at the distance of a third above. We might express the sentence thus: $4 + \overparen{2(+2^*)} + 2 = 10$. Or adopting letters to represent the sections, as in § 821, we should get $A + B + \overparen{C(+C)} + D$.

880. **A melody may therefore be lengthened by the sequential repetition of some of its bars**, and most frequently the bars repeated are the two forming the third *section*. Not infrequently the repeated bars—just like the repeated cadence—will be in a new key, and even slightly varied, as in the minuet of Haydn's P.F. Sonata in G, No. 81, Peters' edition.

We shall see presently that a single bar may be repeated as well as a whole *section*.

881. **Lengthening** may also be produced by **doubling** the length of the notes of the cadence.

Fig. 402.

MENDELSSOHN, 'Greeting.'

Judging from the bar (a) we should have expected the ending to be

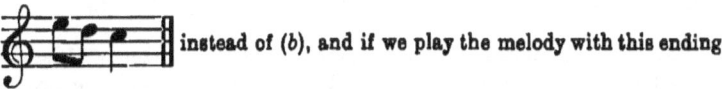

instead of (b), and if we play the melody with this ending instead of that shown above we shall find that it sounds perfectly correct, and that it is eight bars in length. Mendelssohn, instead of ending this way, doubled the value of a bar like (a) and wrote it as at (b). This merely strengthens the feeling of the ending, and the melody is $4 + 5 = 9$ bars.

832. In many cases this doubling is not quite so evident to the eye, as

HOW SENTENCES ARE LENGTHENED

will be seen from the following extract from Wagner's *Lohengrin*. The Bridal Chorus opens thus with a regular sixteen-bar sentence divided into four phrases:—

Fig. 403.

When this is repeated later in the movement, it is repeated exactly until the fourth phrase is reached, which now appears thus:

Fig. 404.

Here the two bars marked (*b*) are a freely lengthened form of the bar (*a*) in fig. 403, the crotchet G becoming a minim, &c. Thus at its repetition the melody becomes 4 + 4 + 4 + 5 = 17 bars.

833. As a rule, lengthening such as that here described is confined to doubling the last bar of the responsive phrase, thus producing 4 + 5 = 9 bars, but it is quite possible to double the length of the cadence-bar in both phrases, producing 5 + 5 = 10 bars. Mendelssohn's song 'New Love' quadruples the length of the cadence in both phrases, producing 6 + 6 = 12 bars. (See also the last two bars of *Songs without Words*, No. 33.)

834. The general effect of doubling the cadence is to produce a phrase of five bars. There are many cases of five-bar phrases where it is not easy to say whether it is caused by doubling a cadence or repeating a bar, and in some cases one is forced to explain the additional bar as being interpolated. We shall return to this again.

835. We must now examine some cases where the lengthening is only apparent.

FIG. 405.

SCHUBERT, P.F. Sonata, Op. 147.

We have here twelve bars, but it is easy to see that the two bars marked *prefix* have no real connection with the melody. Beginning with the third bar we have the sentence already described in § 828 and the two bars of prefix or introduction may be compared to the introductory bars played before the voice part of a song. Indeed, when the above melody reappears later in the movement it is without this prefix. The twelve bars are therefore made up as follows: 2 (Introduction) + 4 + 2 + 4 = 12. (Compare Mendelssohn, *S. w. W.*, Nos. 22, 28, 34, 35.) Sometimes the *prefix* only consists of a single note.

836. It is a good plan in analysing a sentence to examine the whole of the movement from which it is taken. Very often the same sentence occurs more than once, and it is no uncommon thing to find some modification at each recurrence. A comparison of the various forms a composer has given to a sentence will often show clearly how the modifications have been made.

EXERCISES.

1. Analyse and explain the process of lengthening in the first sentence of the following: Schumann's *Album for the Young*, Nos. 13 and 43; Beethoven's P.F. Sonatas, Nos. 4, 17, 12 (last sentence of Scherzo); Mendelssohn's *Songs without Words*, Nos. 4 and 23.

CHAPTER LXIII.

HOW SENTENCES ARE SHORTENED.

837. The commonest method of shortening an eight-bar sentence is **overlapping**, as in the following example:—

HOW SENTENCES ARE SHORTENED

Fig. 406.

Haydn, P.F. Sonata in C.

Here are two eight-bar sentences, the first phrase of each ending with a half-cadence. The second sentence, instead of beginning *after* the first, begins on the last bar of the first, so that the eighth bar serves the two-fold purpose of the eighth bar of the first melody and the first bar of the second melody. This is overlapping, and it shortens two eight-bar sentences (= 16 bars) into 15 bars.

838. This is scarcely a shortening of a melody, however, and if this were the only use of overlapping it would demand very casual notice. But overlapping can take place between two *phrases* (or even two *sections*), *i.e.* the responsive phrase may be begun on the final bar of the first phrase, thus producing a shortened sentence of seven bars instead of eight.

Fig. 407.

Mozart, *Il Seraglio*, Act II.

This sentence is used as the final symphony (§ 871) of a song. It is previously used as the introduction to the same song, and then it is a regular eight-bar sentence, but now it is shortened to seven bars.

The first *phrase* is evidently incomplete. We might easily imagine some ending like this:—

FIG. 408.

This change would make it an ordinary eight-bar sentence, and it is evident that in fig. 407 the **responsive phrase overlaps**[1] by beginning on the last bar of the first phrase.

839. In examining cases of apparent overlapping it is necessary to be careful to find the exact end of the phrase or sentence, *e.g.* in the *Rondo* of Beethoven's P.F. Sonata XIX. bar 38 it looks as if the new melody begins at the beginning of the bar, in which case there would be overlapping. But if we compare bar 104, where the same melody is repeated in G, it becomes clear that the melody begins at the half-bar. The D therefore in bar 38 is the end of a previous sentence and there is no overlapping here.

840. A sentence is often shortened by the **omission of a bar** from one of its phrases.

FIG. 409.

Mozart, ' The Violet.'

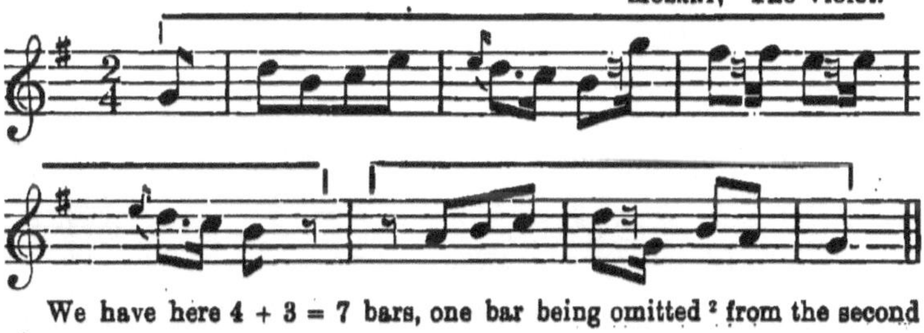

We have here 4 + 3 = 7 bars, one bar being omitted[2] from the second phrase.

---

[1] For some curious effects of overlapping see the accompaniment to Schumann's song ' The Green Hat ' (*Volksliedchen*).

[2] When the second phrase is reduced to three bars it often appears to be caused by a method the converse of that explained in § 831 for lengthening, *i.e.* the notes of two bars are halved in value and thus produce one bar. If the last bar but one in fig. 409 is doubled thus—

and substituted for the one bar, we get a perfectly regular eight-bar sentence. This is also the case in the often quoted example from Schubert's P.F. Sonata, Op. 120 (Andante).

In the next example the sentence is 3 + 4 = 7 bars. It is easy to see by comparing with the second phrase that a bar corresponding to bar (a) is omitted from the first phrase, i.e. bar 3. To make this clearer the motives are marked.

FIG. 410.

HUMMEL, P.F. Sonata in C.

841. A bar may be omitted from each phrase, producing a sentence of 3 + 3 = 6 bars.

FIG. 411.

CLEMENTI, P.F. Sonata.

Let us mark the sections; it is clear that the last two bars of each phrase form a *section*, and so we see that the omitted part is from the beginning of each phrase.

EXERCISES.

1. Analyse the first sentence from the following, explaining the construction: Schumann's *Forest Scenes*, No. 1; Mendelssohn's *Songs without Words*, No. 11; Allegro con moto(₵) from Fantasia dedicated to Moscheles, Op. 28; Mozart's P.F. Sonata in G (No. 5, Novello); Beethoven, P.F. Sonata XVII. (Adagio).

2. Analyse and explain the following :—

CHAPTER LXIV.

EXAMPLES OF RHYTHM.

842. When each *phrase* of a sentence consists of an equal number of bars it is usual to speak of it as being in such and such a rhythm, naming the rhythm according to the number of bars in each phrase. Thus we speak of three-bar rhythm, five-bar rhythm, &c. We shall now give examples of such rhythms, and the student should notice (according to the methods of Chapters LXII. and LXIII.) how the lengthened or shortened phrases are produced.

843. As an example of **two-bar rhythm** we quote 'God Save the Queen.' This consists of three phrases, each of which is two bars.

844. We have already seen (fig. 411) an example of **three-bar rhythm**, *i.e.* where each phrase is three bars in length. It should be noted that where the phrases are lengthened or shortened it is almost invariably the rule for the whole sentence to be repeated. This is so in the example from Clementi. In this way the very *repetition* of what is somewhat irregular assists the

---

[1] The student should refer to the harmony of this. It begins in the sixty-sixth bar of the first movement.

EXAMPLES OF RHYTHM

mind in grasping the melody, and creates a sort of regularity which to some extent restores—as it were—the balance.

845. **Five-bar** phrases occur most frequently as the responsive phrase, and it is somewhat rare to find two five-bar phrases in a sentence. Here is an example:

Fig. 413.

Schubert, P.F. Sonata, Op. 122.

846. We must examine six-bar rhythm a little more closely.

Fig. 414.

Haydn, P.F. Sonata in C minor.

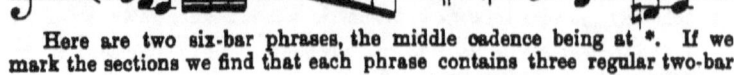

Here are two six-bar phrases, the middle cadence being at *. If we mark the sections we find that each phrase contains three regular two-bar sections. Just as some sentences contain *three* four-bar *phrases* (§ 800) some phrases contain *three* two-bar *sections* (§ 812). We may express this melody therefore as $\overgroup{2+2+2} + \overgroup{2+2+2}$.

It is possible to look upon this and similar melodies in another way. We may consider the third section of the first phrase as a repetition of the cadence contained in the second section (§ 827), though this construction is not nearly so evident in the second phrase. If this view is taken we write $\overgroup{4+2} + \overgroup{4+2}$.

Many six-bar passages take this form. In the next example a different construction is evident.

FIG. 415.   MOZART, P.F. Sonata in F.

Here the six-bar phrases (cadence at *) are clear enough. We cannot, however, divide the phrases into two-bar sections as in fig. 414. It will be seen on referring to the harmony that the bars marked (*a*) are merely repetitions of the same thing. We therefore consider the first section of each phrase as three bars made up of $\overgroup{2+1}$, the one bar being a kind of repeated cadence. The second section of each phrase is made up differently; it is again three bars, but this time it corresponds to the lengthening of a phrase described in § 831. We should, therefore, express this melody as 6 ($= \overgroup{2+1} + 3$) + 6 ($= \overgroup{2+1} + 3$).

847. Occasional examples of **seven-bar** phrases are seen (*e.g.* Haydn's P.F. Sonata in A, No. 26, Peters, where four such phrases come in succession), but as a rule combinations of more than six bars form complete sentences, and as such have been already dealt with.

EXAMPLES OF RHYTHM

848. When the student meets with an exceptional phrase or sentence he will often be assisted in determining its construction *by examining the whole of the movement*, for so deeply ingrained is the feeling for what we have called the normal four-bar phrase that even when a composer has begun with an irregular phrase he very frequently falls, at some part of the movement, into using the same phrase modified so as to fit the four-bar rhythm. There are very many notable examples of this, but we need only quote one, viz. the melody beginning after the first double bar of the last movement of Beethoven's P.F. Sonata I. This melody is ten bars long, and it is immediately repeated in a slightly varied form. Then after a regular eight-bar sentence the first melody comes again, this time *eight* bars long. The second melody is now repeated, and is then again followed by the first melody, which is now only *seven* bars long. Thus in the space of fifty-one bars the same melody occurs four times, the first and second times as a ten-bar melody, then as an eight-bar, and finally as a seven-bar melody. A careful examination of each of these forms will materially assist in deciding the construction of the ten-bar form, and we recommend it as an excellent exercise.

849. To conclude this part of the chapter we will analyse one example of an enlarged sentence.

FIG. 416.

HUMMEL, P.F. Sonata VIII.

This is a melody of eighteen bars beginning in E♭ and ending in B♭. That it is *one* melody and not two is evident, and we must try to explain its construction. First let us look for repetitions (§ 826). The parts of bars 5 and 6 marked (*a*) are clearly repeated in bars 6 and 7. So also the bars marked (*b*). Now for the melody; the first phrase is a perfectly regular one of four bars. In the second phrase the first section (*a*) is repeated, and to restore the balance caused by this repetition a whole new responsive phrase (* . . . *)—lengthened by the repetition of (*b*) to five bars—is added. The melody might end here, but the remaining bars clearly belong to it, and the question arises what relation do these bars bear to the melody? We shall see later (§ 940) that a movement often ends with a **coda** or tail-piece to mark definitely the conclusion. These five bars form a coda to the melody, and it is no uncommon thing to find such a *coda* added to a lengthened sentence. The construction of the coda is simple enough. The two bars (*c*) are repeated slightly varied, and the final bar (*d*) is another varied form of the preceding bar. The whole melody may be summed up thus: **18** bars = **4** (first phrase) + **9** (second phrase) + **5** (coda).

950. Before leaving the subject of Rhythm, we may just draw attention to the occasional interpolation of a single bar of a time different from that of the whole movement. This is sometimes caused by overlapping. Thus in Schumann's song 'Weit, Weit,' which is written in $\frac{6}{8}$ time, at the end of the first phrase of the melody there occurs one bar in $\frac{9}{8}$ time. This is caused thus:—At the end of the first phrase the accompaniment has *two bars* of interlude, but this interlude begins on the last half of the last bar of the melody, thus overlapping.

EXAMPLES OF RHYTHM

Fig. 417.

851. Other cases are caused by lengthening as in § 826 together with the temporary change of time, or by a new rhythmical grouping of a melody when an interpolated bar becomes necessary to restore the movement to its original rhythm. There are interesting examples of this in Dvořák's *Stabat Mater*, especially in Nos. 4 and 11.

852. In some cases a whole melody consists of an alternation of bars in different times. This, as a rule, however, does not affect the rhythm, as is seen from the 'Canzone di Magali,' from Gounod's *Mirella*, which is written in alternate bars of $\frac{9}{8}$ and $\frac{6}{8}$ time. The first sentence is just eight bars, like that described in § 791, the unequal bars merely giving a quaint effect to a perfectly regular melody.

In some cases, like the one just quoted, two bars are combined into one, when we get such signatures as $\frac{5}{4}$, *i.e.* $\frac{2}{4} + \frac{3}{4}$. An example is seen in Chopin's Sonata, Op. 4, mentioned in Pt. I. § 87.

Exercises.

The student should now analyse all the sentences of complete movements, explaining their construction and noting cases of overlapping and extension. The following may be taken to begin with: Beethoven's P.F. Sonatas, VII., Menuetto; XII., Scherzo; XVI., Allegretto; XVIII., Menuetto and Trio; Mozart, P.F. Sonatas, IV. (Novello), Menuetto; VI., Tema; Mendelssohn, *Songs without Words*, Nos. 1 and 8; Schubert's P.F. Sonata I., Rondo.[1]

[1] This, in common with almost all Schubert's instrumental music, will be found extremely difficult from the point of view of rhythmical analysis.

CHAPTER LXV.

KEY-RELATIONSHIP.

853. So far we have only concerned ourselves with *Rhythm*; we must now approach the subject of **Form**. Rhythm is concerned with the construction of musical sentences. Form [1] has to do with the way in which musical sentences or melodies are combined so as to form movements. We might say that **Form in music means the plan on which a piece of music is constructed.**

For example, a *march* or a *sonata* is made up of various tunes: the form of the *march* or of the *sonata* is the way these tunes are used and the relation existing among them which causes the one to be called a march and the other a sonata. The chief relation which binds melodies together into a movement is **key**. This is recognised in the very lowest departments of music. The writer who strings together a number of popular airs makes them recognisable as a *set* by allowing for this element of key. But what is meant by the key of a piece of music? For example, we say that Beethoven's 'Waldstein Sonata' (Op. 51) is in C. Does it mean that the whole sonata is in this key? By no means; but it means that this is the **central key** of the whole, that it begins in C and finally returns to and ends in C, and that all other keys used in the composition have some key-relationship to this central key. It becomes evident from this that before we can study musical form we must thoroughly understand key-relationship.

854. Two keys are said to be related when they consist of all, or nearly all, the same notes, and the more notes common to two keys the more nearly are they related.

Thus the scales of C and G major have all their notes alike except one, F♯; similarly the scales C and F are alike except B♭. We say then that C major is related to G major and to F major.

We saw (§ 128) that every major scale has a *relative minor* which begins on a note a minor third below the old tonic. C *major* is therefore related to A *minor*; G *major* to E *minor*; F *major* to D *minor*. As C major is related to G and F major, it must, through these, be related to their rela-

---

[1] It must not be supposed that Rhythm and Form can be thus separated. A single sentence has its *form* as well as the longest movement, and the principles underlying both are absolutely the same.

tive minors, *i.e.* E minor and D minor. C *major* is therefore related to A *minor*, to G *major*, to E *minor*, to F *major*, to D *minor*. Putting this in general terms, we say the **related keys to a major key** are the *major keys* of the *dominant* and *subdominant* and the *minor keys* of the *supertonic, mediant,* and *submediant.* Proceeding in the same way we shall see that the **related keys to a minor key** are the *relative major,* the *minor keys* of the *dominant* and *subdominant* with their *relative majors, e.g.* C minor is related to E♭ *major,* G *minor,* B♭ *major,* F *minor,* A♭ *major.*

855. The real ground of key-relationship is *chordal,* two keys being related when they have chords in common. When, therefore, we take into consideration the chromatic chords described in Pt. II., Ch. XLIV. and XLV., we obtain other related keys, although the relationship is not so close as in those above mentioned. For example, C is related to A major, because the supertonic chromatic chord in C (D, F♯, A) is the subdominant com. ch. in A.

856. The student should recapitulate Pt. II., Ch. XXXVIII. and XLIX., to see how modulation is brought about. In the majority of cases the modulations used in a melody and in a movement are to related keys, and by far the most usual modulation from major keys is to the dominant, from minor keys to the relative major. But an unrelated key may be used even in a short tune, *e.g.* the second subject of Schumann's trio, Op. 80, modulates to the supertonic *major.* In comparing the keys used, enharmonic notation (Pt. I. §§ 163–173) must be kept in mind. In a long movement, too, a key which is altogether unrelated to the central key may have its justification in the keys surrounding it, *i.e.* it may occur in a compound modulation (§ 667)

CHAPTER LXVI.

Section I. Two-part Form.

857. We are now to see how musical sentences or melodies are combined to make complete pieces or movements. Obviously the simplest form of such a movement is when **two eight-bar sentences** are combined. Of such there are thousands of examples in hymn tunes, simple songs, &c., and we will give two typical examples.

FIG. 418.

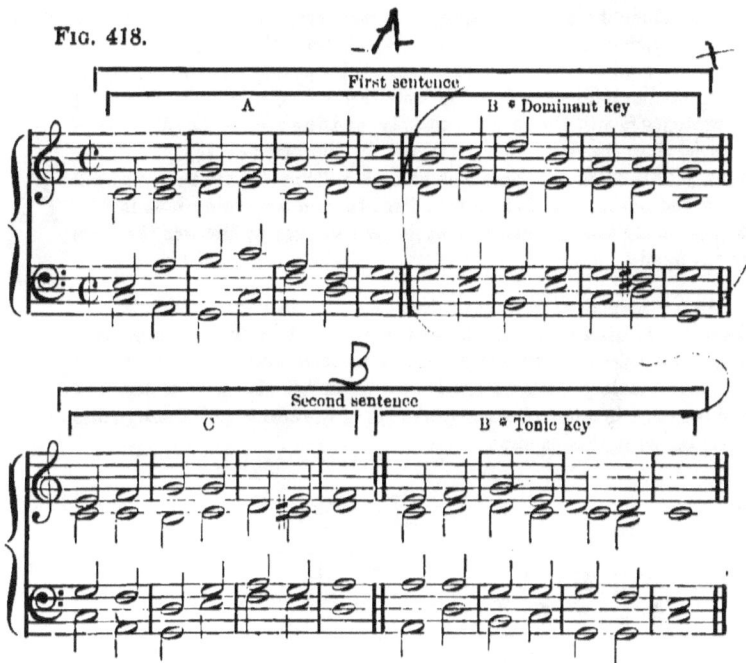

In this example the first sentence modulates to the key of the dominant. The second sentence begins by immediately returning to the tonic key (though it further modulates at the end of the first phrase) and it ends in the tonic key. Now examine the *second* phrase of each sentence; we find they are identical in *melody*; in fact, the final phrase merely repeats in the tonic key the same bit of melody which occurs at the end of the first sentence in the dominant key. We shall see presently that this repetition is not absolutely necessary, but it is easy to see that it gives a great feeling of completeness to the whole tune.[1]

---

[1] It is not often that a complete movement is made up of a single sentence. Mendelssohn's song quoted in fig. 402 is an example. It has, it is true, a few bars of introduction and a final symphony, but the song itself is a single sentence. Such is the case, too, in many old ballads, *e.g.* 'The Bailiff's Daughter of Islington,' 'Barbara Allen,' &c. Complete movements of a single sentence of three phrases (§ 800) are more common than those of two. There is an example in Schumann, Op. 118, No. 2, Air with Variations. Franz's song 'Gleich und Gleich,' Op. 22, No. 1, is a single sentence of four phrases.

858. The student must not imagine that *mere repetition* would cause this feeling of completeness. Play the above tune, beginning with the second sentence and ending with the first. It still consists of two complete sentences, but the total effect is ludicrously incomplete, although the ending of each sentence is still the same in melody, and the reason for this incompleteness is that the tune now ends, not in the original key, but in the dominant. This bears out what was said in § 853, viz. that the principal element which binds a number of melodies into one complete whole is **key**, and the reason for the completeness of fig. 418 is that at the end it comes back to the key.[1]

859. In our second example the first sentence does not modulate. In such cases it is almost invariable that the second sentence begins with modulation (to prevent monotony), but it must eventually return to the original key, and very often we shall find, as in fig. 419, part of the first sentence repeated to add to the completeness of the effect. All these points are to be noticed in this example.

Fig. 419.   Pleyel.

---

[1] A composition *must* begin and end in the same key. Tunes beginning in minor keys often end in the tonic *major*. In longer compositions this is exceedingly common. In shorter pieces it is quite allowable but not so common. There is an example in the hymn tune 'Vox Dilecti,' *v.* n. 1, p. 841.

860. We have drawn attention to the **repetition** of a portion of the first sentence at the end of the second. When the complete tune is short there is less need for this *repetition*, the key alone being sufficient to establish the unity of the piece, and there are hundreds of hymn tunes, airs with variations, &c., in which no repetition whatever occurs.[1] But in **longer pieces it may be taken as a rule that some sort of repetition of part of the first sentence is found at the end.**

Sometimes the first phrase is repeated, as in the following :—

Fig. 420.   Haydn,[2] Quartet, Op. 1, No. 1.

Here the repeated phrase is slightly modified. In many cases only a portion of a phrase—sometimes only the bare cadence—is repeated (*v.* the hymn tune 'Angels' Song ').

861. For a piece of music to give pleasure its form must possess two qualities. It must have sufficient **unity** of design to enable the mind to grasp it as a whole ; and it must have sufficient **variety** to avoid becoming tedious and monotonous. *Unity* is produced firstly by key and secondly by the repetition of some feature. Even the mere similarity (without actual repetition) of a final cadence adds to this feeling. *Variety* is obtained

---

[1] *E.g.* the hymn tunes ' St. Michael ' and ' Tallis.' In general there is less repetition in short vocal forms than in instrumental (*v.* § 1068).

[2] It will be seen that each sentence of this example is repeated. This is not an absolute necessity nor does it alter the construction of the movement ; it still consists of two sentences.

TWO-PART FORM

firstly by using fresh melodies or portions of melodies in contrast to what has already been heard; secondly by using fresh keys.

Let us apply these principles to the Haydn Minuet, fig. 420. The first phrase is in the tonic key, and it is followed by a phrase in *contrast* not only as to melodic form but as to key. The first half of Part II. is more or less founded on the second phrase of Part I. This is an element of unity, but there is also variety, because it is now heard in a new key, and the whole is clinched, as it were, by the very definite repetition of the first phrase with its new ending in the tonic key.

862. This principle of repetition is sometimes applied to large works consisting of many movements. Thus the last movement of Dvořák's *Stabat Mater* is a fugue founded on the chief subject of the first movement, cf. also § 999.

863. All the pieces now analysed have consisted of **two parts**, and on this account compositions of this kind are said to be in **Two-part Form**. As many songs are written in this form it is often called **Two-part Song Form**.

864. Just as an eight-bar sentence may be enlarged without destroying the idea of its being an eight-bar sentence, similarly the *two-part form* may be enlarged at the same time keeping its two-part character, and we must now see how this can be done. The easiest way of doing this is to lengthen the second sentence by repetition of the cadence or some of the other methods described in Chapter LXII. We give an example from Mozart's piano sonatas. In the *Tema* in A (Novello, No. 11) the second sentence is lengthened to ten bars by repeating the cadence (§ 827). Thus the whole stands: Part I., eight bars; Part II., ten bars; total, eighteen bars.

865. Another method, perhaps the commonest of all, is where, instead of the *first phrase* of the second sentence, a whole new sentence is found. In such cases it is almost an invariable rule to repeat the whole of the first sentence after the new sentence thus:—

Fig. 421.

Mozart.

330   RHYTHM, ANALYSIS, AND MUSICAL FORM

If we compare this with fig. 418 we see that we have now exactly the same form as there, only here some of the parts have grown larger.

866. We very often find the second sentence much more enlarged than in the last example, *e.g.* in the *scherzo* of Beethoven's P.F. Sonata II. the second sentence [1] is enlarged to twenty-two bars. With such an enlargement as this it becomes necessary not only to repeat the whole of the first sentence; but, as the great point is to lay stress on the key, to add a few bars of coda to emphasise the key as the final resting-place. The real nature of the coda will be best studied in another place, to which we refer the student (§ 940). The analysis of this scherzo now stands thus:—
Sentence I. in A major = eight bars; Sentence II. in F♯ minor and G♯ minor, ending on the dom. 7th of A major = twenty-two bars; exact repetition of Sentence I. followed by four bars of coda = twelve bars.

867. There is still a further development to be noticed and in some respects the most important of all. Let us again examine fig. 418. It consists of *two* sentences, *four* phrases, which we may write thus: $\widehat{A+B} + \widehat{C+B}$. Now we have seen in § 865 that C and B may each be expanded to a whole sentence. Well, just in the same way **the A phrase and the B phrase** of the first sentence may each be expanded into a whole sentence, and just like the phrases in fig. 418 (which may be taken as a very usual pattern

---
[1] This is a good example of an unusual (at any rate in so short a movement) modulation. The *scherzo* begins in A major; the second sentence goes to G ♯ minor.

in longer movements), sentence A will be in the **tonic**, sentence B in some related key.

868. But this brings us to another question which arises in discussing form, and that is **the principle of Balance or Proportion.** The whole movement must be symmetrical, and when one part is enlarged it is necessary that the other parts should be enlarged too, so as to maintain the balance or proportion which we have spoken of, as being essential to a work of art. We have already seen this in § 849, but the following example will put it beyond doubt :—

Fig. 422.

Menuetto.   Mozart, P.F. Sonata in A.

869. A moment's comparison of this with fig. 418 will show that they are identical in form, but each separate portion of fig. 422 is here seen enlarged. Here is a comparison of the two:—

Fig. 418.	Fig. 422.
First Part.	**First Part.**
{ Phrase A (four bars in *tonic*).	{ Sentence A (ten bars in *tonic*).
{ Phrase B (four bars in *dominant*).	{ Sentence B (eight bars in *dominant*).
Second Part.	**Second Part.**
{ Phrase C (four bars with free modulation).	{ Sentence C (twelve bars with free modulation).
{ Phrase B (four bars in *tonic*).	{ Sentence A (ten bars in *tonic*).
	{ Sentence B (eight bars in *tonic*).

870. As a last example of *Two-part* form we analyse No. 35 of Mendelssohn's *Songs without Words*. A glance will show that the real piece does not begin till the second half of the fifth bar. These opening bars are indeed nothing more than an Introduction, such as is almost always found at the beginning of a song; and in this case, as also in most songs, this Introduction is repeated at the end of the piece.[1]

The real tune, then, begins in the fifth bar, and it is (A) an eight-bar sentence in B minor; then follows (B) a sentence lengthened to ten bars, beginning in D major and modulating to end on the inverted half-cadence of B minor; after this sentence A is repeated, but now it is lengthened to ten bars by two repetitions of the final cadence bar; the whole is then concluded by a repetition of the introductory symphony. This analysis might be put into tabular form, thus:—

Introduction . . in B minor	5 bars
First Part.	
Sentence A . . . in B minor	8 bars
Second Part.	
Sentence B . . . in D major, returning to B minor	10 bars
Repetition of Sentence A in B minor	10 bars
Conclusion . . in B minor	4 bars

871. A passage used as *introduction* or *conclusion* to a song or other similar piece of music is often called a **Symphony**[2] or **Ritornello**. Such *symphonies* often occur in the course of a song or similar piece; an example

---

[1] A comparison of this introduction and the final symphony will show that it is in each case merely a four-bar phrase—the introductory one being lengthened by two beats at the beginning, as in § 835.

[2] This use of the word *symphony* must be carefully distinguished from that explained in § 1009.

will be seen in Mendelssohn's *S. w. W.*, No. 28, where the same symphony is used four times—at the beginning, at the end, and twice in the course of the piece. Such passages do not—as far as form is concerned—belong to the piece, and they are in no sense absolutely necessary, *e.g.* the song analysed in § 870 would be complete without *introduction* and *conclusion*, though, of course, they add to its effect.

EXERCISES ON SECTION I.

1. Hymn tunes: 'Tallis's Canon,' 'Nicæa,' 'Melcombe,' 'Benediction,' 'St. Michael,' 'St. Mary.'

2. Songs: 'Hearts of Oak,' 'The Vicar of Bray,' 'Sally in Our Alley,' 'Bay of Biscay,' 'The Banks of Allan Water,' 'Cherry Ripe.'

3. Schumann's *Album for the Young*, Nos. 2, 4, 8, 10, 15, 43.

4. Chopin's Mazurkas, Nos. 4, 16, 24, 40.

5. Mendelssohn's *Christmas Pieces*, Nos. 1, 2, 3; *Songs without Words*, Nos. 4, 6, 9, 11, 16, 22.

6. Mozart's P.F. Sonatas, No. 4 (Menuetto); No. 11 (Tema).

7. Beethoven's P.F. Sonatas, No. 1 (Menuetto); No. 2 (Scherzo); No. 10 (Andante); No. 14 (Allegretto).

SECTION II.—Three-part Form.

872. Let us now carry the development of Form a little further. Suppose we already have a two-part movement, which we will call A, similar to those examined in the last section. This is, of course, complete in itself, and probably there will be some sort of repetition at the end to establish its unity. If now we wish to continue the movement A, obviously the simplest way will be to add a fresh melody, or set of melodies, which we will call B. It is clear that B must be contrasted with A, or the whole will become monotonous. The contrast may be in melodic outline, or in key, or in both. But what are we to do when B is finished? We must return to the original key in such a way that the final part gives the idea of completing the whole, and this (at any rate, in a long movement) can only be done by repeating either the whole or a part of A. The movement will then consist of three parts, A+B+A, and it will be in **Three-part Form**.

873. The air 'Lascia ch' io pianga,' from Handel's *Rinaldo* is a good example of Three-part Form. We give the melody of it, indicating the sentences by means of capital letters.

FIG. 423.

Sentence A is eight bars in E♭ ; B is six bars in B♭, consisting of three two-bar phrases, exactly like the first sentence of 'God save the Queen.' Then A is repeated in E♭. This ends the first part, and it is clear that this is complete in itself, and the movement could very well end here.

The second part consists of a sentence (C) of twelve bars ; it opens in C minor and ends in G minor. It should be noticed that the contrast spoken of in § 861 is chiefly that of key, the melodic outline being somewhat like that of sentence B. There is a further element of contrast in its *length*. Had it been an ordinary eight-bar sentence the contrast would have been much less complete. The remainder of the movement consists of a repetition of $\overline{A + B + A}$.

The analysis of 'Lascia ch' io pianga' may be shown thus :

First Part. $\begin{cases} A & \text{in} & E♭ & \text{(8 bars).} \\ B & \text{in} & B♭ & \text{(6 bars).} \\ A & \text{in} & E♭ & \text{(8 bars).} \end{cases}$

Second Part. C in C min. and G min. (12 bars).
Third Part. A + B + A exactly as in the *First Part*.

874. It will be observed that the *symphonies* of the song are omitted. As a general rule, it may be stated that the symphonies of a song are entirely outside its *Form*—*i.e.* the song would be complete *without* them. Such is the case here, where indeed they do nothing but repeat the sentence A. The chief object of such symphonies is to give the singer time for breathing. There are cases in which symphonies must be considered as an intrinsic part of the song. This will be seen by examining Bishop's

song, 'Bid me discourse.' After the voice has sung an eight-bar sentence, a symphony begins to repeat the same sentence, and after two bars the voice joins it, taking up the sentence where the symphony left it, and it is easy to see that this symphony is part of the Form of the song. Such is the case, too, in the next two symphonies of the same song. But in that which comes at the end of the first part it is merely a breathing-place, and has no absolute connection with the song.

875. This may be taken as a typical example of a *three-part movement*, but just as we found that the different parts of a two-part movement could be extended, so too with the parts of a three-part movement. The part which we have marked C very frequently consists of two lengthened sentences, indeed, it is very often a complete two-part movement in itself.

876. Another example of Three-part Form is Purcell's song, 'I attempt from Love's sickness to fly,' which may be analysed thus:

Introductory Symphony[1]	. . . .	8 bars.
First Part. { A in G	. . . .	12 bars.
{ B in E min.	. . .	11 bars.
{ A in G	. . . .	12 bars.
Symphony[1]	. . . . .	6 bars.
Second Part. C in A min., and in D	.	10 bars.
Third Part. A in G	. . .	12 bars.
Final Symphony[1] .	. . . .	4 bars.

The only point of note here is that in the third part the first sentence (A) only is repeated, and not the whole of the first part. This is not uncommon, but in more elaborate movements, especially in instrumental music, it is almost a universal rule to repeat the whole of the First Part.

877. The last example we analyse is instrumental, viz. the 'Marcia Funebre,' from Beethoven's P.F. Sonata XII. Sentence A is an ordinary eight-bar sentence beginning in A♭ minor, and ending in the relative major, C♭ major. Sentence B begins in C♭ minor, written enharmonically as B♮ minor (*v*. Part I., §§ 166–173 ; Part II., 566–571 ; 661). It is an eight-bar sentence modulating to D major.[2]

---
[1] These might be omitted from the analysis.
[2] From the point of view of modulation the two sentences are alike. A begins in A♭ minor, and goes to the relative major C♭ major; B begins in C♭ minor (written as B♮), and goes to the relative major E♭♭ major (written as D♮ major).

338 RHYTHM, ANALYSIS, AND MUSICAL FORM

878. If the student will now examine the four bars following sentence B, viz.:

FIG. 424.

he will find that the four bars do not form a phrase or any part of a sentence (they are really modified repetitions of *one* bar). It will be seen by referring to the music that this passage is used to modulate back to the original key in which sentence A will be repeated, and therefore it merely *joins* B on to A repeated. Such a passage is often called a Link.

After the *Link* of four bars, sentence A is repeated, but now it is extended to 10 bars, and it ends in the tonic key, A♭ minor. This concludes the First Part.

The *Second Part* consists of two four-bar (§ 806) sentences, both of which are repeated, and both are in A flat major. The *Third Part* repeats A, B, the link, and finally A again exactly as in the First Part, and then follows a coda of seven bars, the final chords having the *Tierce de Picardie* (ii. § 865).

879. The whole analysis may be shown thus:—

First Part.
A	in A♭ minor to C♭ major	8 bars
B	in B minor to D major	8 bars
Link		4 bars
A (repeated)	in A♭ minor	10 bars

Second Part.
C (twice)	in A♭ major	4 bars
D (twice)	in A♭ major	4 bars

Third Part.
A + B + *link* + A (repeated) as in Part I.	30 bars
Coda	7 bars

It will be well to sum up three-part form.[1]

880. The **first part** will always be complete in itself, beginning and ending in the same key, and very often there will be some sort of repetition exactly as in two-part form.

The **second part** is added as a **contrast**; it is therefore almost

---
[1] Often called *aria form* (§ 1069).

always in a new key, and occasionally it has a new time-signature. (An example is quoted in § 955.)

The second part, like the first, may be, and often is, complete in itself, beginning and ending in its own key as in the 'Marcia Funebre,' analysed in § 879. But as it always leads back to a repetition of the first part, it often modulates at the end, so as to facilitate the return, and not infrequently a *link* will be found both before and after the second part.

The **third part** is always a repetition—often slightly varied—of the whole or part of the first part. A coda may be added.

881. The second part of a movement in three-part form is often called an **Episode** (v. § 973), and a movement in three-part form is often called an **Episodical Movement**, or a *Movement of Episode*. This form is used, not only for Songs, but for a great number of instrumental pieces, such as Marches, Nocturnes, Polonaises, Impromptus, and in particular for the slow movement of a sonata (§ 953).

882. **Note on the use of Double Bars.** In Hymns and Chants a double bar is often placed at the end of each *phrase*. On the other hand, in some classes of music, double bars are sparingly used, and in analysing such the student must be careful to notice the end of each melody or subject. As a rule the definite final cadence will make it perfectly clear. It should also be remembered that very frequently a whole melody is *written out again entirely*, whereas it might have been written once and marked 'repeat.' Such a passage is not to be counted as two, but must be regarded as one, just as if it had double bars and the 'repeat.' For example, see Mendelssohn's *Songs without Words*, No. 19, where (in the second half) a passage of nineteen bars (corresponding to the second part of fig. 421) is written twice.

EXERCISES ON SECTION II.

1. Schumann's *Album for the Young*, Nos. 11, 18, 29.
2. Schubert's Impromptu in A ♭, Op. 142.
3. Chopin's Polonaise in A, Op. 40; Waltz No. 9; Mazurkas Nos. 5, 48.
4. Mozart's P.F. Sonata No. 10 (Andante).
5. Beethoven's P.F. Sonatas No. 2 (Largo appassionata); No. 4 (Largo); No. 6 (Allegretto); No. 8 (Adagio).

CHAPTER LXVII.

THE SONATA, SONATA FORM, CYCLIC FORM.

We might continue to trace the development of form historically, but it will now be better to turn our attention to what is to be considered as the most important of all forms—**Sonata Form**.

883. The word *sonata* is derived from the Italian *suonare* (or *sonare*)=*to sound*, and it was first applied to music which was to be *played* in contradistinction to *cantata* which meant music to be *sung*. A sonata is a composition consisting of either two three, or four movements, one [1] of which (sometimes more than one) is written in what is known as sonata form. By sonata form is meant a certain arrangement of a movement according to a definite plan to be presently described.

884. The majority of sonatas consist of three movements, a *quick* movement, a *slow* movement, and a final *quick* movement. Where a sonata has *four* movements the additional movement is a *minuet and trio* (or a *scherzo*) usually placed after the slow movement. When a sonata has only two movements it omits the slow movement.

885. In modern music the name sonata [2] is only applied to compositions for one or two instruments. Thus there are sonatas for piano, for violin, for organ, &c.; sonatas for piano and violin, for piano and 'cello, &c. Where a composition exactly on the plan of a sonata is intended to be performed by more than two instruments, some other name is used, thus **Trio** (for *three* instruments), **Quartet** (*four*), **Quintet** (*five*), **Sextet** (*six*), **Septet** (*seven*), **Octet** (*eight*), **Nonet** (*nine*). A similar composition for a whole orchestra is called a **Symphony**; a composition for one or more solo instruments and orchestra is called a **Concerto**. All such compositions are virtually *sonatas* as regards form.

886. The term sonata was in use before the development of that special form now known as Sonata Form was completed, and consequently in older music we often find compositions called sonatas, which have little in

---

[1] There are occasional exceptions to this. Beethoven's P.F. Sonata XII. has no movement in sonata form.

[2] A sonatina is a 'little sonata.' It is on the plan of a sonata, but shorter and slighter, and simpler in style.

common with the modern sonata, and having no movement in sonata form (*v.* § 988).

887. So far we have only been analysing single movements. In the sonata we are concerned with a composition in which several movements are to be combined so as to produce one total effect. And just as each portion of a single movement has to be considered with reference to the others, so in a sonata each complete movement must bear some relation to the other movements. We see that the element of contrast is provided for by using the series of movements in contrasted tempi, *quick, slow, quick*. There is further the element of key. The slow movement is always in some related key. But there must also be **unity**, and the first essential of unity in a sonata is **key**, just as it was in the very simplest examples of two-part form. The first movement of the sonata must be in a definite key, and though the slow movement is contrasted in key, the last movement *must return to the original key*.[1] There must further be unity in idea, *i.e.* each movement must be thoroughly in keeping with the others. This is sometimes attained by using a similar melody for each movement (*v.* § 999), but more frequently the connection between the movements is merely in style and character.

888. As a sonata is a *series* or *cycle* of movements belonging to each other, its form viewed as a whole is often called **cyclic form**.

We now proceed to describe Sonata Form.

889. A movement written in Sonata Form is in three parts. The first part consists in the main of two distinct melodies or *subjects*. The two subjects are not in the same key, and a passage—called the *bridge passage*—is used between the two subjects to modulate to the key of the second subject. The part so far described, *i.e.* first subject, bridge passage, second subject, is called the **Exposition**.

The exposition is followed by the **Development**. This does not consist of new subjects, but it is made up by using portions of the melodies already used in the exposition. These melodies are not merely repeated, but are treated according to certain methods to be presently described. The development therefore grows, or is *developed* out of old material.

The final section is called the **Recapitulation**. In it the exposition is repeated, but with both its subjects in the same tonic key.

---

[1] In the case of Sonatas in minor keys the finale is very often in the tonic *major*. The converse case, where a sonata begins in the major and ends in the tonic minor, is so extremely rare as to be practically non-existent. Dussek's P.F. Sonata, Op. 10, No. 3, E major, ending in E minor, and Mozart's P. and V. Sonata in A major, ending in A minor, are, however, two examples. For a similar example in vocal music, where it is commoner, see Franz's 'Aus meinen grossen Schmerzen,' Op. 5, No. 1.

890. **Sonata**[1] **Form** is most frequently used for the first movement of a sonata, and on this account it is often called *First Movement Form*.[2]

We now describe in detail each section of sonata form.

SECTION I. The Exposition.

891. **The First Subject** is a well-defined melody in the tonic key. It may be a single sentence (eight bars in B.[3] X.; twelve bars in B. XX.); or it may be of considerable length (B. XVIII. twenty-nine bars).

The first subject usually ends with a perfect cadence; it may, however, end on a half cadence, as in B. XIX., bar 9. The first subject is as a rule entirely in the tonic key, though simple modulations are sometimes found, *e.g.* in the final *Allegro* of B. XXVIII., the first subject, which is thirty-two bars long, modulates to the dominant, afterwards returning to the tonic.

892. The **Bridge Passage**[4] is used to **modulate** to the key of the second subject. It is as a rule of a much less definite character than the *subjects*, and very often it is made up of repetitions or sequential imitations of portions of the first subject. It may, however, be entirely new matter of a very melodious character, as in B. V. 32-56. The bridge passage may be very short (B. VIII., where it is six bars); but it may be also of considerable length (B. XV., fifty bars).

893. **Examples of First Subjects and Bridge Passages.**—(*a*) In B. IX. the first subject ends with a full cadence (with overlapping) on the first beat of bar 13. The B. P. begins by repeating the first two bars of the first

---

[1] It is also called **Symphony Form, Binary Form** (because founded in the main on *two* subjects), and **Movement of Continuity** (because there is a close connection between each part of the movement, there being no strongly contrasted episodes, § 973).

[2] When the first movement is not in sonata form the term *sonata quasi una fantasia* is generally used (*v*. B. XIII.).

[3] As it is very important that the student should examine all the examples given, those in this section are for convenience taken almost exclusively from Beethoven's P.F. Sonatas, referred to as B. with Roman numerals. Unless otherwise stated the first movement of each sonata is referred to.

[4] This part of the movement is often called **Episode**. It will be seen from § 973 why the term Bridge Passage is to be preferred.

subject, but it soon begins to modulate and ends on the dominant of the new key in bar 22.

(b) In B. VII. the first subject ends in bar 17 with a full cadence. The B. P. begins in the same bar by repeating a varied form of the first subject, but after three bars it modulates and ends in bar 23 on the dominant of the new key.

(c) In B. I. the first subject ends in bar 9 on a half-cadence. The B. P. begins by repeating the first section of the first subject in a new key so that it modulates at once. It ends in bar 21 on a half-cadence in the new key.

894. The student will have little difficulty in determining the end of the first subject and the beginning of the B. P. if he remembers that the function of the first subject is to establish the key; that of the B. P. is to lead away from the new key. The first subject keeps to its key and establishes it by its cadence; the B. P. modulates..

There is very often overlapping at the beginning and end of a bridge passage.

895. **The Second Subject.** It has been said that the second subject is in a new key. The principle at work is exactly the same as in a single melody which modulates (§ 857); Up to the time of Beethoven the following rule was in universal use:—

(a) In **major** movements the second subject is in the key of the **dominant**.

(b) In **minor** movements the second subject is in the key of the **relative major** or less frequently in the **dominant minor**.

Thus (a) a movement in **D major** would have its second subject in **A major**; one in **B♭ major**, second subject in **F major**.

(b) A movement in C minor would have its second subject in E♭ major or else in G minor; one in A minor, second subject in C major or in E minor.

896. Beethoven and subsequent musicians frequently modify this rule of keys, but nevertheless it must still be considered as the general rule. Before mentioning what other keys are used it will be best to describe the second subject.

897. The **second subject** should come as a contrast to the *first*, *e.g.* in B. IX. the *first subject* (bars 1–13) is characterised

by *leaps*; the *second* (beginning at bar 22) moves by *single steps*. But it must be remembered that, as a sonata is a movement of continuity (p. 342, n. 1), striking contrasts are not sought, and the *second subject* must be thoroughly in keeping with the character of the *first*.

898. In most cases the *second subject* is of considerable length, and is capable of division into several definite portions, each of which often ends with a perfect cadence. This has led some theorists to speak of a *third* and a *fourth* subject, while others speak of all the portions of the second subject except the first as **Tributary subjects**. But a very little experience will show the student that though in the majority of cases the second subject is divisible into sections, yet in idea it is all one, and so we shall use the term **second subject** to cover all these portions.

899. The sonata writers before Beethoven often used some part (or some striking figure) of the first subject in the first section of the second subject. This will be seen by comparing the beginning of the two subjects of Clementi's Sonata in B♭, which he played in his contest with Mozart [1] in 1781.

Fig. 425.
(a) Beginning of *First Subject*, in B♭.

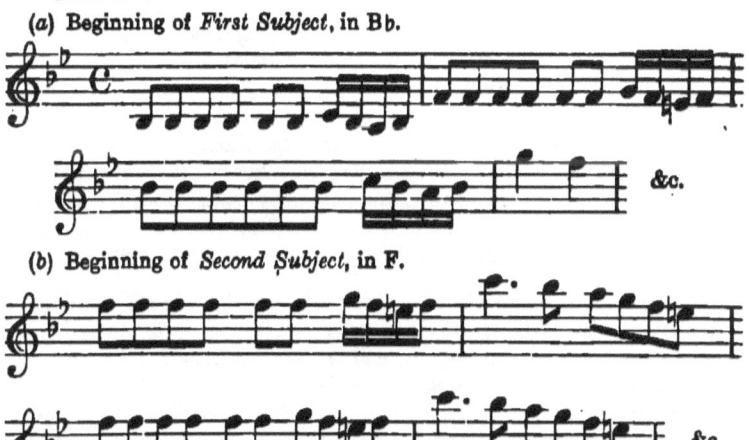

(b) Beginning of *Second Subject*, in F.

This method is frequently followed by Haydn and Mozart, and a much later example is seen in Mendelssohn's P.F. Sonata, Op. 106, written in 1827.

[1] Mozart used this afterwards (1791) as the chief subject of his overture to *Die Zauberflöte*.

900. In the majority of cases, however, even in older writers, the *second subject* is new, and not derived from the first. We now give examples of *second subjects*. In B. X. the *second subject* consists of three sections; the beginning of each is shown below:—

FIG. 426.

The first section[1] (*a*) is an eight-bar melody; (*b*) which begins by overlapping with (*a*) is fifteen bars long. Notice that this part of the second subject (which is in D) has a transient modulation (at *) to the dominant of the new key. This is far from uncommon. (*c*) is seventeen bars long—and this brings us to the end of the *exposition*, and to the double-bar. To mark the end of the exposition we almost invariably find the final cadence strengthened by repetition, or ornamented by some striking figure. In the case we are examining the exposition might·end at bar 59—the remaining bars being merely a repetition of the cadence (§ 827).

901. Another common way of ending the *exposition* should be noticed here. We saw in § 827 how the end of a simple melody is strengthened by repetition. In the same way the end of the *exposition* is often made up of portions of melodies or figures previously used. Thus in B. IX. the four bars immediately before the bar marked 1 are clearly founded on the opening bars of the sonata. Such an ending is called a **Codetta**, a term which will be understood by comparison with § 940.

902. Incidental modulation in second subjects. In general all the sections of a second subject begin and end in the same key, but there is often considerable modulation, chiefly to nearly related keys, in the course

---

[1] The student should note that some writers call (*a*) the *second subject*, and (*b*) and (*c*) *tributary subjects*.

of the subjects. In B. VI. in F the second subject is in C (bar 19); it modulates to G (bar 29), back to C (bar 38), to C minor (bar 41), and back to C major (bar 47), in which key it concludes. In Mendelssohn's Sonata for 'Cello in B♭, Op. 45, the second subject is perfectly regular in F, but it modulates to C major, G minor, D minor, and back to F.

903. The only difficulty the student is likely to find is in determining the various sections of the second subject. It must be stated that to a certain extent it is a matter of opinion. Some authorities argue that each section must end with a perfect cadence; others that whenever there is a clear beginning of fresh matter then we have a new subject, although no full cadence has completed a previous section. In deciding the student should be guided by the evidence of connection of idea in the several sections. To illustrate these points let us take the second subject of B. XI. This clearly begins in bar 23, and ends at bar 31. The *second section* beginning in bar 31 is repeated at bar 39, but this time it is interrupted at bar 44 with so distinct a figure that we must consider this bar 44 as beginning a *third section*, which ends at bar 57. From bar 57 to the double bar is evidently a *Codetta* [1] founded on the *second section* of the *second subject*, and (in the last two bars) on the opening of the *first subject*.

904. The end of the exposition is usually, and formerly was always, indicated by a double-bar and repeat marks. As the subjects of the exposition are used in the second part it was thought necessary to impress them on the mind by repetition. But in modern sonatas this is frequently neglected, and there are many examples where no double bar [2] is used. There will, however, be little difficulty even in these cases in finding the end of the first part, for there is usually either a repeated or a prolonged cadence in the key of the second subject.

Further Rules for the Key of the Second Subject.

905. We must now note cases where the key of the second subject does not conform to the rule of § 895. These may be divided into two classes: (*a*) where the second subject begins in an unusual key, but ends in what may be called the normal key; (*b*) where the second subject throughout is in an unusual key. One or two examples will make this clear.

---

[1] The term Codetta is often used somewhat freely. It is quite possible to consider bars 57-62 as a *fourth section* of the second subject. Bars 63-70 are undoubtedly Codetta.

[2] Do not be led astray in such cases by double bars, which are often found in the *development* when a new key signature is used to avoid the use of too many accidentals, *v.* Beethoven's Appassionata XXIII.

(a) In B. II. in A major the second subject begins (bar 59) in E *minor*, and modulates through G major, B♭ major, D major, E major, and finally ends in E major. In B. XXV. in G major the second subject opens (bar 24) in A *major*, but in bar 36 it modulates into the normal key D, and so ends. As an example of a sonata in a minor key we may take B. VIII. in C minor. The first section of the second subject begins (bar 41) in E♭ *minor*, and in bar 65 there is a full cadence in D♭ major. This subject is then repeated slightly modified, and makes its way through E♭ minor, F minor, and C minor to E♭ major, the normal key, in which the part ends.

(b) As an example of the second class of abnormal second subjects, we quote Beethoven's great Hammerclavier Sonata,[1] Op. 106, No. 29, in B♭, where the second subject (beginning in bar 63), though it touches other related keys, is practically entirely in G major. It is a curious coincidence that Mendelssohn's Op. 106, quoted in § 899, is a P.F. sonata having exactly the same keys for first and second subject, viz. B♭ and G major.

906. We may conclude this part of the subject by tabulating the keys in which second subjects occur.

In **major keys** the *second subject* is usually in the key of the **dominant**, but it may also be in the *submediant major*, in the *mediant major* or *minor*, and occasionally in other less closely related keys.

In **minor keys** the second subject is usually in the key of the **relative major** or **dominant minor**, and occasionally in the *submediant major*.

907. The first movement is not infrequently preceded by an Introduction—always in slow [2] time. It is not an intrinsic part of sonata form, but it adds to the impressiveness of the form. It may be short—four bars in Beethoven's P.F. Sonata XXIV., Op. 78, but at times it is of great length and importance—in Beethoven's Symphony No. VII. sixty-two bars.

908. The *Introduction* in some cases announces subjects or significant phrases or figures which are afterwards used in the sonata. In Beethoven's P.F. Sonata XXVI., Op. 81a, the whole of the allegro may be said to be founded on the first four bars of the Introduction. The first three notes in particular are important, the second subject (bar 34), the codetta (bars 46–53), being founded on them. They are even more noticeable in the

---

[1] The pianoforte trio in B♭, Op. 97, also has the second subject in G.

[2] A slow section at the beginning of a sonata is not of necessity an Introduction. In Mozart's Sonata for P. and V. in C (No. 2, Peters), the first subject and bridge passage are *adagio*, while the remainder of the exposition is *allegro molto*. In Dussek's Op. 10, No. 2, the first movement in regular sonata form is marked *Grave, adagio non troppo*. So also Mozart's P.F. Sonata in E♭, No. 4, is *adagio*.

development and in the coda (especially throughout the last seventy-five bars).

Another example is seen in Schubert's Octet, where part of the *Introduction* is used again just before the Recapitulation.

In most cases, however, the materials of the *Introduction* are not used again in the movement. The Introduction in these cases serves to rouse the attention of the hearer for what is coming.

909. In analysing the exposition of a sonata the following plan may be followed:

ANALYSIS OF MOZART'S P.F. SONATA IN A MINOR.

First Subject, bars 1-9. A nine-bar melody, the nine bars being the result of the repetition of one of the motives of the second phrase.

Bridge Passage, bars 9-22. The B. P. (which begins by overlapping with the end of the First Subject) is made up chiefly out of the materials of the First Subject. In bars 16 and 17 there is a two-bar phrase on the dominant of C minor; this is repeated in bars 18 and 19. Bars 20-22 consist entirely of repetitions of the half-cadence on which the B. P. ends.

Second Subject, bars 22-45 in C, the relative major key. It consists of two sections: Section I., bars 22-35; Section II., bars 35-45. The second section is a six-bar melody repeated with the parts inverted and slightly modified.

Codetta, bars 45-49, founded on the first four notes of the First Subject with a bass suggested by a figure of the B. P. in bar 11. Ends in C major with double bar and repeat.

EXERCISES IN SECTION I.

1. Analyse as in § 909 the exposition of the first movement of the following sonatas:

(*a*) Mozart, No. 5 in G; No. 6 in D; No. 16 in C; No. 2 in F; No. 12 in F; No. 14 in C minor.

(*b*) Haydn, No. 5 in C; No. 11 in G; No. 2 in E minor; No. 8 in B♭.

(*c*) Beethoven, No. 20 in G; No. 19 in G minor; No. 5 in C minor; No. 4 in E♭; No. 7 in D; No. 8 in C minor; No. 18 in E♭; No. 17 in D minor.

2. Point out where the exposition ends (and then analyse) in the first movement Beethoven's P.F. Sonatas No. 23 in F minor; No. 27 in E minor; No. 28 in A; No. 31 in A♭.

Section II.—The Development.

910. The part of a movement in sonata form immediately following the *Exposition* is made up out of the subjects and melodies used in the exposition. To merely repeat such melodies would simply cause monotony and tedium. They must therefore be repeated with such modifications that they appear to us *in a new light*, and so produce a new impression and a new pleasure. As this new pleasure is founded on matter heard before, we are led to compare the two, and so a higher pleasure than mere sensuousness comes in—an intellectual pleasure—and it is this element of sonata form which make it so important. This method of using musical subjects is called **Development**, and this portion of sonata form is called the **Development**. As in the development a composer is practically free to follow his own fancy, it is often termed the **Free Fantasia**.

911. Though *development* is most used in the development section of sonata form this is by no means its only use. Even a short melody can consist of developed portions. We have already seen this in Fig. 396, where a whole melody is made up by repeating a little figure with slight modifications at each repetition. At each repetition the figure appears in a new light, and the whole melody grows, as it were, out of one little figure.

912. Perhaps the first and most obvious means of thus presenting old ideas or melodies in a new light is transposition. A melody may be given in a new key; or it may be placed higher or lower.

At first sight it might appear that mere transposition offers nothing new. But everything is to be considered in relation to its surroundings. When, therefore, in Beethoven's P.F. Sonata II. the exposition ends in E major, and then, after touching on E minor, gives in C major the bold subject which opens the sonata, the effect is striking, although the repetition is identical with the original in everything except key.

913. A subject may be changed as to mode from minor to major, or *vice versa*, and this is perhaps one of the most commonly used devices.

914. The harmony may be changed while the melody is unaltered. As an example let the student examine the trio in Beethoven's P.F. Sonata XV. The same melody occurs six times in succession, but each time with varied harmony.

915. The subject may be **ornamented** by the addition of shakes, runs, &c., or by a florid accompaniment, or it may be altered in expression by the use of signs of emphasis, &c.

916. A subject may be altered with regard to time and accent. This may be merely bringing an accented portion to the unaccented part of the bar, as in Haydn's Symphony in C (Salamon, No. 1), where the figure (*a*) taken from the first subject is used in the forms (*b*) and (*c*).

FIG. 427.

917. Or the time may be changed, *e.g.* from $\frac{2}{4}$ to $\frac{6}{8}$ (which, however, is only a form of ornamenting a melody); or by a more radical change, *e.g.* from $\frac{2}{4}$ to $\frac{3}{4}$ as in the following, from Grieg's P.F. Concerto, Op. 16 :—

FIG. 428.

(*a*) First Subject of Finale.

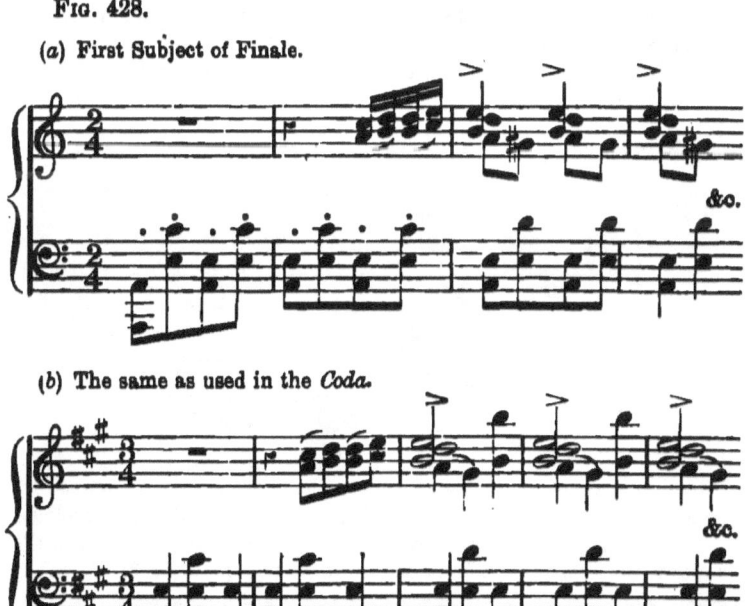

(*b*) The same as used in the *Coda*.

THE SONATA, SONATA FORM, CYCLIC FORM 351

918. The methods so far described are more or less superficial. We now proceed to describe one which is more important. This is done by taking a small portion of the subject and treating it in a variety of ways, to show, as it were, what it is capable of. This will be best understood by examination of the development of Beethoven's P.F. Sonata II. The sonata is in A major, and opens with a bold subject, after which comes the following :—

FIG. 429.

(a) Bars 9-13.

The first forty bars of the development (counting from the change of key-signature) are founded on the opening phrase. This leads us through C, A♭, F minor, ending on the dominant of F. Then (bar 40) comes the passage (a) fig. 429 in F, afterwards repeated in the left hand, and ending in F. All this (40-50) is now repeated, ending this time in D minor (bar 60). Then comes the following :—

FIG. 430.

(b) Bars 60-62.

It is easy to see that this is merely the first portion of extract (a) used by imitation. It is in three-part harmony. The middle part includes the small notes, and so is an exact imitation of the upper part, while the lower part stops short at F. The phrase (b) is now repeated in G minor, C major, and F major, in which key it is continued by repeating the last three notes of the extract (marked α), first directly, then (at β) inverted thus :—

352   RHYTHM, ANALYSIS, AND MUSICAL FORM

Fig. 431.
(c) Bars 68-71.

This brings the key to D minor again. Then the whole extract (c) is repeated twice, first ending in A minor, secondly in E major. The remainder of the development is founded on the same passage (a), but it is not necessary to describe it further. Thus sixty bars of development are made up by working the figures of two bars (a).

919. Another method of development is to take a portion of a theme as in § 918 and treat it in double counterpoint,[1] as in the following example from Beethoven's P.F. Sonata, Op. 28, No. XV. :—

Fig. 432.
(a)

(b)

---

[1] When two parts are written in such a way that they still sound satisfactory when the upper part is placed below the lower, *i.e.* when they are

The phrase used above is taken from the end of the First Subject, bars 7-10. A melody used thus in double counterpoint is often made the means of modulation, and then the ending may be slightly modified at each recurrence, as in the Finale of Dussek's P.F. Sonata in C minor, Op. 35, No. 3.

920. A melody may be treated in canon (§ 1033), as in the example from Haydn's Symphony in Bb, No. 9 of the Salomon set.

FIG. 433.[1]

921. The subject of the *canon* is taken from the second section of the second subject.

The extract will serve to illustrate another important point. When a fragment of a melody is developed it is quite usual to find the fragment inverted, they are said to be in double counterpoint. In the same way we may have three parts in *triple* counterpoint, &c. In the Finale of Mozart's Jupiter Symphony we have an example of five melodies, which are all invertible, *i.e.* in *quintuple counterpoint*, v. Pt. II., § 701.

[1] There are other parts to this, but they either double the parts shown above or complete the harmony.

finished off into a complete sentence by a new ending. Thus the fragment (a) used above is simply two bars – afterwards repeated a third higher —to which three bars (*... *) of entirely new matter are added. Of course such a new ending must be perfectly in keeping with that which it completes. There are almost innumerable examples of this procedure, but we may mention in particular Beethoven's great Hammerclavier Sonata, Op. 106, beginning at bar 19 of the development.

922. A melody, or a fragment of a melody, may be treated **Fugally** (§ 1045). This is less common in P.F. sonatas than in larger works, but the whole of the development of Beethoven's Op. 101 (Finale) consists of a somewhat freely developed fugue. Among examples in larger works may be mentioned the first movement of Beethoven's Quartet, Op. 59, No. 1, and Haydn's Clock Symphony (Finale), in both of which cases there is the opening of a double fugue.

923. In all the cases yet seen the development has been made up out of materials previously heard, but there are cases where **entirely new matter** is introduced. We have already seen (§ 921) how a fragment of an old melody may have a *new ending*. It is but a step further to introduce an entirely new melody, provided such new matter is thoroughly in keeping with the rest of the music.

As examples of entirely new melodies we quote Beethoven's P.F. Sonata, Op. 10, No. 1, beginning at bar 13 of the development; and Op. 14, No. 1, beginning at bar 5 of the development. A long and important section of the development in Schumann's P.F. trio, Op. 63, first movement, is new. The term *Episode* (§ 973) is often applied to new melodies introduced into the development.

924. Summary of the Methods used in Development.

A *subject* may be treated in the following ways:—

(a) **Transposition** to a new key, or to a higher or lower octave.
(b) The **mode** may be changed, major to minor or *vice versa*.
(c) It may be differently **harmonised**.
(d) It may be ornamented by shakes &c.
(e) The accent or the time may be changed.
(f) Small portions of the melody may be worked by imitation and sequential repetition.
(g) **Double counterpoint, canon, and fugue** may be employed.
(h) An **Episode**—new matter—may be introduced.

925. It must not be supposed that all these methods will be followed in the same sonata, or that they will be carried out in any specified order. The only necessity is that whatever development is used shall be consistent with the spirit of the exposition. More than one of the methods may, however, be used at once, *e.g.* a melody may be newly harmonised, and then used sequentially through a series of keys.

The development will not employ all the materials of the exposition. Two or three fragments will, as a rule, be found sufficient to supply all the material required. These fragments may be taken from any part of the exposition. In Mozart's P.F. Sonata in D, No. 9, eighteen bars of the development are founded on a *codetta* of two bars; the next eight bars are founded on part of the second subject, the remaining thirteen bars on a part of the first subject.

The development may be very short, *e.g.* in Beethoven P.F. Sonata XX. it is only fourteen bars long; in No. XXI. it is seventy bars long, while in symphonies and similar works it is often much longer.

926. There are cases where there is practically **no development** (*v.* also § 958). The sonata for P. and V., by Mozart, quoted on p. 347 n. 2, has in the place occupied by the development a sort of *Link* of ten bars, merely leading back to the original key.

927. With regard to the **keys** used in the development, practically any key is allowable. But it will be found that (*a*) the keys used in the *Exposition* are in general avoided except when they are used in passing from one key to another; (*b*) the same key is not as a rule used twice, except transitionally.

928. We now give examples of the way in which a development may be analysed. We take as the first example Mozart's P.F. Sonata in A minor. The bars are numbered from the beginning of the Exposition.

The whole development is founded on the following fragments:—

FIG. 434.

(*a*) Beginning of 1st subject, bars 1-9. (*b*) Fragment of 2nd subject, bars 41-3.

The development opens with a reproduction of four bars of the first subject in C major. At bar 54 the dominant chord of F is reached, and this is repeated in three successive bars, apparently hesitating between F major and D minor. In bar 57 this chord (the dominant of F) is changed enharmonically into the German sixth in E minor, in which key the real development begins. The next twelve bars consist of repetitions of the following fragment :—

FIG. 435.
(c) Bars 58-61.

It will be interesting to note the origin of this. The fragment (*d*) is clearly the first three notes of (*a*). By breaking up the crotchet in (*d*) into a dotted quaver and a semiquaver we get the rhythmic figure 𝅘𝅥𝅮. 𝅘𝅥𝅯 𝅘𝅥𝅮. 𝅘𝅥𝅯 which is the foundation of the remainder of extract (*c*). The fragments (*e*) and (*f*) are merely variations of (*d*); they retain the rhythmic figure, at the same time being greatly modified in melodic outline and in harmony. The third and fourth bars of (*c*) are free sequential imitations of the second bar.

The extract (*e*) occurs on a pedal bass in E minor; then the whole extract is repeated in A minor (bars 62-65) and in D minor (66-69).

The remainder of the development is founded on (*b*) fig. 434. It is treated sequentially in C major and A minor (70-72), and finally transferred to the left hand in A minor (74-77). The bass of bars 70-72 is suggested by the bass of the codetta, *i.e.* the last five bars before the first double bar (bars 45-49). The development ends in bar 80 on the dom. chord of A minor.

929. As a second example, we analyse the development of Beethoven's P.F. Sonata No. III., Op. 2, No. 3 in C major.

The development is, with the exception of one passage, constructed out of the following materials :—

FIG. 436.
First Subject, bars 1 and 2.   Bars 6 and 7.
(*a*)   (*b*)   (*c*)

Second Subject, bars 77-79.

It opens with example (*d*) in C and F minor; then the figure of four notes with the shake in example (*d*) is repeated four times on each of the notes of the dominant seventh of E♭. Here follows a long series of arpeggios founded on the Bridge Passage, bars 13 and 14. This takes us through E♭ (bars 98-99), C minor (bars 100-101), F minor (102-103); then by enharmonic change in F♯ minor (104-107), and D major (108-109). Now comes a shortened form of the first subject example (*a*) in D major, but in bar 114 the fragment (*c*) is worked in G minor. It is followed by a syncopated passage which is worth our careful attention.

The whole sonata abounds in beautiful effects of syncopation, and all these are derived from the first half of bar 6 quoted above at (*b*). Example (*b*) is not, of course, strict syncopation, but by the entry of the bass the accent is thrown to the second beat and we get the spirit if not the letter of syncopation as explained in Part I., § 83. This leads us to G major in bar 128. Then follows a repetition of bars 114-117 in C minor and major and again in F minor, but this time the syncopated passage is lengthened, and it ends on the dominant of C major. The remaining bars (130-139), on a dominant pedal, are founded on example (*a*), with imitation between treble and tenor. In bar 136 the dominant seventh is struck, and with this sustained in the left hand the right hand repeats (*c*) in example (*b*) on the descending notes of the dominant seventh, reaching the re-entry of the first subject in bar 140.

EXERCISES.

The student should now analyse the development of those sonatas mentioned at the end of Sect. I. p. 348, stating the origin of the matter, the method pursued in the working, and the keys passed through.

SECTION III.—THE **Recapitulation** AND **Coda**.

930. As the final section of a movement in sonata form repeats—with certain modifications—the Exposition, it is called

the **Recapitulation or Reprise.** The chief point of difference is that, while in the Exposition the first and second subjects are in different keys, in the Recapitulation *both subjects are in the* **tonic key** (though the *mode* may be changed). This will be best seen in tabular form:

	Exposition		Recapitulation	
	1st Subject	2nd Subject	1st Subject	2nd Subject
Major keys	Tonic	Dominant	Tonic	Tonic
Minor keys	Tonic minor	(a) Relative major or (b) Dominant minor	Tonic minor	(a) Tonic minor or (b) Tonic major

931. The second subject of a minor movement is most frequently in the relative major. In the Recapitulation this usually reappears in the *tonic minor*. But in many cases the change from the relative *major* to the tonic *minor* cannot be made without completely changing the character of the melody, and therefore it is a very common practice, especially in modern music, to give the second subject in the Recapitulation in the tonic major. There are very many examples of this, *e.g.* Beethoven's P.F. Sonata, Op. 10, No. 1 (Finale), and the fifth Symphony (*first movement*), Schumann's two Sonatas for P. and V., &c.

We must now see how unusual keys in the Exposition (§ 905) are represented in the Recapitulation.

932. When a subject in the Exposition has incidental modulation we generally find a corresponding modulation in the Recapitulation, *e.g.* Beethoven's Sonata in F for horn, Op. 17, the second subject in C modulates to E minor in the Exposition; in the Recapitulation it is in F modulating to A minor, the modulation in each case being to the mediant minor.

933. When the second subject is in a **series of keys** the corresponding series of keys is often, though by no means always, found in the Recapitulation. Thus in Beethoven's P.F. Sonata in C, Op. 2, No. 3, the second subject is in G minor, C minor, D minor, G minor, A minor, G minor, and G major in the Exposition; in C minor, F minor, G minor, C minor, D minor, and

C minor and C major in the Recapitulation. It should be noted that all the keys in the Exposition are related to the final key G major in exactly the same way that the keys of the Recapitulation are related to the final key, C major. This is by no means always the case, and the student must be prepared for considerable irregularity in this respect. A single example will suffice. Beethoven's eighth Symphony in F; First Movement, second subject in D major and C major in the Exposition; in B♭ major and F major in the Recapitulation. The last movement of this symphony is quite regular, *e.g.* second subject in A♭ and C in the Exposition, in D♭ and F in the Recapitulation.

934. When the whole of the second subject is in an unusual key there is often an apparent irregularity because the Recapitulation must end in the tonic key. This will usually, but not always, be easily explained if we compare the irregular keys of the Exposition with what would have been the regular one. Thus in Beethoven's P.F. Sonata in C, Op. 53, the second subject is in E major and minor in the Exposition. The regular key would have been G major, and thus we might very well have had the series E major, E minor, *G major*. When we come to the Recapitulation we find the corresponding series A major, A minor, C major. It is as if the Exposition only gives a portion of the series which is given complete in the Recapitulation. So again in Beethoven's P.F. Sonata in G, Op. 31, No. 1, the second subject of the Exposition in B major, B minor (related to *D major*, the regular key) becomes in the Recapitulation E major, E minor, and G major.

935. There is one case of irregularity of key in the second subject where the Exposition has been perfectly regular. That is, where the second subject appears twice in the Recapitulation, first in a new key and then in the regular key; *e.g.* in Beethoven's P.F. Sonata in C minor, Op. 10, No. 1, the second subject is in E♭ major; in the Recapitulation this is given first in F major and then in C minor.

936. **Irregularity in the key of the First Subject.** In order to preserve the same key-relationship between first and second subjects [1] in Exposition and Recapitulation the first subject is occasionally introduced in the Recapitulation in the subdominant, *e.g.* Mozart's P.F. Sonata in C, No. 16, where the Recapitulation opens in F; Schubert's Sonatina for P. and V. in A minor, Op. 137, No. 2, where the Recapitulation opens in D minor. This causes the second subject to appear in a key a fifth higher than the first both in the Exposition and Recapitulation.

---

[1] In Mozart's P.F. Sonata in C, No. 10, there is an irregularity in the second subject in the Recapitulation which is, no doubt, due to the same idea; the second subject is partly introduced in the dominant and then turned aside, as it were, into the regular tonic key.

937. Inversion of subjects in the Recapitulation. In a few cases the Recapitulation has the second subject placed before the first. One of the best-known examples of this is Mozart's Sonata in D for P. and V. Another example is seen in Mozart's P.F. Sonata, in D, No. 9. There is a very modern example in Dvořák's String Quartet in E♭, Op. 51.

Sometimes there is a partial inversion; *e.g.* in Dussek's P.F. Sonata, Op. 9, No. 1, an important section of the first subject is placed after the second subject.

938. To reproduce the Exposition in the Recapitulation with no change but that of key would be monotonous, and we very often find variety brought about (a) by ornamenting or varying[1] some of the melodies, (b) by shortening some of the matter of the Exposition.

The first may be dismissed with a reference to the Recapitulation (first subject) of Mozart's P.F. Sonata in G, No. 5.

The shortening may be produced by shortening a melody, as in Beethoven's P.F. Sonata in C, Op. 2, No. 3, where the first subject is cut down from thirteen to eight bars. But shortening is more usually caused by the omission of some part of the Exposition. In Dussek's Op. 9, No. 2 (Finale), the first subject (fifty bars) is omitted and the bridge passage is shortened by nineteen bars. In his Op. 9, No. 3, eight bars of the first subject, the whole of the B. P., and the first section of the second subject are omitted, and in his Op. 10, No. 2, all the first subject and B. P. are omitted.

When a whole subject is omitted from the Recapitulation it is usually because that subject has been prominently brought forward in the development, when it would be tedious to use it again in the Recapitulation.

939. Occasionally there is considerable modification of the subjects in the Recapitulation. Let the student compare the first subject of Beethoven's P.F. Sonata, Op. 31, No. 2, with bars 148-157, where a *recitative*-like passage is added. In the same sonata part of the second subject appears in bars 194-196 in an inner part with a pedal note in the highest part. This is due to the fact that the compass of the pianoforte in Beethoven's time (the highest note then being F *in alt*) did not allow the exact transposition of the original second subject of bars 60-62.

940. Coda. In most cases the movement in sonata form ends with a more or less exact reproduction of the ending used for the exposition, only of course in the tonic key. But such an ending for a long and important movement often sounds tame

---

[1] A very good example of the ornamentation of a subject on its re-entry is seen in Mozart's P.F. Sonata in D, No. 6 (Polonaise), where the same subject occurs six times, each time differently varied.

and unfinished, and therefore it is very usual—especially in modern works—to add another section after the recapitulation, to bring the work to an end in a more striking manner. Such an ending is called a **Coda**. The word is derived from the Italian *coda*=a tail, and its appropriateness will be easily recognised, for a coda is simply a *tail-piece*. The diminutive of *coda* is **Codetta**, which therefore means a little coda. As we have already seen, a simple melody can have a coda (§ 849).

We have already used the term *codetta* in speaking of the end of the exposition (§ 901). Sometimes, however, such an ending is called a *coda*, but it seems desirable to limit the use of each word. We shall apply the term *codetta* to the end of the exposition, and also to the end of the recapitulation, when it merely repeats in a new key the ending of the exposition—*e.g.* the end of Mozart's P.F. Sonata in A minor (cf. § 909). When, however, at the end of the recapitulation there comes a section different both in importance and in matter from the ending of the exposition we shall use the term coda, and it is this section which we now propose to describe.

941. The simplest form of coda is seen in Mozart's P.F. Sonata in E♭, No. 4, where three bars reminiscent of the first subject are added, and named *coda*. But in many cases the coda assumes great length and importance. As an example, we analyse the coda of Beethoven's P.F. Sonata in C, Op. 2, No. 3, the development of which is analysed in § 929.

The recapitulation ends with the last section of the second subject (quoted in fig. 436 (*d*)), omitting, however, the passages in broken octaves (bars 85-91), but instead of a full cadence in C we get, in bar 219, an interrupted cadence on A♭, and here begins the coda. For fourteen bars we have a series of arpeggios, evidently suggested by the opening of the development, leading through A♭, F minor, G minor, D minor, C minor to C major (bar 233), in which key there is a long **Cadenza**[1] founded on a figure of the first subject (*v.* fig. 436 (*a*)). This leads to four bars of the

---

[1] A **Cadenza** is a passage usually of a brilliant and showy character, of no definite form, often made up by development out of the materials previously heard. A cadenza is not commonly found in solo sonatas, though among other examples may be mentioned Beethoven's 'Moonlight Sonata' (last movement), Mozart's P.F. Sonata, No. 9 (last movement), and Clementi's Sonata in C, in which latter case, however, it is introduced just at the end of the recapitulation.

first subject followed by another phase of the syncopated passage described in § 929, bars 238-252 being clearly traceable to bars 120-129 of the development. The remaining six bars now give out that part of the last section of the second subject which was interrupted by the entry of the coda.

It will be seen from this that the coda when important consists of development, but, of course, the development of the coda is not a mere repetition of the development proper, but rather another view as it were of the materials of the sonata. It may be said to sum up the sonata, just as a speech might be summed up in concluding, by drawing attention to the salient points.

942. In some few cases entirely new materials are used in the coda just as in the ordinary development. An example of this is seen in Beethoven's P.F. Sonata, Op. 57, Finale. So also Schumann's Sonata for P. and V., Op. 121 (second movement).

943. **How to find the beginning of a Coda.**—In some cases the second part of a movement is repeated, and when in such cases a coda is added the beginning of it is readily seen from the double bar with repeat marks. Such is the case in Mozart's P.F. Sonata in C minor (No. 14), in the Finale of the 'Jupiter Symphony,' and in Beethoven's Sonata for 'cello in G minor Op. 5, No. 2. But in most cases the Coda follows on the recapitulation without any special warning, but there will be little difficulty in seeing where it begins, if we compare the end of the recapitulation with the end of the exposition. Let us take as an example Beethoven's P.F. Sonata, No. 4, Op. 7. It is easy to follow the recapitulation up to bar 307. It follows the lines of the exposition very closely, especially in the last twenty or thirty bars. But in bar 307 instead of giving the bars corresponding to the last three bars of the exposition, it leaves the key abruptly, thus interrupting the cadence, and here begins the coda.

It has been mentioned that the coda is a sort of second development section, and it is interesting to note that in many cases the opening of the coda is very similar to the opening of the development, though it soon assumes a character of its own. This is the case in the sonatas mentioned in §§ 941-3 and in many others.

944. We have now completed our account of **Sonata Form**, but before leaving it we ask the student to again examine the examples of two-part song form discussed in Chapter LXVI. Each of these bears a certain resemblance to a movement in sonata form, *e.g.* fig. 420, the first half contains two well-defined phrases, one in the tonic, the other in the dominant. The first four bars of the second half are clearly founded on the second part of the first half—a sort of rudimentary development—and the last four bars form a sort of *recapitulation*, though not a complete one. When we examine fig. 422 the resemblance to sonata form is still more

striking. Indeed, if the first part had a bridge passage and the bars after the first double-bar were developments of previous materials it would be a short but complete example of sonata form.

945. Movements in sonata form though not so named.

Many movements not so named are written in sonata form. Such is No. 15 of Clementi's *Gradus ad Parnassum*, which, though an excellent exercise on thirds and sixths, is none the less in regular form. There are examples of such unnamed sonatas which seem to present the form in its most condensed state. No. 6 of Mendelssohn's *Christmas Pieces* is one; and before analysing it we will just recapitulate the essential features of this form.

These are:—

(a) **Exposition**, *i.e.* first subject, second subject in related key with a definite end in the new key.

(b) **Development**, which, however, may be very short.

(c) **Recapitulation**, *i.e.* first and second subjects both in the tonic key.

946. We now analyse Mendelssohn's *Christmas Pieces*, No. 6.

Exposition, first subject in F (bars 1-15) ending in the dominant, there is no bridge passage; second subject in C (bars 15-25).

Development (founded on bars 1, 2, and 28-29) in the keys of F, B♭, G minor, D minor, ending on the dominant of F, bar 41.

Recapitulation, first subject in F now in the bass (bars 41-57); second subject in F (bars 57-68), ending on an inverted cadence.

Coda (bars 68-98), founded on the same matter as the development, but very differently treated.

Exercises on Section III.

1. Analyse the codas in the first movement of the following Sonatas by Beethoven:—No. 25 in G major; No. 15 in D major; No. 9 in E major; No. 10 in G major; No. 21 in C major; No. 23 F minor; No. 26 in E♭ major.

2. Analyse the *recapitulation* of the first movements mentioned in Question 1, p. 348.

3. Analyse the following movements by Mendelssohn: *Songs without Words*, Nos. 3, 5; Op. 7, No. 7; Op. 16, No. 2.

CHAPTER LXVIII.

THE SLOW MOVEMENT; MODIFIED SONATA FORM.

947. When a sonata has more than two[1] movements the second[2] one is most frequently a slow movement. It is in contrast to the first movement, not only in rate of movement but in character and in key.

948. The **key of the slow movement** may be any of the keys related to the first movement; but, as a matter of principle, the related key which has been used for the second subject of the first movement is usually avoided. The most frequently used keys are: For major keys, the key of the **subdominant**; for minor keys the major key of the **submediant**. Examples of other keys than these are Beethoven's P.F. Sonatas, I. in F minor, with slow movement in F major (tonic major); III. in C, with slow movement in E (mediant major); VII. in D, with slow movement in D minor (tonic minor), &c. The dominant is not often used, though Mozart has it in two P.F. Sonatas, Nos. XVI. and XIX.

Sometimes the key is enharmonically related; thus in Dussek, Op. 44, in E♭ major the slow movement is in B♮ = C♭ major, *i.e.* in major key of the flattened submediant, and exactly the same relation is found in Beethoven's E♭ concerto ('The Emperor'). So also Beethoven's Op. 106 in B♭, with slow movement in F♯ (= G♭) minor.

949. The **Form** of the slow movement is not at all restricted. It may be (*a*) in **song form**; (*b*) in **sonata form**, with or without certain modifications; (*c*) an **air with variations**; (*d*) a **rondo**.

950. As the subjects of air with variation and rondo form will be dealt with in subsequent chapters it will only be necessary here to refer to examples, *e.g.* slow movement as (*a*) air with variations, Mozart, No. XX.; Beethoven, No. X. (*b*) Rondo, Mozart, Nos. XVI. and XVIII.; Beethoven No. XVI. The slow movement of Schumann's P.F. Quintet, Op. 44, is in sonata-rondo form. It should be added that this use of rondo form is not very common.

---

[1] In some cases when there are only two movements the finale partakes of the nature of the slow movement and the usual finale, thus Dussek, Op. 47, No. 2, the finale is called *Rondo con espressione, Andantino con moto*.
[2] In Schumann's 'Rhenish Symphony,' Op. 97, the slow movement stands third. So also Beethoven P.F. Sonata XIII.

THE SLOW MOVEMENT; MODIFIED SONATA FORM 365

951. (a) **Slow Movements in Song Form.** Song form has already been described in Ch. LXVI. Except in small works simple two-part song form is not much used in slow movements. Dussek's Op. 30, No. 2, may be analysed as an example, thus: *Andante quasi larghetto* in F :—

First Part.
(A) Eight bars in F, ending in the dominant (repeated).
Second Part.
{ (B) Six bars in C minor, A♭, and D♭ major, ending on dominant of F.
(A) Eight bars repeated with slight variation, ending in tonic } repeated.
Coda.
(C) Three bars in F.

952. Beethoven's Op. 27, No. 1 (*Adagio con espressione*) presents an even simpler example. It is constructed thus :—(A.) Eight bars in A♭, ending on a half-cadence. (B.) Nine bars in E♭, C minor, E♭, overlapping with (A.), repeated in A♭. Here in bar 24 the movement really ends, but it is followed by three bars of cadenza, which serve to connect the slow movement with the finale. It is by no means uncommon to find at the end of a slow movement such a connecting section. Another example is in Haydn's second P.F. Sonata, where five bars are added.

In some cases the slow movement merely serves as an *Introduction* to the finale. It then has all the characteristics of an *Introduction* (§ 908); *e.g.* Haydn's P.F. Sonata VII. This would be in two-part form, but, instead of the repetition explained in § 860, it ends on a half-cadence, and so introduces the finale.

953. **Three-part form** (§ 880) is of very frequent occurrence in slow movements.

One of the most familiar examples is that in Beethoven's P.F. Sonata VIII. It is thus analysed :—
First Part.
(a) Eight bars in A♭ (repeated).
(b) Twelve bars in F minor, C minor, ending in E♭.
(a) Repeated in A♭.
Second Part.
(c) Eight bars in A♭ minor, to E major.
(c) Partly repeated in E major, but interrupted to lead back to the
Third Part, which consists of (a) twice repeated and a
Coda of seven bars.

954. The character of a slow movement lends itself to ornamental variation, and in almost all cases the subjects which are repeated appear considerably varied at each reappearance.

955. As a rule a three-part slow movement is all in slow time, but occasionally the second part is in a quicker time. A good example of this is Beethoven's Quartet in G, Op. 18, No. 2, where the first part is Adagio in $\frac{3}{4}$ time, the second part Allegro in $\frac{2}{4}$ time (founded entirely on the coda of the first part), and the third part goes to the original tempo and signature.

In very much extended movements links (§ 878) and bridge passages are often met with.

956. Before leaving this part of the subject two curious examples may be noted. The slow movement of Mozart's P.F. Sonata in C, No. VII., is as follows :—

First Part.
   (A.) Eight bars in F given three times, ending on a half-cadence, and then a fourth time on the tonic, at each re-entry much varied.

Second Part.
   (B.) Twelve bars in C and F, followed by (A.) twice repeated.

The second part is then repeated in full with variations, and the movement closes with four bars of *coda*.

This is clearly in two-part song form, but the first section is given out four times instead of the usual two.

957. The slow movement of Haydn's Symphony in B♭ resembles what is sometimes called a **strophic song** (§ 1070). Thus: first verse, sixteen bars in F; the second verse exactly repeats the first; the third verse in A♭ like the first and second, but slightly modified; the fourth verse is in F slightly modified, after which come seven bars of coda, which may be very well compared to the final symphony of a song.

958. Slow movements in sonata form are usually made much shorter than first movements—partly because a well-developed movement in slow *tempo* would be too long—and this shortening is generally brought about by *omitting the whole of the development section*. Such a movement is said to be in **modified sonata form**, which therefore consists of *exposition* and *recapitulation*, only, with or without *coda*.

It will easily be seen from this that in modified sonata form the subjects are heard with less intervening matter, and it becomes necessary to do something to avoid the consequent monotony. The subjects are, therefore, very frequently varied [1] on their reappearance in the recapitulation.

---

[1] This is not entirely due to the cause stated. The object of the slow movement is to add feeling and sentiment to the sonata, and this lends itself more to ornamentation.

THE SLOW MOVEMENT; MODIFIED SONATA FORM 367

As an example of modified sonata form, we analyse the Adagio in B♭ from Beethoven's P.F. Sonata in D minor, Op. 31, No. 2.

Exposition.—First S. in B♭ . . . . . . bars 1–17.
        Bridge passage to dominant . . . bars 17–30.
        Second S. in F . . . . . . bars 30–38.
        Link on dominant pedal . . . . bars 38–42.
Recapitulation.—First S. in B♭ much varied . . . bars 43–59.
        Bridge passage modified to remain in tonic bars 59–72.
        Second S. in B♭ . . . . . . bars 72–80.

Coda.—Founded on the link (bars 80–88), and on the first and second S. combined (bars 89–103).

It will be seen that we apply the term *link* to five bars which take the place of the development. These are in no sense a development, being really a reiteration of the dominant chord preparatory to returning to the first subject.

959. There are, however, many slow movements in which there is a full development. As such movements present no difficulty in analysis, it will be sufficient to refer to examples like Mozart's Sonatas, Nos. III. and XV., and Beethoven,[1] Nos. XI. and XXIX.

960. As a rule, the double bar and repeat marks at the end of the exposition are rarely (and in 'modified' movements never) used in slow movements. Mozart's Sonata No. III. has them, however, and No. XV. has repeat marks both at the end of the exposition and recapitulation.

961. In some cases the slow movement in sonata form is somewhat free in the choice of the key of the second S.—*e.g.* Beethoven's P.F. Sonata IV. has S. M. in C, second S. in A♭. As an example, we analyse Schubert's Op. 120, *Andante.*

Exposition.—First S. in D major . . . . . bars 1–15.
        No bridge passage.
        Second S. in F♯ minor ending on interrupted cadence bars 16–26.
Development on first S. . . . . bars 26–39.
Recapitulation.—First S. in D . . . . . . bars 40–50.
        Second S. in D minor ending in D major . . bars 50–60.
Coda founded on first S. . . . . bars 60–65.

EXERCISES.

The student should now analyse the slow movements of the sonatas mentioned in the exercises on pp. 348, 363.

---

[1] Sonata No. VII. has a slow movement in sonata form, in which an episode takes the place of the development. This episode is afterwards largely used in the coda.

CHAPTER LXIX.

THE MINUET AND TRIO; THE SCHERZO.

962. The third movement of a sonata is usually the Minuet and Trio. Originally the Minuet was a somewhat slow and stately dance in triple time (most commonly $\frac{3}{4}$), though after Haydn's time its character became gayer, and its pace was much quickened. It consists of two parts, each of which is repeated. After the minuet, what is virtually a second minuet is added, contrasted in style with the first. In the earlier examples it was the rule to write the second minuet in *three-part harmony* to heighten the contrast, and from this fact it was called Trio, and this name is still used, although the method of writing it in three-part harmony is discontinued. Like the minuet, the trio is in two sections, each being repeated, after which the minuet is played again, this time without repeats. In some cases a coda is added to conclude the whole. As the minuet is invariably repeated after the trio, the two must be considered as forming one whole, from the form point of view. They are clearly an example of three-part form. In some cases a second trio is added, when the whole stands thus: Minuet; first trio; M.; second trio; M.; with very often a *Coda*. This, as will be seen from the next chapter, then becomes a *Rondo*. Schumann in particular is fond of this form; there are examples in his P.F. Quintet and Sonata for P. and V., Op. 121.

963. The **key of the minuet** is usually that of the first movement, though it is not uncommon to find tonic major in place of minor, as in Beethoven's 'Moonlight Sonata' in C♯ minor, when the minuet (here called simply *allegretto*) is in C♯ (written as D♭) major.

It may be in a related key, as in Dussek's Op. 44 in E♭, where the minuet is in A♭ minor (written as G♯), ending in A♭ major.

The trio may be either in the same key as the minuet, or in a related key.

964. In **form** the simplest examples of the minuet consist of two eight-bar sentences, *i.e.* two-part song form. An example of such a minuet is given in fig. 420. But in many cases this form is much enlarged on the methods described in §§ 864–868. In its most developed state this form bears a very great resemblance to a movement in **sonata form**, and, indeed, many minuets

may very well be looked upon as **miniature sonata movements**. This will be made clear by one or two examples:—

Fig. 437.

Minuet, HAYDN, P.F. Sonata XIV.

The first part of the minuet is an eight-bar sentence, the first half of which is very definitely in the tonic key, and the second half in the dominant. It would be going too far to call these phrases first and second subjects, but it is clear that they stand in exactly the same relation to each other as first and second subjects. The second half of the minuet opens with six bars—not of new matter, but of a kind of development, and after this comes the whole of the first section, but now phrase A. and B. are both in the tonic key. The whole minuet is clearly then a miniature sonata form.

965. The minuet from Mozart's P.F. Sonata in A, fig. 422, is even a clearer example, for here in place of phrases A. and B. the first part consists of Sentence A. in the tonic and Sentence B. in the dominant. The rest of the minuet is exactly on the same plan as that of Haydn's, but the development part is considerably longer.

A similar example in a minor key is seen in Beethoven's P.F. Sonata No. I. in F minor. This minuet may be thus analysed :—

First Part.
    Phrase A. in F minor, four bars. Phrase B. in A♭ major (rel. maj.), ten bars.

Second Part.
    Development, fourteen bars, in A♭ major, B♭ minor; phrases A. and B. repeated (with modification), both in F minor, followed by two bars of coda.

966. Since Beethoven's time the place of the minuet is often occupied by the **Scherzo** (Italian *scherzo*, a jest [1]). In form the scherzo is in many cases identical with the minuet, and indeed the term is used more to express a certain style of movement characterised by greatly increased pace, by sudden surprises, or by the use of ever-recurring figures.[2] It may be written not only in triple but in duple time, *e.g.* Beethoven's 'Eroica Symphony.'

967. In form the scherzo is most frequently in what we have called miniature sonata form; but it is usually much more enlarged than the minuet. A very good example is in Beethoven's Sonata III. Here the first part consists of a definite eight-bar subject in C and a second subject of eight bars in G clearly founded on the first. Then we have twenty-three bars of development. The first part is now heard again, but modified so as to get both subjects in C, and the whole concludes with a nine-bar coda.

When the scherzo takes the place of the minuet it is followed by a trio, after which the scherzo is repeated and followed often by a coda.

In larger works the scherzo is often extended into a full and well-developed sonata movement. Perhaps the best example is the scherzo of Beethoven's Ninth Symphony.

---

[1] There are, however, serious scherzos, *e.g.* the scherzo in Schumann's Sonata in D minor for P. and V.

[2] That the scherzo does not merely take the place of the minuet is amply proved by the fact that some sonatas contain both scherzo and minuet, *e.g.* Beethoven's P.F. Sonata XVIII., Schubert's Octet, &c.

968. The scherzo is sometimes written as a separate movement (without a trio). It is then usually in full sonata form, as in Beethoven's P.F. Sonata XVIII. Mendelssohn has employed the *Modern Rondo form* (§ 981) in the scherzo of the D minor trio and in that of the *Midsummer Night's Dream* music.

EXERCISES.

Analyse the minuet (or scherzo) and trio in the following sonatas: Haydn, VI., XI., and XII.; Mozart, IV.; Beethoven, I., II., VII., XI., XII., XV., XVIII.

CHAPTER LXX.

RONDO FORM.

969. The Final Movement of a sonata is naturally in the same key as the first, though in the case of sonatas in minor keys it is not at all uncommon to find the **Finale in the tonic major,** *e.g.* Beethoven's P.F. Sonata XIX. and his Fifth Symphony.

970. As regards **Form** the Finale may be in (*a*) **Sonata Form**; (*b*) **Rondo Form**; (*c*) **An Air with Variations**; or, (*d*) less frequently, a **Fugue**. We have already described (*a*), and subsequent chapters will deal with (*c*) and (*d*). For the present, then, it will be sufficient to mention examples. Beethoven's P.F. Sonatas Nos. V. and XIV. have finales in sonata form; Nos. XXX. and XXXII. have an air with variations, and No. XXXI. has a fugue. We now proceed to deal with Rondo Form.

Rondos may be divided into two classes, and it will be convenient to examine them separately.

SECTION I. **Rondo Form.**

971. The study of Rondo Form takes us back to the point in the development of Form which we left in Chapter LXVI. We saw there that, given a complete tune A, we may add another contrasted tune B provided we return to A as a conclusion. This process may be carried on as long as we wish, provided we return to A after each fresh addition. Thus we get a movement made up as follows: A B A C A &c., and such a movement is termed a **Rondo**, which may be thus defined:

In **Rondo Form** there is **one principal subject** which occurs at least three times, and between each appearance of the principal subject there are introduced other subjects or passages, called **episodes,** _in contrast_ with the principal subject. After the final appearance of the principal subject a _coda_ may (or may not) be added.

972. An example will make this perfectly clear. The Finale of Haydn's P.F. Sonata IX. in D may be analysed thus :—

A, **Principal Subject** $\begin{cases} (a) \text{ 8 bars in D repeated} \\ (b) \quad ,, \quad ,, \quad ,, \end{cases}$

B, _Episode_ in D minor $\begin{cases} (c) \text{ 8 bars in D minor repeated.} \\ \begin{cases} (d) \quad ,, \quad \text{in F major} \\ \quad \text{4 bars of Link} \\ (c) \text{ 8 bars in D minor} \end{cases} \text{repeated.} \end{cases}$

A, Principal Subject, varied two sentences, of 8 bars each repeated.

C, _Episode_ in A minor $\begin{cases} (e) \text{ 8 bars in A minor repeated.} \\ \begin{cases} (f) \text{ 10 ,, ,, ,,} \\ (e) \text{ 8 ,, ,, ,,} \end{cases} \text{repeated.} \end{cases}$

A, Principal Subject varied, two sentences of eight bars each repeated. After this the P. S. is again used with further variation, each part being again repeated.

973. This may be taken as a very typical example of the Rondo up to the time of Beethoven, and it deserves careful study. First, it should be noticed that a Rondo is a movement implying contrast. In a movement in sonata form continuity of thought and idea is aimed at. The second subject there, though in a sense contrasted with the first, is more a counterpart and a completion of the first, but in a Rondo the sections other than the principal subject are added entirely _for the sake of contrast._ Such subjects are termed Episodes. An **Episode** may therefore be defined as **a subject of secondary importance added as a contrast to a principal subject.** The contrast may be that of key as in the above example, or of style, or of tempo, or all three. In many cases the episode is distinct in itself, beginning and ending in its own key, _e.g._ each of the episodes in the above are complete pieces which might occur as separate movements fulfilling all the requirements of Ch. LXVI. On the other hand, many episodes are indefinite in character and very frequently they end on a half-cadence to lead back more conveniently to the Principal Subject.

974. The next point to be noticed is that as the Principal Subject occurs so frequently it would become tedious if repeated without any change. In

all except the earliest writers, therefore, the Principal Subject is varied at each reappearance. The same principle sometimes causes the P. S. to reappear in fresh keys. Thus in C. P. E. Bach's Rondo II. (Third Collection, Baumgart Edition) in G major the P. S. appears once in C♯ major. From this same cause, too, when the P. S. is long only a portion of it will sometimes recur after the episodes.

975. Rondo Form was the earliest form used for long movements, and as regards Form pure and simple it varied little from the time of Couperin (1668–1733) to Haydn or even Mozart. Some of the earlier examples are noticeable for their simplicity and rigidity and for the number of the episodes, e.g. La Favorite¹ by Couperin has a P. S. of eight bars in C minor with five episodes,² all in C minor. Episodes 1, 2, and 3 are each eight bars long, No. 4 is thirteen and No. 5 is sixteen bars. The P. S. is not written out afresh each time, but the sign D.S. is used and the end of the P. S. and of each episode is marked by a pause ⌢.

976. The Rondo by Haydn analysed in § 972 is the type of this class, i.e. the P. S. three times and two episodes, and practically the only modification which it underwent before Mozart and Beethoven was in the direction of lengthening the Principal Subject and the episodes. In some cases an air of continuity is given, and the rigidity of the Haydn model is avoided by leading to and from the episodes by passages resembling Bridge Passages.

977. A good example is Dussek's *Rondo à la militaire*, Sonata XXV., Op. 47, No. 1. Here the P. S. is twenty-eight bars long, and it concludes with a very striking *codetta*. The first episode (which is marked *minor*) opens in D minor, but it ends in F major, with the codetta used at the end of the P. S. The codetta is then used as a Bridge Passage leading through G minor and D minor to the original key, when the P. S. is repeated exactly as at first. The second episode in G major is altogether new, and is twenty-four bars long, after which the P. S. is again repeated exactly as at first.

978. In the slow movement of Mozart's P.F. Sonata in D (No. IX.) a curious example of Rondo occurs. The movement is in G, and the P. S. is twelve bars long. A *link* of four bars leads to the first episode in D. The latter part of this episode consists of a portion of the P. S. now in D with a new ending, after which the P. S. is repeated in the original key (G), just as at first. The old link, now shortened to two bars, is again used to lead to the second episode. This episode is identical with the first, including the use

---

¹ Published in convenient form in No. 10 of *Les Maîtres du Clavecin* (Litolff).

² Couperin labels each episode with the name *Couplet*, numbering them 1, 2, &c. Rameau (1683–1764) sometimes uses the word *Reprise* in the same way.

of the P. S., but it is all in G. The final section consists of the P. S. in G, ornamented and lengthened out by means of repeated cadences to nineteen bars.

There are two points to be noted in this example. First, that it is by no means uncommon to find in an episode a reference to the P. S. The second point is more important. As the second episode repeats the first exactly, it is quite possible to consider this movement as in Song Form. We, however, prefer to consider it as a Rondo on this ground. The object of an episode is to give variety, and this is sufficiently attained here by means of *key contrast*. If the second episode were in the same key as the first we should unhesitatingly class this movement with that described in § 956.

979. The only difficulty the student is likely to find in analysing Rondos of this type is in determining the end of the P. S. The P. S. is always complete in itself, and it is usually in two-part form. Now, we have seen (§865) that in this form we often find a sentence in a given key, a second sentence in a complementary key, and a return to the first sentence and key. But the three sentences form *one melody or subject*. Such an example is seen in the slow movement of Beethoven's P.F. Sonata XV.; here the first melody consists of three parts (a) eight bars in D minor, (b) eight bars in A minor, (a) repeated. Now, in some cases it is not easy to decide whether the whole of this or the first eight bars is the principal subject. If the whole twenty bars is the P. S. the movement is in three-part form; if the first eight bars is the P. S., then the movement is a Rondo. In this special case there is no difficulty, because the whole of the twenty-four bars is repeated after an episode. But in cases of a long P. S. it is common to repeat only a portion after the first episode, and in these cases it is a question of opinion whether the movement is a Rondo or not. The slow movement of Beethoven's P.F. Sonata VIII. is a notorious example. It opens with (A.) an eight-bar sentence in A♭, which is immediately repeated; then comes (B.) a sentence beginning in F minor, ending in E♭ major, and this is followed by a repetition of (A.). Now comes an undoubted episode (C.) beginning in A♭ minor and going through E♮ major (=F♭), and finally leading to A♭, in which key sentence (A.) is repeated twice with variations. The movement ends with seven bars of coda. The question arises, is sentence (B.) an independent episode, or is it merely a continuation of (A.)? In the first case the movement is a Rondo; in the second it is merely an example of three-part form.

980. There are cases where movements which the composers have named Rondo do not conform to the definition[1] of a Rondo given in § 971.

---

[1] The definition is perfectly logical and correct, but there is no doubt that some of the earlier writers like Mozart and Dussek used the term Rondo to signify a movement in which one little melody occurs several times, and in many cases their use of the term *Rondo* merely implies this without any definite reference to construction in other respects.

In most cases this is in examples somewhat analogous to that just described. Thus the Rondo of Dussek's P.F. Sonata, Op. 39, No. 2, is clearly in three-part form, and here there cannot easily be two opinions, because the whole of the first subject (37 bars) is repeated after the episode.

Mozart's Rondo in D is in sonata form, but as the second subject is merely a transposition of the first, and this is used largely in the development, the subject is constantly cropping up, and so the term Rondo is not very inappropriate.

Section II.—The Modern Rondo or Sonata-Rondo.

981. Mozart (frequently) and Beethoven [1] (almost always) use a form of Rondo which bears so great a resemblance to sonata form that it is commonly called **Sonata-Rondo** or **Rondo-Sonata**. It may be described thus: the **first part** has a *first subject*, and a *bridge passage* leading to a *second subject* in the complementary key exactly as in sonata form; but instead of ending in the complementary key it always returns to the *first subject* in the original key, in which the first part ends. The **second part** consists, in the majority of cases, of an *episode* in a related key, generally with very little or even no development. The **third part** has the *first subject, bridge passage*, and *second subject*, but now both subjects are in the tonic, and this is commonly followed by a coda, in which the *first subject* is usually referred to or even repeated entirely.

As in the older Rondo, the first subject which is most repeated is often varied at each reappearance.

982. As an example of Sonata-Rondo we analyse the finale of Beethoven's P.F. Sonata, No. II.

    First Part (A.) First Subject in A (1-16).
                      Bridge Passage (16-26).
               (B.) Second Subject in E (26-40).
               (C.) First Subject in A (41-56).
    Second Part (A.) Episode in A minor(57-94), leading by means of a short codetta to,

---

[1] Beethoven occasionally uses the older form, as in the P.F. Sonata No. XXI. (the 'Waldstein').

Third Part (A.) First Subject (varied) in A (95-110).
Bridge Passage (110-118).
(B.) Second Subject in A (118-130).
Coda founded chiefly on (A.) with a slight reference to the episode (C.) and ending with a final repetition of the first sentence (A.) considerably varied.

983. Not infrequently the *second part* instead of being an episode is made up of development. Such is the case in Beethoven's P.F. Sonata, No. XXVII., Op. 90; Mozart's P.F. Concerto in C; Mendelssohn's *Midsummer Night's Dream* music (Scherzo), and Weber's Rondo in E♭.

EXERCISES.

Analyse the *Finale* of the following sonatas: Haydn, II., III.; Mozart, III., VII., VIII., IX., X., XIII., XVI.; Beethoven, III., IV., VIII., IX., XI., XV., XVI., XX., XXI., XXVII., and Schumann's Fantasiestücke, Nos. 2 and 4.

CHAPTER LXXI.

THE HISTORY OF THE SONATA AND SONATA FORM.

984. The earliest efforts in music were vocal, and the earliest use of instrumental music was to support the voices by playing the same parts. A very little consideration will show that vocal music is much less dependent on pure form than instrumental. For in vocal music the words supply the hearer with a means of understanding the music, and thus the form of vocal music depends not so much on any general underlying principles as on the form of the words. The **History of Form** is then a history of instrumental music; for purely instrumental music, having no assistance from words, must be arranged on some plan or design in order to be intelligible. One of the most essential elements in form is repetition of some kind. We have already shown how important this is even in short tunes like those in § 860, and in long compositions repetition is absolutely necessary. The repetition may be that of a short figure, which is repeated throughout a movement on various degrees, or the repetition of a subject as in a fugue. In the earlier examples of instrumental music the form element was almost entirely represented by these methods of repetition.

985. As instrumental music began by playing the voice parts of vocal music, it was only natural that in the earliest attempts at independent in-

strumental music the methods of vocal music should be followed and developed. The most effective way of combining voices is to give each voice a melodious part which shall be distinctive and well contrasted with the others. And such was the case in early instrumental works. Each part had its own well-defined melody, *i.e.* the music was contrapuntal (II. § 698), and the whole effect was produced by the combination of many melodies or parts. Such music is termed polyphonic (= many voiced). Early instrumental music was essentially polyphonic, and it derived its feeling of unity and form from the repetition of figures or subjects. Of this description were the various *toccatas, canzoni*, and *fantasias* written for the organ [1] by writers like Frescobaldi (1580-1640).

The highest development of polyphonic music is the fugue, which reached its culminating point in the works of J. S. Bach (1685-1750).

986. Besides the effect produced by the combination of several independent melodies, there is another fact to be taken into account, viz. the harmonic effect, or the effect produced by chords and successions of chords without any reference to the interest of the individual parts. No doubt this was observed early, but by the end of the sixteenth century the harmonic effect of music was becoming more and more recognised. As the feeling for harmony grew, the interest in the individual parts was lost, and by degrees the melody was given to one (the upper) part alone, while the others merely added a groundwork of chords on which the melody rested. Thus the music consisted of *one* melody with a supporting harmony, and such music is called homophonic (= one-voiced).

987. When instrumental music became homophonic it lost to a large extent the element of form which characterised polyphonic music, viz. the repetition of figures and subjects in different parts. Henceforth another element of form comes into play, viz. contrast and balance of keys. Thus, after beginning in a given key, another key is proceeded to by way of contrast, and the balance is restored by returning to the original key.[2] This is an essential quality of modern music which may be said to date from the time when this element became paramount.

988. There is another important aspect of form—viz. that of rhythm—and for the origin of this we must go to the dance tunes. As early as the middle of the sixteenth century a very clear form of dance tune—both from the harmonic and rhythmic point of view—was in vogue, and by the middle

---

[1] The advancement of instrumental music is clearly connected with the advancement of skill in making instruments. Owing to its importance in connection with the church, the organ was the earliest instrument to attain a moderate perfection. Hence the earliest compositions were for the organ.

[2] The key element is not, of course, absent from polyphonic music, but there it plays a somewhat different part.

of the seventeenth century it became a common practice to write sets of dance tunes, not for dancing purposes but as purely instrumental music. One of the earliest composers to do this was the Frenchman Couperin (1668-1733), who called his sets by the name of **Ordres**. Couperin's *ordres* were taken as models by others, and in Germany similar sets of dance tunes were called **Suites**. By degrees the dance tunes in the suites were developed, and while maintaining their distinctive rhythmic qualities they were greatly lengthened. Sometimes movements of a type not connected with the dance were introduced and then the set was called a **Partita** (§ 1059). Gradually the suites and partitas lost more and more the traces of the dance forms which had originally characterised them, becoming sets of movements which depended on themselves for being understood, without the help of words or the suggestions of the dance. Such sets of movements were called **Sonatas**, and thus the original meaning of sonata is *a group of movements of* **abstract** [1] **music.** The earliest sonatas consisted of several movements, usually all in the same key, but varied in character and tempo. It is to be noted, however, that the earliest examples had no movement in what we now call sonata form, a form which was not definitely fixed until the time of Haydn. The sonata did not lose the traces of the dance tunes of the *suite* and *partita*, from which it was descended, all at once ; in fact, there is practically little difference [2] in the constituent movements of the partita and many early sonatas. In Corelli's time a distinction was drawn between the **Sonata da Chiesa**, *i.e. church sonata*, and the **Sonata da Camera**, *i.e. chamber sonata*, the church sonata consisting of more dignified and solemn movements suitable for church performance, while the chamber sonata was of a livelier description, and usually contained some dance numbers. This will be readily understood by comparing the movements in Corelli's Sonata da Chiesa, Op. 1, No. 1 (*grave, allegro, adagio, allegro*), with his Sonata da Camera, Op. 2, No. 1 (*largo, allegro, corrente, gavotta*).

989. All sorts of composers helped, no doubt, in the development of the sonata, but certain names must be singled out as marking important epochs. These are (*a*) the Italians **Corelli** (1653-1713), **Tartini** (1692-1770), **D. Scarlatti** (1683-1757); (*b*) the Germans **Biber** (1638-1698), **Kuhnau** (1667-1722), **C. P. E. Bach** (1714-1788), **J. Haydn** (1732-1809), **Mozart** (1756-1791), **Beethoven** (1770-1827).

---

[1] In music with words the words show clearly the meaning of the music. So also a hearer listening to a dance tune would form a mental picture of the movements of the dance connected with each phrase of the music. The dance thus supplies as it were a key to the music. Music which has to depend (for being understood) on its own *form* or plan without any outside assistance or suggestion is called **abstract** music.

[2] Compare the movements of J. S. Bach's Violin Sonata IV. (*allemanda, corrente, sarabanda, giga, chaconna*) with the suite described in § 1060.

990. The movements comprised in a sonata have varied considerably at different periods. Thus most of Corelli's had four movements, generally in the order *slow, quick, slow, quick* as regards tempo. Tartini's Sonata *Il trillo del diavolo* is in three movements, though the last movement is in five short sections in alternately slow and quick tempo. By the time of C. P. E. Bach three movements became the rule. These were usually (1) a vigorous *quick* movement, (2) a *slow* movement, and (3) a *quick* movement, which last, however, was of a less important character than the first movement. Haydn and Mozart adopted this plan, though both composers added a fourth movement, the *minuet*, in their symphonies. Beethoven and composers since his time have generally though not invariably adopted the four-movement form for sonatas, and with Beethoven the *scherzo* often takes the place of the minuet.

991. Another point must be noted. In early works all the movements of the sonata are in the same key. By C. P. E. Bach's time the principle of key contrast was at work, and while the first and last movements were of necessity in the same key (though not always the same mode) the slow movement was in a contrasted key.

992. The origin and development of Sonata Form.—We are now to consider how the type of movement, which we now call Sonata Form, arrived at its present state. We have said that unity is given to a movement by some sort of repetition. The earliest examples were contrapuntal, and repetition of a figure was so persistent that the movement was clearly of the same *texture* and was easily recognised as such, and very often the only thing approaching to repetition of subject was the repetition of the final cadence (§ 827). This is usually the case in Corelli. But Corelli often advances beyond.

There is a curious example in the *Giga* of his Sonata IX. for violin. It opens with a distinctive melody in A major, which we will call (*a*). This modulates to the dominant, in which key the first part ends. The second part opens with a slight reference to (*a*) repeated three times; the last time with a very distinctive new ending in C♯ minor. This new ending we will call (*b*). The part (*a*) now reappears in the tonic key, and the movement ends with the part (*b*) in the tonic key. It almost looks as if Corelli had arranged his Giga in sonata form, but had put his double bar in the wrong place.

993. Before sonata-writing had progressed very far there was in common use a form of movement which had a very definite plan. It was divided into two halves. The first half set out with a well-defined figure and modulated to a contrasted key (the dominant for major keys, the relative major for minor keys) in which it ended. The second half, of course, completed the balance of key by returning to the original key, and to add to

this feeling of balance the figure which ended Part I. in the new key was used, *in the tonic key*, to end Part II. The first movement of Tartini's *Il trillo* is a clear example of this. Sometimes the first half of Part II. was made to correspond with the first half of Part I. as well as the correspondence of the second half of each part, as in the third movement of Kuhnau's Bible Sonata,[1] No. I. By the time of D. Scarlatti a very definite type of movement was in use to which the name Old Sonata Form has been given. In old sonata form the movement opens with a subject A modulating to a new subject B in a new key. This ends Part I., which is repeated. Part II. opens with A now in the new key, and gradually working back to the original tonic it ends with B in the tonic key. Thus the plan in a major key would be:

Part I. A in tonic, B in dominant :|| Part II. A in dominant, B in tonic :||.

An example of this form may be seen in the March in Handel's *Judas Maccabæus*.

994. By degrees a rough sort of development was added in Part II. between the two subjects, and then, on the principle explained in § 868, both A and B were repeated in the tonic key. But, as in this case, A occurs three times, the plan arose of omitting the repetition of A at the beginning of Part II., thus giving us our modern sonata form. These may be shown in a table where A and B stand for contrasted subjects :—

Old sonata forms.

(1.) A in ton., B in dom. :|| A in dom., B in ton. :||

(2.) A in ton., B in dom. :|| A in dom., development; A and B in tonic :||.

Modern sonata form.

(3.) A in ton., B in dom. :|| Development; A and B in tonic :||.

995. The modern form was fairly well established by the time of C. P. E. Bach,[2] though all three forms may be found in his works, and even in Haydn's.[3]

996. Haydn adopted the sonata form of C. P. E. Bach, but he extended and enlarged the different sections of it, and—what is even more important—he was the first to use definitely melodic subjects. In earlier composers the 'subjects' consisted of well-defined figures rather than of subjects in the modern sense. In place of these figures Haydn used a

---

[1] Kuhnau published in 1700 six sonatas for the harpsichord to illustrate Bible stories. The first and second of these (I. David and Goliath, II. Saul and David) have been recently republished, edited by J. S. Shedlock (Novello & Co.).

[2] See Set I., Sonatas V. and VI., and Set II., Sonata I. in Baumgart's edition of C. P. E. Bach. The slow movement of Haydn's Sonata XXII. is in the old form (1).

genuine subject in the shape of a melody.'¹ **Mozart's** form, with one exception, was no advance upon Haydn's. His influence, however, is distinctly felt in the style of the melodies he employs; in other respects his influence on sonata form is best studied in connection with the symphony and concerted music (§§ 1008-18). The exception referred to, in which Mozart distinctly advanced upon Haydn's work, is in the application of the sonata form to the rondo (*v.* Rondo of P.F. Sonata XIII.).

997. **Beethoven** took up the sonata where Haydn left it, and carried it forward to almost the highest possible point of perfection. His influence may be summed up as follows; (1) He enlarged the key-system of the sonata. Previous to his time the second subject was invariably in the dominant, the relative major, or the dominant minor (§ 895). Beethoven used many other keys with the happiest results. (2) In Haydn and Mozart the 'subjects' of the sonata are clear and definite, and very often the connecting matter, *i.e.* bridge passages &c., is the merest padding, of little musical importance. With Beethoven all parts of the movement are factors in the total effect, the bridge passages are logically necessary, and, in fact, the movement becomes one organic *growth*. (3) With Beethoven the coda became an important and highly characteristic part of the form. (4) Further, Beethoven's work is marked by a much deeper feeling. This is especially noticeable in the slow movements. (5) Out of the old minuet Beethoven developed the highly organic Scherzo. (6) Above all, Beethoven's 'developments' are characteristic. Here each part seems to *grow* out of what has gone before, and he knows how to show to the full what effects a ' subject' is capable of producing.

Since Beethoven's time many composers have produced sonatas, but, with the exception of Brahms, it cannot be said that anyone has advanced (or even maintained) the *form* as used by Beethoven, though writers of the romantic school have added to its power of expression.

998. Of all moderns, Beethoven's mantle seems to have fallen on Brahms (born 1833). In certain respects he has advanced on Beethoven's form. In the highest music of the sonata type not only must each movement be perfect in itself, but the collection of movements constituting the sonata must be mutually related, and thoroughly in keeping with each other. The whole sonata should be the working out of one supreme idea. Just as Beethoven made each portion of the sonata movement of importance, so Brahms has endeavoured to work each movement of the sonata into one organic whole.

999. This is an important aspect of the subject, and as it is in this direction that the further advance of sonata form must move, it is worth

---

¹ Dr. Parry explains this as being the result of Haydn's early associations. The son of a wheelwright, he was, no doubt, well acquainted with folk-songs from his childhood, and it was this influence which caused him to insist so strongly on the melodic interest in his sonatas.

382 RHYTHM, ANALYSIS, AND MUSICAL FORM

a moment's consideration. The organic unity of a series of movements may be made clear in several ways. (*a*) Each movement may be clearly an expression of the same feeling, a unity which is not easy to define, but which becomes very evident, nevertheless, in the best works of Beethoven. (*b*) A movement may be founded on a fragment of a preceding movement (compare § 955). Of this there are examples as early as Haydn and Mozart. (*c*) A striking feature from one movement may be woven into a later movement. An example is seen in Beethoven's P.F. Sonata, Op. 101, where part of the first movement is used to lead into the Finale. Schumann does this on an even more organised plan. In the Sonata for P. and V., Op. 121, the principal figure of the Scherzo is woven into the following slow movement in a remarkable manner, and with the most conspicuous success. So, too, in the P.F. quintet, the opening phrase in the development of the first movement is used as a link in the following movement. (*d*) Finally, several movements may be founded on varied forms of the same subject, or the same idea. This is often called the **transformation of themes**.[1] There are examples in all the great modern composers, especially in Berlioz and Liszt and Wagner. An example from Brahms's Symphony in D will make this clear (cf. fig. 428).

Fig. 438.

(*a*) The subject of the Allegretto.

(*b*) The same subject transformed in the following Trio.

---

[1] Edward Dannreuther points out (*Macmillan's Magazine*, July 1876, p. 201) that in Beethoven's P.F. Sonata, Op. 109, the leading theme of each movement is characterised by the same feature, *i.e.* an ascending third (or tenth) followed by a descending third.

CHAPTER LXXII.

ORCHESTRAL MUSIC, CONCERTED MUSIC.

1000. We have already seen that instrumental music was first employed to support the voices, and in time independent pieces of music were given to the orchestra to act either as an introduction to the opera or as ritornellos between the songs. Such pieces were at first called by the name *symphony*. Thus in Handel's opera *Faramondo* the Introduction to Acts II. and III., in each case a piece of about eighteen bars, is called *sinfonia*. Orchestral music had its origin, therefore, in the opera overture, which we now proceed to describe.

SECTION I.—The Overture.

1001. The overture (Fr. *ouverture* = opening), as its name implies, is an instrumental composition played as an introduction to an opera, oratorio, or similar piece. We shall see presently that in recent times overtures intended for concert use have been written.

As regards the *form* of the overture it is necessary to draw a distinction between the old overture and the modern. Of the old form there are two types—the French and the Italian.

1002. The French Overture was perfected by Lulli (1633–87), who was superintendent of music at the Court of Louis XIV. Lulli's overtures consisted of (*a*) a slow movement, (*b*) a quick fugal movement, (*c*) a movement in some of the dance forms (*e.g.* often a minuet) though in many cases the third movement was dispensed with.

Handel adopted the Lulli form of overture. Thus in *Samson* the overture has three movements: (*a*) *Pomposo*, (*b*) *Allegro* (fugal), (*c*) *Minuet*. In the *Judas Maccabæus* overture we have: (*a*) *Largo*, (*b*) *Allegro* (fugal), after which there is a reminiscence of the opening *Largo*. The *Messiah* overture has the two first movements, and it is said that a minuet exists which was intended to form the third part of this overture.

1003. The Italian Overture, which was due to the labours of **Alessandro Scarlatti** (1659–1725), the father of D. Scarlatti (§ 989), consisted of (*a*) a quick movement, (*b*) a slow movement,

(c) a quick movement. As an additional element of contrast the *slow movement* was scored for fewer instruments than the two quick ones, sometimes indeed for strings only.

The importance of the Italian Overture lies in the fact that it became the model [1] on which the modern Symphony was framed, for the earlier symphonies had three movements, contrasted exactly like the Italian Overture.

1004. The Modern Overture is usually a single movement (with very often an Introduction) in sonata form or in the shortened sonata form described in § 958.

Beethoven's *Egmont* Overture is a good example. It has an *Introduction* leading to an *Allegro* in full sonata form, ending with a long coda, where the pace is quickened, the tempo altered, and there is abundance of new material.

1005. The overture to a dramatic work ought to be thoroughly in keeping with the spirit of the work, and as early as Gluck (1714-1787) means were taken to make the connection as close as possible. This may be done in several ways. The overture may run, without having a finish of its own, straight into the first number of the opera, as in the case of Mozart's *Die Entführung aus dem Serail*. Another method is to introduce some significant part of the music of the opera into the overture.[2] Mozart was probably the first to do this with any frequency. In *Die Entführung* he introduces, in place of a development section, thirty-four bars (Andante) of the first song of the opera. In the Introduction of the *Don Juan* Overture he brings in some of the very significant statue music from the Finale of Act II. Beethoven also followed this in the Introduction to the Overture 'Leonora, No. 3,' where Florestan's 'Dungeon Song' is used.

Weber uses themes from his operas in constructing the overture, but in a slightly different way. He uses the themes as *subjects* for a regularly constructed overture, as in *Der Freischütz*.

1006. Many modern opera overtures are simply constructed by stringing together a number of the principal melodies of the opera. With rare

---

[1] That is as regards *order* of movements, which of course is the *form* of the composition as a whole. As regards the form of the individual movements of a symphony, that arose from the same elements as the movements of the sonata proper.

[2] Mendelssohn's overture to the *Midsummer Night's Dream* is a converse example. The overture was written in 1826, and when, seventeen years later, Mendelssohn added incidental music to the whole play, he used parts of the overture.

exceptions such overtures have little artistic value, though they are often very effective. Examples of such are Bishop's 'Guy Mannering,' Hérold's 'Zampa.' As a most masterly example of such an overture Wagner's 'Die Meistersinger' may be cited.

1007. The **concert overture** is an independent composition intended for concert use, and written in the style and form of a modern overture. In many cases the concert overture is intended to illustrate some poem or story. While keeping to the classical model the composer uses significant subjects or melodies and works these in such a way as to suggest or depict the crises of the story.[1] Among composers of concert overtures are **Mendelssohn** ('Hebrides,' 'Calm Sea and Prosperous Voyage,' 'Fair Melusine'), **Schumann** ('Hermann and Dorothea,' 'Manfred'), **Sterndale Bennett** ('Parisina,' 'The Naiads,' 'The Wood-Nymph'), &c.

Section II.—The Symphony.

1008. We have seen how the term Symphony was first used for the interludes in operas. The term was further applied to any introductory instrumental movement, e.g. the first movement in J. S. Bach's second 'Partita' is so named.

When musicians had become accustomed to writing independent movements in operas, it was but a small step to write such movements for separate performance unconnected with opera, and naturally, in doing so, they began by moulding their compositions on the plan of the opera overture. The modern symphony must, then, trace its origin to the Italian form of overture, i.e. a composition of three movements. There were innumerable symphonies written before Haydn's time, but he is looked upon as the father of the modern symphony. At the same time, part of this credit is due to Mozart, whose three greatest symphonies (the G minor, the E♭, and the 'Jupiter') were written in 1788, while Haydn's finest series was not begun until 1791. Haydn and Mozart added a fourth movement—the minuet. Beethoven in his nine symphonies carried symphony-writing to the highest point of perfection (compare § 997). Among more modern symphony-writers may be mentioned Mendelssohn, Schubert, Spohr, Schumann, and Brahms.

---

[1] Music which is intended to illustrate a definite story in this way is often called **programme music**. It is as it were written to a certain programme. Examples of such are Beethoven's 'Pastoral Symphony,' Spohr's Symphony, 'Die Weihe der Töne.'

D D

1009. In its modern sense a symphony is a composition of (generally) four movements written on the same plan as a sonata, and intended to be performed by an orchestra. It is sometimes described as a sonata for an orchestra.

The first point to be noted is that the movements of a symphony are in general on a larger scale than the corresponding movements of a sonata. This will be readily understood when we consider the greater variety of effects at the composer's service. But mere length would not make a symphony. The musical subjects used must be important in themselves, and fit to bear this grander treatment. Indeed, the term *symphonic* is often applied to music of a grand or sublime character, to imply that it is fit for use in a symphony.

1010. As regards form, the symphony is exactly similar to a sonata. The first movement is in sonata form and in quick tempo; the second is a slow movement; the third a minuet and trio, or a scherzo; and the finale a quick movement which may be in any of the forms used for the finale of a sonata. The whole symphony may be preceded by an *introduction* (§ 907), which is sometimes of considerable length and importance (*e.g.* Beethoven's seventh symphony has sixty-two bars of introduction).

1011. The four-movement symphony may be taken as that most commonly and in modern times almost exclusively used. Some of Haydn's and many of Mozart's earlier works, however, are in three movements, *e.g.* Mozart's Prague Symphony in D has no minuet and trio. It has—exceptionally for Mozart—an Introduction of thirty-six bars. Very occasionally there are five movements, *e.g.* Schumann's Rhenish Symphony (E♭), which has an imposing movement in slow time before the finale.

The order of the second and third movements is sometimes reversed, as in Schumann's symphony just quoted, which has a scherzo for the second movement.

The student should now analyse symphonies. The best to begin with are those of Haydn[1] (especially those composed for Salamon's concerts No. 1 in C, No. 7 in D, No. 8 in E♭, No. 9 in B♭, No. 11 in D), and Mozart[1] (the G minor, the E♭, and the 'Jupiter').

---

[1] All those mentioned can be obtained in score at a very slight cost in Peters' edition.

Section III.—The Concerto.

1012. A Concerto, in its modern meaning, is a composition consisting of three[1] movements, written for one or more solo instruments with an accompaniment for orchestra. In form a concerto is a sonata with certain modifications. The first movement is in sonata form; the second, a slow movement; the finale, most frequently a Rondo.

The solo instrument has the chief part of the work in a concerto, and usually this is of a kind to show the highest executive ability. The orchestra is used in two ways: (*a*) It plays an accompaniment to the solo. In this part sometimes only a few instruments are used, or even only one, and at times the orchestra is entirely silent, the solo instrument being heard alone. (*b*) The orchestra is used as a whole, either as a contrast to the solo instrument—*i.e.* there is a sort of dialogue between orchestra and solo instrument—or to play what might be very well compared to the introduction and ritornellos of a song. Any portion of a concerto in which the orchestra is employed as a whole, and not merely as accompaniment, is called a **Tutti** (*Italian = all*). The term **Tutti** is, however, more especially applied to those orchestral portions which are used at the beginning or between the important sections of each movement.

1013. The first movement of a concerto is in sonata form, but with certain modifications, which we must now examine. The form of the concerto was fixed by Mozart, and the first movement is arranged as follows: *Tutti*, *solo* (**Exposition**); *tutti*, *solo* (**Development**); *tutti*, *solo* (**Recapitulation**); *tutti* (in which the solo often joins). It must be understood that there are often other short *tuttis* besides those here indicated, and of course the solo parts have a certain amount of accompaniment. As regards the tuttis the first is the longest (in Beethoven's Op. 15 it is ninety-six bars), and from a structural point of view the most important. It is not an introduction in the sense of § 907, but it prepares the way for the solo by giving out the first and second subjects of the concerto; in other words, the first tutti is an exposition with this difference, that very often (though by no means always) the first and second subjects are *both in the tonic key.* Thus in sonata form as used in the concerto *there are two expositions*—one for the orchestra, the other for the solo instrument. The remaining tuttis are constructed out of the materials of the concerto.

---

[1] Sometimes there is a sort of short intermezzo between the second and third movements, but this is by no means a movement, being really an introduction to the Finale, *v.* Mendelssohn's concerto for violin, and that in G minor for piano.

1014. In the earlier concertos the orchestra and the solo instrument were treated very much apart, but the modern tendency is to treat the two as one whole, and this has led to the freer use of the orchestra, to the shortening of the tuttis, and, above all, to the absolute omission or very great curtailment of the first tutti. Beethoven is usually credited with originating the method of omitting the first tutti, but this is not quite accurate. His piano concertos Op. 58 in G and Op. 73 in E♭ (the 'Emperor') opens, it is true, with the solo, but the regulation first tutti is taken up after a few bars. In the case of Op. 73 this solo might very well be called an *Introduction*. Mendelssohn was the real innovator in his Op. 25, in which the piano enters after six bars of simple prelude. This practice has been generally followed by modern writers, *e.g.* in the P.F. concertos of Schumann (A minor), Grieg (A minor), and Hiller (F♯ minor).

1015. Another feature of the concerto is the Cadenza. This most usually occurs after the Recapitulation.[1] The orchestral tutti is brought to a pause usually on the $\tfrac{6}{4}$ on the dominant, whereupon the cadenza is played as a solo. In the cadenza the player was expected to show his technical facility and also his ability in using the material of the movement in a sort of second development. As a rule, therefore, it was left[2] to the player, who either improvised it or previously prepared it. As an instance of an improvised cadenza, it may be mentioned that when Mendelssohn played Beethoven's concerto in G for the Philharmonic Society in 1844 he played the cadenza three times at the rehearsal (owing to some mistake on the part of the orchestra), each time a different cadenza, and when the performance came, he electrified the band by again playing a completely new one.[3] But there are manifest dangers in leaving the cadenza to the player's judgment. Beethoven began (E♭ concerto) the practice of writing the cadenza out in full. This plan has been followed by modern writers, *e.g.* Schumann and Grieg.

Mendelssohn in his two piano concertos omits the cadenza altogether, and in his violin concerto it is written out in full.

1016. The slow movement of a concerto is most frequently in song form, often with a brilliant solo part. The finale is a Rondo or an air with variations.

1017. Concertos may be written for more than one solo instrument, *e.g.* Brahms' **Double Concerto** for violin and 'cello, Beethoven's **Triple Concerto** for violin, 'cello, and piano.

---

[1] In Mendelssohn's violin concerto it is just before the Recapitulation.
[2] Both Beethoven and Mozart wrote cadenzas (published separately) for their concertos.
[3] Quoted from Grove's *Dictionary of Music and Musicians*, vol. ii. p. 285.

Section IV.—Concerted Music. *(Chamber Music)*

1018. Music written for two or more instruments, with only one player to a part, and where each part is of equal importance, is called **Concerted**[1] **Music or Chamber Music.**

This will be best understood by comparison. In a symphony each string part is played by several players, in the case of the first and second violin parts, by as many as fourteen players in the largest orchestras. In a string quartet there is only one player to each part, and the quartet is therefore concerted music. Again, the ordinary violin solo has usually a pianoforte accompaniment. In many cases this pianoforte part has no individual significance, being merely used to support the solo part. On the other hand, it only needs a moment's hearing of Beethoven's 'Kreutzer' Sonata for P.F. and V. to recognise that both instruments are equally important in producing the result, and the 'Kreutzer' is concerted music.

Concerted music is written for almost any combination of instruments for strings, strings and piano, strings, piano, and wind instruments, &c.

1019. The form of concerted music is usually that of the four-movement sonata. In some cases there are additional movements, *e.g.* Beethoven's string trio in E♭, Op. 3, has six movements: 1. Allegro con brio; 2. Andante; 3. Minuet and trio; 4. Adagio; 5. Minuet and trio; 6. Finale Allegro.

1020. The most important section of concerted music is undoubtedly the **String Quartet.** It is said to have been invented by Boccherini (1740–1805) but as in the other forms of the sonata and symphony it was securely placed on its present important footing by Haydn and Mozart. Haydn's early quartets are slight in character, and it was not until after Mozart published (in 1782) the six magnificent quartets which he dedicated to Haydn that the older master gave to the world his best efforts in this direction. Beethoven, taking up the string quartet where Haydn and Mozart had left it, carried it to the highest point of perfection. His seventeen quartets are among the grandest examples of the highest class of music.

The string quartet has always appealed to the greatest composers, and since Haydn's time there is scarcely a composer of high standing who has not written examples.

---

[1] This term is also applied to the sections of an opera where more than two of the solo characters are actively engaged in the same scene.

CHAPTER LXXIII.

VARIATIONS, THE FANTASIA, &C.

1021. Variations.—The use of variations may be said to date from almost the very beginning of instrumental music. We shall presently see how they were freely used (under the name of *Doubles*) in the old suites (§ 1061), and when a melody is introduced more than once in the course of a movement it is almost invariably modified or varied in some particular. But we are using the term here in a much more important sense, referring to pieces in which the whole interest lies in the varying of a given subject or theme. Such an **air with variations** may form part of a larger work (especially the slow movement or finale of a work in sonata form), or it may exist as a separate piece, and it is worthy of note that all the greatest musicians from Bach to Beethoven and Brahms have had a predilection for this form of composition. In an *air with variations* a subject or theme, generally a melody in two-part form, is made the groundwork. There are various ways in which variations may be written.

1022. (*a*) The **melody** may be **ornamented** by the addition of passing notes &c., or by the free use of arpeggios, at the same time keeping the original harmony and rhythmic character. This is the easiest kind of variation to write, and it has so often been done in a perfunctory way by second-rate writers as to cast an undeserved stigma on variations in general. In the hands of a good composer a merely ornamental variation may be very charming.

(*b*) The harmony being retained, a new melody may be built upon it.

(*c*) The melody may be retained while the harmony is completely altered.

(*d*) The tempo may be changed from duple to triple, &c., or the rhythmic character may be completely changed, giving to the original subject the character of a march or a polonaise, &c.

(*e*) The theme may be treated contrapuntally, *i.e.* with imitation or worked as a fughetta or fugue.

(*f*) The highest kind of variation, however, passes beyond the mere outward variation and consists of presenting the same musical thought in a different aspect.

The same key [1] is maintained throughout a set of variations, though change of mode, from minor to major or *vice versa*, is common.

---

[1] A solitary exception is Beethoven's Op. 34 in F. For each succeeding variation a key a third below the key of the last is used until the final variation returns to the original. Thus F, D, B♭, G, E♭, C, and F.

VARIATIONS, THE FANTASIA, &c.

1023. The greatest writers of variations have been J. S. Bach, Haydn, Mozart, Beethoven, Weber, Chopin, Mendelssohn, Schubert, Schumann, and Brahms.

1024. Fantasia.—The word fantasia means fancy, and it is applied to compositions in which the composer follows his fancy and is less bound down by a fixed form than in many other works. But it must not be imagined from this that a *fantasia* is without form. A fantasia usually consists of several sections, each of which is independent of its neighbours as regards form. A section frequently interrupts a previous one, and very often a brilliant cadenza is used. The whole, however, is united into one whole in spirit. Mozart's Fantasia in D minor is a beautiful example. This opens with eleven bars of prelude (*Andante*) leading to an *Adagio*, which in form resembles the old sonata form (§ 994), but it is interrupted by cadenzas. The last section of the fantasia is in D major (*Allegretto*) which is simply a melody made up of two eight-bar sentences with a long coda.

There are many modern fantasias on operatic airs. These merely string together a number of melodies contrasted as to key and character, with a certain amount of original matter (often of a worthless character) to connect them.

1025. There are a great many smaller instrumental forms, Nocturnes, Songs without Words, &c., and others to which fanciful names are given. These are almost invariably in song form (Ch. LXVI.) or rondo form (§ 971) and will present little difficulty in analysis.

The student should now examine variations in the pianoforte works of Mozart, Beethoven, Mendelssohn, and Schumann, and Fantasias by Mozart, Mendelssohn, and Schumann.

CHAPTER LXXIV.

IMITATION, CANON AND FUGUE; FUGUE AND SONATA FORM COMBINED.

1026. When a melodic phrase or figure, after having been heard in one part, is repeated in *another* part or parts, there is said to be **Imitation**. Imitation may be at any interval above or below—in the unison (fig. 445), octave (fig. 489), fifth (fig. 440), &c.

1027. When the imitation is exactly like the pattern, the steps between the notes of the melody being alike in quality as well as in name, the imitation is said to be **strict** (fig. 439). When the steps of the pattern melody are only imitated in name and not in quality, the imitation is **free**.

Strict imitation at the octave below.

Fig. 439.   Martini.

Free imitation at the fifth below.

Fig. 440.   Handel, *Xerxes*.

At (*a*) the melody moves by two major seconds; at (*b*) the imitation moves by a minor and a major second.

1028. There is a freer imitation still where the general form only is imitated, a leap being imitated by a leap (but not necessarily the same interval), &c. In practical music free imitation is much more frequent than strict.

1029. Imitation may be by **contrary motion**, *i.e.* where the pattern *ascends* the imitation descends, and *vice versa*.

Imitation by contrary motion.

Fig. 441.   Mozart, P.F. Sonata.

1030. The imitation may begin in such a way that the accented beats of the pattern become unaccented and *vice versa*. This is termed **imitation with reversed accents**, or *per arsin et thesin*.[1]

Imitation with reversed accents.

FIG. 442.

ASTORGA, *Stabat Mater*.

&c.

1031. Imitation may be by **Augmentation**, where the notes of the imitation are of greater length than in the pattern, or by **diminution** where the notes of the imitation are of shorter length than in the pattern.

Imitation by augmentation.

FIG. 443.

BACH, *Wohltemperirtes Clavier*.

&c.

1032. There is a kind of imitation in which the pattern is imitated by beginning at the end and going backwards. This is called by a variety of names, *e.g.* **Retrograde, Al rovescio, Per recte et retro,** and **Cancrizans** (= crab-like).

1033. When imitation is continued throughout a complete phrase or melody it is said to be *canonic*, and a composition containing such imitation is called a **Canon**—a Greek word meaning 'rule.'

1034. Canons are divided into finite and infinite. In a **Finite** canon the imitation ceases when each part has once given out the whole of the

---

[1] *Arsis* = raising, *i.e.* up-beat; *thesis* = putting down, *i.e.* down-beat. *Per arsin et thesin* is also sometimes applied to canons (§ 1033), which proceed by contrary motion.

pattern. In a finite canon the parts may end (as they began) successively, as they finish the pattern. Such is the case in the three-part canon shown in fig. 433. As this is a somewhat awkward way of ending, it is a common practice to let the part or parts which have first finished the pattern continue with a part not intended to be imitated, in order to bring the whole to a satisfactory conclusion. Such a continuation is called a *Coda*. and usually it is necessary to let all the parts take part in the Coda.

Finite Canon with Coda.

Fig. 444.

1035. A canon, however, may be so arranged that as each part finishes the pattern, it returns to the beginning without interrupting the imitation. Such a canon is called Infinite or *Perpetual*, and it can be continued as long as is wished. A pause is sometimes written over a convenient ending point, or a coda may be added. The example in fig. 445 might end at the pause.

Infinite Canon.

Fig. 445.

1086. Canons may be in any number of parts and at any interval. Canons are spoken of according to the number of parts and the number of subjects or patterns imitated. Thus a canon 2 in 1 means that there are two voice parts, and one subject as in figs. 444-5. The canon shown in fig. 433 is 3 in 1, *i.e.* three parts and one subject. Similarly we speak of 4 in 1, 5 in 1, &c. Sometimes two subjects or patterns are imitated at the same time by two or more other parts. Such canon would be called 4 in 2, *i.e.* four parts in two subjects.

1087. Canons are often accompanied by other parts not in canon, but merely completing the harmony. In the tune used for the Evening Hymn known as *Tallis's Canon*, the treble and tenor are in canon (at a bar's distance), while the alto and bass have free parts.

1088. All the methods of imitation explained in §§ 1026-32 may be applied to canons, and thus we get *canons* by *contrary motion*,[1] by *Augmentation*, by *Diminution*, *Cancrizans*,[2] &c.

1089. When a canon is written out in score, as in fig. 433, it is called an open canon. Formerly another method of showing a canon was much used. The *subject* of the canon was written once, the number of parts given, and the points of entry indicated by some sign placed *above* when the new entries were in a higher voice and *below* when in a lower. A canon written in this way is called a close canon.[3]

Close Canon, 4 in 1.

FIG. 446.

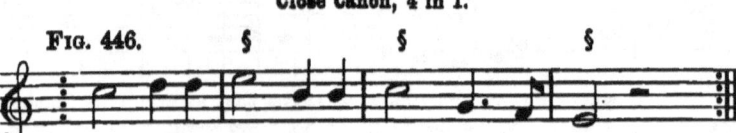

This canon is for four voices. When the first voice reaches the sign § the second voice will enter, beginning, of course, with the beginning of the subject. When the first voice reaches the next sign, the third voice enters, &c. In the above case all the entries are at the unison. If the entries were at some other interval, a figure indicating the interval would be placed beside the sign §.

---

[1] Examples of this will be seen in the minuet of Dussek's sonata, Op. 77, and in No. 10 of Clementi's *Gradus ad Parnassum*.
[2] When Haydn took his degree of Doctor of Music at Oxford in 1791, he sent in as his 'Exercise' a three-part canon cancrizans.
[3] There are other ways of writing a close canon, for which the student must consult books like Albrechtsberger's 'Thoroughbass,' Part III. The subject has now, however, no practical importance.

1040. Close canons also used to be written, but with all indications as to entry of voices and intervals omitted. These were intended as puzzles and were called **enigma** or **riddle canons**, in the solving of which a musician had to use all his ingenuity. Sometimes a sort of motto (usually in Latin), was prefixed to give some hint as to the method of procedure.

1041. An **infinite canon** is sometimes made to modulate so that each repetition is a tone or a semitone higher. If this is continued long enough we shall in time reach the starting key again, and therefore such canons are called **circular canons**.

1042. It is possible to write a canon subject in such a manner that it can be treated canonically in more than one way. Such a canon is called **polymorphous**.

1043. The simplest kind of canon is what is known as a **round**. In a canon the entries may be at any interval, and they need not be at the same distance of time, but in a round the canon is at the unison and each voice completes a whole phrase or even a sentence before the next entry. The entries, too, are all at the same distance of time.

Round for three voices.

Fig. 447.

Arnold.

The figures at the end of each line indicate which line is to be next sung. The first voice opens, and when it has finished the first line it proceeds to the second, while the second voice begins at the beginning; when the first voice reaches the third line the second voice will be beginning the second, and the third voice the first. As each voice finishes the last line it begins at the beginning again, and so the round can go on as long as we please.

1044. When a Round is written to humorous words, or with a play on words, it is termed a **Catch**. When Hawkins and Burney published their histories of music, in 1776, the rivalry between them was made the subject of a catch in which perfectly harmless words were made, when sung, to sound like ' Sir John Hawkins! *Burn his* (= *Burney's*) History ! '

1045. A Fugue is a composition consisting chiefly of the repetition and imitation of a *Subject* developed according to certain rules.

The term is said to be derived from the Latin *fuga* = *flight*, because as the parts enter in succession there is the appearance of flight and pursuit among the parts.

The points to be noted in a fugue are *subject, answer, counter-subject, episodes, and stretto.*

1046. The **subject** is a short theme (rarely more than eight bars), of a character suitable for use in imitational passages. The fugue opens with one part (or voice) which announces the subject. When the first part has finished [1] the subject the second part enters with the *answer*.

1047. In general the **answer** is simply a transposition of the subject to the key of the dominant. When the answer is an exact transposition of the subject it is called a *real answer* (fig. 448), and a fugue with a real answer is called a *real fugue.*

Fig. 448.

Subject.

J. S. Bach, *Wohl. Cl.* II. 9.
Real answer.

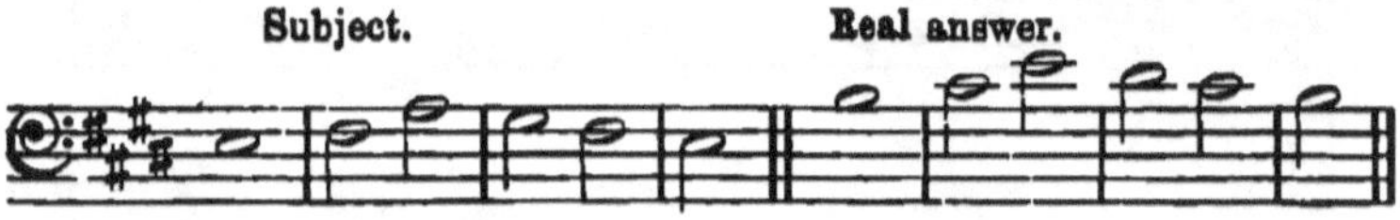

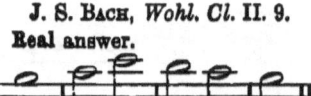

1048. Very often, however, certain modifications of the subject are necessary in the answer, when it is called a *tonal answer*, and a fugue with a tonal answer is called a **tonal fugue**. These changes are necessitated by the rule that, generally speaking, the *tonic* in the subject must be represented by the *dominant* in the answer and *vice versa*. These changes are usually necessary

(*a*) When the subject begins or ends on the dominant;

(*b*) When the subject skips (especially through the third of the key), to the dominant ;

(*c*) When the subject modulates.

---

[1] Sometimes the answer enters before the subject is finished, so that subject and answer are heard together. Such a fugue is called a *close fugue*, *v.* Bach's *Wohltemperirtes Clavier*, II. 3.

Examples of tonal answers.

FIG. 449.

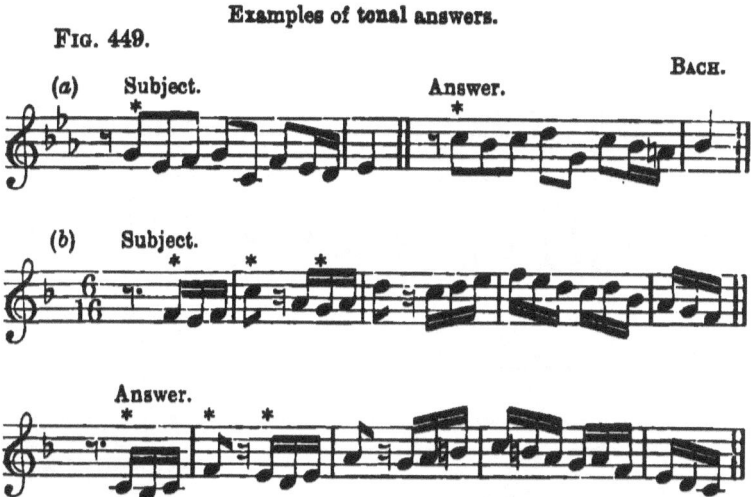

In a tonal answer all modifications are made in approaching and leaving the dominant or tonic.

1049. While the second part is giving the answer, the first part accompanies it with a suitably contrasted counterpoint, which is called the *counter-subject* (fig. 450). The C.S. should be written in double counterpoint (p. 352, n. 1), so that it may be used either above or below the subject or answer.

1050. When the second part has finished the answer, the third part enters with the subject in the original key, and the second voice now uses counter-subject, transposed of course. During this time the first voice usually gives out an additional counterpoint, filling up the harmony. If the fugue is in four parts, the fourth voice will now enter with the answer, the third voice taking the C.S. while the other two voices have free parts to complete the harmony

1051. When each voice has in turn had the subject or the answer, the first section of the fugue, called the **exposition**, is usually at an end. Sometimes, however, the exposition is wholly or partly repeated, and it is then called the *counter-exposition*, in which the voice that had the subject in the exposition will now have the answer, and *vice versa*.

Very frequently it is necessary to add a short passage between subject (or answer), and the counter-subject. Such a passage is called a **codetta**, fig. 450 * . . . *.

IMITATION, CANON, AND FUGUE 399

Exposition of a three-part fugue.

Fig. 450.

J. S. Bach, *Wohl. Cl.* I. 11.

1052. A fugue consists of three sections. The first section is the *exposition*, where the only keys used are the tonic and dominant; the second section comprises the entries of subjects in fresh (related) keys, and the final section returns to the original key. Partly to give variety and partly to provide means of modulation, **episodes** are introduced between the sections and between the various parts of the middle section. An episode is most effective when constructed from materials supplied by the subject or counter-subject, such material being very often worked sequentially. Fig. 451 shows an episode from the fugue in fig. 449. The figure (*a*) is the last bar of the subject, and it is freely imitated in the highest part; this, sequentially repeated, leads us to D minor in which the next entry of the subject comes.

Fig. 451.

In the second and third sections the subject may be treated by augmentation,[1] diminution, or inversion.

1053. The word **Stretto** is derived from the Italian *stringere* (= to draw close), and it is applied to those portions of the fugue in which the subject and answer follow each other at shorter intervals of time than in the exposition. In Fig. 450 the answer follows the subject after four bars. Fig. 452 shows a stretto from the same fugue where the subject and answer are at two bars' distance. Some fugue subjects are capable of many combina-

---

[1] Fugues worked out with great strictness and full of imitational and canonic devices were formerly called **Ricercare** or **Ricercata**, both of which terms mean 'sought out.' The terms are also applied to fugues containing no episodes.

IMITATION, CANON, AND FUGUE 401

Fig. 452.

Example of Stretto.

&c.

tions in stretto. A stretto may occur at any point after the exposition, and when there are several stretti the closest should be reserved for the last. Some fugues are entirely without stretto (Bach's *Wohl. Cl.* II. 1); others, on the contrary, are almost entirely made up of stretto (Bach's I. 1).

1054. Towards the end of a fugue it is a common practice to introduce a pedal point (§ 648), usually the dominant in the bass (fig. 452). Sometimes both tonic and dominant pedals are used, in which case the dominant must occur first.

1055. Fugues may be written on two, three, or more subjects. They are then called double or triple fugues, &c. In such cases the several subjects are written so as to be capable of being worked together.

1056. A **Fughetta** is a short fugue worked with less elaboration than an ordinary fugue. Schumann's *Album for the Young*, No. 40, is an example.

1057. Sometimes a passage, without actually being a fugue, resembles a fugue in style of subject and in entry of parts. Such passages are called fugato.

1058. **Fugue and Sonata Form combined.**—Certain movements are sometimes described as being a combination of fugue and sonata form. It

E E

would be more correct, perhaps, to describe them as in sonata form, but with subjects which lend themselves easily to fugal treatment. In fact, the main interest lies, no doubt, in the contrapuntal effects, but the movements are laid out in sonata form. Beethoven's P.F. Sonata, Op. 10, No. 2, Finale, is a good example. It has an exposition with two subjects in regular keys; a development and a recapitulation with repeat marks at both double bars. It is thus clearly in sonata form. When, however, we examine the subject and treatment we see an unmistakable resemblance to fugue. In the first place, the first subject is distinctly fugal in character and style (compare it with the finale of the 'Moonlight Sonata'), and in the exposition the parts enter in succession just as in a fugue. There is a considerable amount of contrapuntal treatment throughout, especially in the Recapitulation, where double counterpoint is freely employed.

Still more striking examples will be seen in Mozart's overture to *Die Zauberflöte*, the Finale of the string quartet in G and the Finale[1] of the 'Jupiter Symphony.' These are all in sonata form with much fugal working. The 'Jupiter' Finale is, indeed, a colossal example of contrapuntal working.

CHAPTER LXXV.

THE SUITE; THE PARTITA; DANCE FORMS.

1059. Early in the seventeenth century the practice of writing sets of dance tunes as independent instrumental music was much in vogue. These sets went by various names. In England they were called *Lessons*, or *Suites of Lessons*; in Italy, *Sonate da Camera*; in Germany, *Parties, Partitas*,[2] and *Suites*. Among writers of such pieces may be mentioned Corelli, Purcell, Kuhnau, Mattheson, J. S. Bach, and Handel, and among these J. S. Bach must be singled out as the one composer who brought the suite to its highest perfection.

1060. A Suite consists of a series of dance tunes almost

---

[1] Mozart's pupil, Hummel, uses the same subject fugally in his P.F. Sonata, Op. 20.

[2] According to Mattheson, a contemporary of J. S. Bach and Handel (quoted in Peters' edition of Bach's Partitas), *Partita* originally meant *part* of a suite. A distinction between suite and partita is sometimes made according to which a partita includes movements of a freer character and not in dance rhythm; while a suite consists, with the exception of an *Introduction*, entirely of dance movements. This distinction cannot always be maintained (cf. Bach's first Partita).

invariably in the same key,¹ but contrasted in tempo and in rhythmic character. In the best examples there were always four movements, *Allemande, Courante, Sarabande*, and *Gigue*, to which might be prefixed an introductory movement called by various names—viz. *Prélude, Préambule, Ouverture, Symphonie* (§ 1,000). Between the sarabande and gigue other dances were often introduced, especially the *Bourrée, Minuet, Gavotte*, &c. In Handel's suites, which are not by any means strict examples of the form, a fugue is very frequently used. We now give examples of the movements in suites.

J. S. Bach's first French suite contains *Allemande, Courante, Sarabande, Minuet* I. and II., *Gigue*. Bach's first English suite contains *Prélude, Allemande, Courante* I., *Courante* II., with two variations, *Sarabande, Bourrée* I. and II., *Gigue*.

1061. The same form is usually followed in each of the movements comprised in the suite. Each movement consists of two parts, both of which are repeated. Part I. opens with a figure in the tonic key, and proceeds to a related key in which that part ends. Part II. opens in the related key and leads eventually back to the tonic in which it ends. Unity is secured not so much by repetition as by an all-pervading rhythmic character or figure (§ 984).

We now describe the chief dances used. It is impossible for us to find space to give examples. The student, however, can easily get these for himself in the works of Bach and Handel.

1062. The **Allemande** is a somewhat quick movement in $\frac{4}{4}$ time, beginning with an incomplete bar. It is marked by constant movement in semiquavers.

The **Courante** is in $\frac{3}{4}$ or $\frac{3}{8}$ time, rather quick, and marked by much cross-accent.

The **Sarabande**, originally a Spanish dance, is a slow movement in $\frac{3}{4}$ or $\frac{3}{8}$ time. It begins on the first beat of the bar, and perhaps the most noticeable feature is that the second beat of each bar is often emphasised.

The **Gigue** is a lively dance usually characterised by the division of its beats into three quavers. It is therefore most usually in $\frac{6}{8}$ or $\frac{12}{8}$ time.

---

¹ There is an exception in the second minuet in Bach's fourth English suite.

The **Gavotte** is in $\frac{4}{4}$ time, beginning with two crotchets before a full bar. Its time is moderate. A second Gavotte called a **Musette** is usually added.

The **Bourrée** is in ₵ time, beginning on the last crotchet of a bar with a more flowing character than a Gavotte. A second Bourrée is sometimes added.

The **Minuet** is a moderately slow,[1] stately dance in $\frac{3}{4}$ time. A second minuet is often added.

The Allemande, Courante, Bourrée, and Sarabande are sometimes followed by variations called Doubles, v. J. S. Bach's first English Suite [2] and his Second Sonata for Violin Solo.

1063. Other movements in Suites were the *Polonaise, Burlesca, Scherzo, Toccata, Passepied, Loure, Rondeau, Caprice, Rigaudon, Passacaglia, Chaconne.*

Of these we describe the Passacaglia and the Chaconne.

1064. The **Passacaglia** (Fr. *Passecaille*) and the **Chaconne**, which are very similar to each other, are in reality series of variations on a Ground Bass (II. § 660). The only real difference between them is that in the Chaconne the theme is always kept in the bass, while in the Passacaglia it may be used in an upper part. Among the best-known examples we may cite the Passacaglia in C minor of J. S. Bach for organ with twenty variations and a fugue, and that of Handel in the seventh Suite with fifteen variations; the Chaconne of J. S. Bach in the fourth Sonata for Violin alone in D minor with thirty variations, and that of Handel in G in the second Book of Suites with sixty-two variations.

The Finale of Brahms' Fourth Symphony, Op. 98, is a modern example of the Passacaglia with thirty-three variations.

1065. Suites have been written in modern times. In them an attempt is usually made to catch something of the spirit of the old dance forms, while using modern methods. As an example we may mention **Raff's** (1822–1882) Suite in E minor, Op. 72, which consists of *Preludio, Menuetto, Toccata, Romanza,* and *Fuga.*

---

[1] When Haydn introduced the minuet into his symphonies he made it into a quick movement, which has not very much in common with the older minuet.

[2] In the second and third English Suites the variation to the Sarabande is called **Agréments**, a term which, however, usually means merely grace notes, *e.g.* trill, mordent, &c.

CHAPTER LXXVI.

VOCAL MUSIC.

1066. We have already pointed out that the form of vocal music is dependent on the words. This is so to such an extent that in one form of vocal music, the *recitative*, the most elementary requisite of pure music, viz. that of beginning and ending in the same key, is no longer imperative, *e.g.* 'Thy rebuke' (Handel's *Messiah*) begins in A♭ and ends in B♮.

1067. In **Recitative** the words are declaimed or recited very much as an elocutionist would recite them, but the inflections of the voice are in definite musical intervals. There are three kinds of recitative. In the simplest kind, **Recitativo secco**, the invention of which is usually attributed to Peri about 1600, the words are declaimed as just explained, the only rhythmical effect being the natural accent of the words, the singer being free as regards time. *Recitativo secco* was supported by the barest accompaniment of chords, usually played on the harpsichord.[1] An example of this is seen in 'There were shepherds' (Handel's *Messiah*).

Sometimes the accompaniment was given to the orchestra, and then it assumed larger proportions, even playing at times short interludes to add to the effect, the voice part, however, being merely declamatory. In this case it was called **Accompanied Recitative**.

A third kind of recitative is when the accompaniment is made so important that it must be played in strict time, though the voice part still retains its declamatory character. Such is called **Recitativo a tempo**. It will easily be seen that accompanied Recitative often becomes of necessity Recitativo a tempo. There is a good example in 'For, behold, darkness' (*Messiah*).

1068. But while Recitative is practically free as to real form, it must be remembered that in most cases the 'words' for music are themselves on a clear and definite plan,[2] so that by merely following the words the music acquires a form. Add to this too that the form element is strong in musicians and it will become

---

[1] At one period it was the custom to play these chords arpeggio on a 'cello, a practice happily now gone out of fashion.
[2] Even where the words are in ordinary prose the feeling of the musician almost always makes them fit into a rhythmical plan by repetition and prolongation &c. Examine the words of 'Why do the nations' (*Messiah*).

easy to understand that in the main the same principles[1] of form apply equally to vocal and to instrumental music.

1069. Songs are most frequently written in *two* or *three part* form, which we have already described (§§ 857–81). There are innumerable examples in national songs and in the songs of classical writers, Haydn, Mozart, Beethoven, Mendelssohn, Schumann, Schubert, Franz, Brahms. The three-part song form is sometimes called the **Aria form**, because it is so often used for *Arias*, and sometimes the **Scarlatti form** because its invention is due to Alessandro Scarlatti (§ 1,003). Handel's 'Why do the nations' is a good example. There is a first part, a second part, and a third part, which, as is very often the case in older examples, is merely a Da Capo of the first part.

1070. When the words of a song are arranged in a number of equal strophes or verses the song is called a **strophic song**, and as a rule the music for each verse will be the same. Sometimes in a strophic song the same melody is retained throughout but each verse has a different accompaniment, as in Beethoven's 'Kennst du das Land.' Sometimes one of the verses of a strophic song will be in a new key or each verse may have trifling modifications, to better express the sentiment of the words, as in Franz's 'Aus meinen grossen Schmerzen,' Op. 5, No. 1.

1071. The larger instrumental forms were formerly frequently used in songs, *e.g.* 'Rejoice greatly' (*Messiah*) is in old *rondo* form (§ 971), and there are many examples of songs in *sonata* form, *e.g.* Mozart's *Die Entführung aus dem Serail*, Nos. 8, 10, and 17, &c. A modern example of a song in sonata form is Mackenzie's 'Unto my charger' (*Rose of Sharon*).

1072. A song sometimes consists of more than one movement. In such cases it is usually best to consider each movement as a separate form. Thus in 'Batti, batti' (Mozart's *Don Juan*) there is a section in $\frac{2}{4}$ time. This is complete in itself and in three-part form, but instead of ending on the tonic it leads to a section in $\frac{6}{8}$ time, which may be regarded either as a coda to the $\frac{2}{4}$ section or as a separate piece in two-part form.

1073. A series of songs dealing with the same subject and often containing the development of some story is called a **Song Cycle** (German, Liederkreis). The earliest example is Beethoven's Op. 98, 'An die ferne Geliebte,' consisting of six songs. In this song cycle the songs are all connected by instrumental interludes; but this is not usually the case. Thus in Schubert's 'Die schöne Müllerin,' Op. 25, each of the twenty songs is

---

[1] The principle of *repetition* (§ 860) is by no means so imperative in vocal music.

musically independent, though they form one complete whole[1] as regards subject. Sir A. Sullivan has written a delightful song cycle, 'The Window, or the Songs of the Wrens,' consisting of eleven songs, the words being by Lord Tennyson.

1074. In opera the term **Scena** or **Scena and Aria** is applied to the music employed (for one solo voice) in working out one complete episode of great dramatic intensity and importance. A scena consists of a recitative followed by an aria consisting of two sections, the first in slow and the second in quick tempo. 'Gott! welch Dunkel hier' (Beethoven's *Fidelio*) is a good example. Weber excelled in this form. Among his examples may be mentioned 'Wie nahte mir der Schlummer' (*Der Freischütz*).

Scenas have been written for concert use and they are then sometimes called **Concert Arias**. Two of the finest examples are Beethoven's 'Ah perfido' and Mendelssohn's 'Infelice.'

1075. Among other vocal forms the following are to be noted:—

Anthem, a composition to sacred words, in one or more movements. An anthem may contain solos, or some parts of it may be arranged to be sung with only one voice to a part, such sections being marked 'verse.' The parts sung by the whole choir are marked 'full.'

A *full anthem* means one entirely for the whole choir, while a *verse anthem* contains portions to be sung by one voice to a part.

Ballad, a song of a simple character, the words of which contain a short story.

Cantata. (a) In old music a piece for a solo voice resembling a scena, generally consisting of two airs with recitatives between them.

(b) In modern music, a short work for soli and chorus with accompaniment intended for representation without scenery, *i.e.* a short opera or oratorio.

Chorale, a form of hymn tune used by the Lutherans in Germany.

Chorus, a composition for several voices, with or without accompaniment, to be performed by several singers to a part. In general a chorus has its chief interest and unity in its contrapuntal character.

Glee, a composition for several voices, generally in two or more movements to be sung with only one voice to a part (cf. *Part Song*).

Madrigal, a secular vocal composition generally in one movement for at least three-part chorus. It is very contrapuntal in character.

---

[1] In Beethoven's and Sullivan's cycles unity is attained by using the same key for the first and the last songs. Beethoven also uses the subject of the first song in the last.

Mass, the name given to the musical setting of the Roman Catholic Church service. It comprises the following parts, *Kyrie*, *Gloria*, *Credo*, *Sanctus*, *Benedictus*, and *Agnus Dei*. Each of these is musically independent.

Motet a sacred composition after the style of a madrigal.

Opera, a dramatic composition for voices and orchestra to be performed with scenic effects. It comprises overture (for orchestra), solos, duets, terzets, quartets, &c., and choruses. At the end of each act there should be a grand *finale*, which, in the working out of one great crisis, may include recitatives, songs, and choruses; *v.* finale to Act I. *Don Juan*.

Oratorio, a composition to sacred words for solo voices, chorus, and orchestra, to be performed without the aid of scenery.

The **Part Song** differs from the glee in being written for a chorus, and it is generally homophonic (§ 986) in style, *i.e.* it has one striking melody (in the upper part usually), the other voices merely completing the harmony.

Plain Song, traditional music used in the service of the church, written in the old church modes.

INDEX.

The references are to paragraphs except where page is specified.

Abbreviations, 220-222
Abstract music, p. 378, n. 1
A cappella, 60
Accent, 40, 61-63, 785
— displacing of, 84-86, 810
Acciaccatura, 226, 542
Accidentals, 88-97, 131; p. 52. n. 1
Acoustics, 149
Added sixth, 585
Agréments, p. 404, n. 1
Alla breve, 60
Allemande, 1062
Al rovescio imitation, 1032
Alt, in, 26
Altered diatonic minor, 123
Alternation of time-signature, 852
Altissimo, in, 27
Alto, 22
— clef, 19
Amphibrach 825
Analysis of Exposition, 909
Anapæst, 825
Ancient music, notes in, 38
Andante, p. 86, n. 2
Anthem, 1075
Anticipation, 544
Appoggiatura, 225, 542
— double, 228
Aria form, 1069-74
Arpeggio, 223, 347, 658, 659
Augmentation, 1031
Augmented intervals, 185, 193
— progression by, 429, 430
— triad, 642-7
— sixth, 629-39
— — derivation of, 631
— — inaccurately written, 639
— — on the minor second, 633-7
— — used in modulation, 661
Auxiliary notes, 539-41
Balance in form, 868
Ballad, 1075
Bar, 41
Bar-line, 41
Barring, method of, 806-11
Bass, 22, 320
— clef, 5
— figured, 321-5
— voice, compass of, 300

Beat (grace-note), 227
Beats, 45
— dividing bars into, 46
Beethoven's influence on sonata form, 907
Binary form, p. 342, n. 1
Bis, 213
Boccherini and the string quartet, 1020
Bourrée, 1062
Brahms and sonata form, 998
Breve, 37
Bridge passage, 892-4
C, middle, 13
—, tenor, 28
Cadences, 450, 461, 462, 787-8
— ending on dom. 7th, 796
— imperfect, 459, 789, 793
— in counterpoint, 750
— interrupted, 460, 789, 793
— inverted, 463, 789
— middle, 694, 790
— perfect, 453, 787-9
— plagal, 456, 789, 794
— use of, 452, 1793-99
Cadential endings, 795
— repetition, 827
Cadenza, p. 361, n. 1, 1015
Cancrizans imitation, 1032
Canon, 1033-44
— finite, 1034
— infinite, 1035
— in sonata form, 920
Canons, how named, 1026
Cantata, 883, 1075
Canti fermi for exercises, p. 287
Canto fermo, p. 262, n. 1
Catch, 1044
Chaconne, 1064
Chamber music, 1018
Changing notes, 543
Chorale, 1075
Chord, broken, 223
— close, extended, 84
— common, 278, 312, 357
— definition of, 275
— firm, 223
— method of building, 276
— root of, 276
Chorus, 1075
Chromatic chords, 594

F F

INDEX

Chromatic common chords, 595
— fundamental discords, 600-18
— minor scale, 124
— scale, 174
— — origin of, 623-8
— semitone, 161
Circular canon, 1041
Clefs, 5, 18, 19, 22, 23
— form of, 21
Close, 788
— canon, 1039
Coda to a melody, 849
— to a composition, 866
— in sonata form, 940
— new matter in, 942
— to find beginning of, 943
Codetta in sonata form, 901, 940
— in fugue, 1051
Concert aria, 1074
— overture, 1007
Concerted music, 1018
Concerto, 1012-17
— double, triple, 1017
— use of orchestra in, 1015
Consecutive fifths, 434-6
— fourths, 442
— hidden, 440
— octaves and unisons, 437-9
— seconds and sevenths, 443
Consonance, 203, 271
Continuity, p. 342, n. 1
Contrapuntal, p. 263, n. 1
Contrary motion, 286, 1029
Contrast and balance of keys, 987
Convenient notation, 589
Counterpoint, 691
— combined, 778-84
— compared with harmony, 698
— double, 701
— fifth species, 770-77
— figuring, 736
— first species, 731-40
— fourth species, 762-9
— free and strict, 704
— laws of progression in, 706-22
— quadruple, quintuple, triple, 752
— second species, 741-9
— third species, 754-61
Counter-subject, 1049
Counting bars, 298
Couplet, p. 373, n. 2
Courante, 1062
Crossing of parts, 432
Crotchet, 29
Cyclic form, 888
Da capo, 212
Dactyl, 825
Dal segno, 212
Dance tunes, sets of, 988
Dashes, 216
Demisemiquaver, 29
Development, 910-528
— change of time in, 917
— keys used in, 927
— methods of, 924
Diatonic, 101
— discords, 547
— intervals, 181, 182

Diatonic semitones, 160
Diminished intervals, 194
— — progression by, 431
— octave, 449
— seventh, 566-73
Direct, ↙, 622
Discord, fundamental, 390, 619
— secondary, 414, 574
Dissonance, 203, 271
Dissonant, 271
— triads, 640-6
Distribution of a chord, 284-5, 687
Dominant, 138
— seventh, 372, 407
— — allowed to rise, 400
— — decides the key, 388
— — exceptional resolution of, 485-7
Doppio movimento, 60
Dot, 32, 36, 210, 216
Double bars, use of, 42, 882
— sharp, 90, 206 (e)
Double counterpoint, 701
— — in sonata form, 919
Doubles, 1062
Doubling, 280, 327, 362, 377, 727
— in a second inversion, 336
Duple time, 47
Duplet, 74
Eighth note, 30
Eleventh, the dominant, 581-6
— figuring of, 582
Enharmonic, 167-173, p. 204, n. 1
— changes in diminished seventh, 567
— modulation, 570-3, 661
Enigma canon, 1040
Episode, p. 342, n. 4; 881, 973
— defined, 973
— in fugue, 1052
— in sonata form, 1052
Episodical movement, 881
Essential discords, 547
Exercises, method of writing, 300
Exposition in fugue, 1051
— in sonata, 891-908
Extended sentence, example of, 849
F clef, 7
False relation, 445-9
— — of the tritone, 722
Fantasia, 1024
Fifths, 186
— augmented, 206 (c)
Figure, 824
Figuring, 321-5, 345, 376, 527
— in counterpoint, 736
— use of accidentals, 363, 371
— — — horizontal line, 406
Finale, key of, 969
— form of, 970
First inversions, 319, 326
— in succession, 329-32
First movement form, 890
Flat, 91, 248
— double, 92
Foot in poetry and music, 825
Form defined, 853
— requisites of, 861, 868
— three-part, 872-81
— two-part, 857-71

INDEX

Fourths, 185
— with the bass, 335
Free Fantasia, 910
French sixth, 630
Fugal treatment, 922
Fugato, 1057
Fughetta, 1056
Fugue, 985, 1045-57
— counter-subject, 1049
— double and triple, 1055
— episode, 1052
— stretto, 1053
— subject and answer, 1046-7
— tonal, 1048
— and sonata form combined, 1058
Fundamental note, 154
— discords, 390
— — and the chromatic scale, 619
— — to find root of, 565, 620
G clef, 5
Gavotte, 1062
Generator, 154
German names of notes, 140-1
— sixth, 630
Gigue, 1062
Glee, 1075
Grace notes, 224, 542
Great stave, 14
Gregorian tones, 245, 371 a
Ground bass, 680
Half-note, 30
Harmonic effect, 986
— combinations in strict counterpoint, 723-6
— minor scale, 124
— series, 155, 389
Harmonics, 154
Harmonising a melody, 669-96
Harmony, 273
Hidden consecutives, exceptions to, 316, 440
History of sonata, 984-99
— of form, 984-88
Homophonic, 986
Iambic, 825
Imitation, 1026-32
— strict and free, 1027
Impromptu, 881
Instrumental music, early, 984
Intensity of sound, 153
Interpolation of a bar with different time-signature, 850-1
Intervals, 178
— alteration of chromatic to diatonic, 198
— augmented, 185, 193
— chromatic, 181, 191, 253
— compound, 179
— consonant, 203-5, 272
— diatonic, 181-9, 253
— diminished, 186, 194
— dissonant, 203-5
— inversion of, 200-2
— major and minor, 182
— simple, 179
— table of, 189, 197
— to find key of, 206
— to find name of, 190, 199
Introduction in sonata form, 907
— to a song, 870-871
Inversion of intervals, 200-2, 268
Inversion of order of subjects in recapitulation, 937

Inversions, 318
— first, 326, 367
— of augmented sixths, 636
— of dominant sevenths, 391
— second, 334, 370
Italian sixth, 630
Key, 628, 853
— at beginning and end of a composition, p. 327, n. 1 ; p. 341, n. 1
— compared with scale, 118
— contrast, 987
— how to tell the, 145
— importance in form, 858
— of finale, 969
— relative, 127, 132
Key-note, 111, 116
Key-relationship, 853-55
— — enharmonic, 948
Key-signature, 107, 110, 115, 133
Largo, 38
Laws of part-writing, 428-49
Leading-note, 138, 298, 433
— in counterpoint
— seventh, 562
Legato, 215
Leger line, 8
L. H., 241
Lengthening of cadence, 831
— of sentences, 82
Lessons, 1059
Liederkreis, 1073
Link, 878
Lunga pausa, 214
Madrigal, 1075
Maelzel's metronome, 244
Major and minor keys in compositions, p. 341, n. 1
— mode, p. 46, n.
— scale, 102
— sixth in minor mode, 353
— third, doubling of, 328
March, 881
Mass, 1075
M. D., 241
Measure, 44
Mediant, 138
Melodic outline, 821
Melody, 273
— how to harmonise, 669-96
Metronome, 244
Mezzo-soprano, 246
— staccato, 216
Mi contra fa, p. 265, n. 1
Middle cadences, 790
— C, 13
Miniature sonata form, 964
Minim, 29
Minor mode, p. 46, n.
— scale, 120, 348-52
— — altered diatonic or melodic, 125
— — chromatic or harmonic, 125
— — diatonic, 125
Minuet in sonata, 962
— form of, 964
— key of, 968
— (the dance), 1062
M. M., 244
Mode, p. 46, n.
Modes, Gregorian, 371 a

Modern rondo, 981
Modification of subjects in recapitulation, 939
Modified sonata form, 958
Modulation, 471-88, 661-8, 798, 856
— compound, 667
— enharmonic, 556, 661
— extraneous, 666
— in second subjects, 902
— natural, 476
— on a pedal, 652
Mordent, 234
— inverted, 235
Motet, 1075
Motion, contrary, oblique, similar, 286
Motive, p. 308, n. 1; 819
— incomplete, 306, n. 1
M. S., 241
Movement in sonata form, 945, 990
— of continuity, p. 342, n. 1
— of episode, 881
— of one sentence, p. 326, n. 1
Musical sounds, 1
— Terms, 236-244
Names of notes of scale, 250
Natural, 93
Neapolitan sixth, 598
New ending to old melody, 921
— matter in development, 923
Ninth, dominant, 548-56
— inversions of, 557-61
— — method of writing, 613
— supertonic, 611
— tonic, 615
Nocturne, 881
Nonet, 885
Notes, 4
— ancient shapes of, 38
— French and German names of, 139-143
— names of, 2
Octave, 3, 25, 151, 218, 219
Octet, 885
Old sonata form, 993-4
Omission of notes from a chord, 282, 378, 729
Open canon, 1039
Opera, 1075
Oratorio, 1075
Orchestral music, 1000-1017
Order of flats, 114
— of sharps, 108
Ordres, 988
Organ point, 648
Origin of sonata form, 992
Ornamentation of subjects in recapitulation, 938
Overlapping of parts, 432
— of sentences, 837-39
Overtones, 154
Overture, 1001-7
— concert, 1007
— French, 1002
— Italian, 1003
— modern, 1004-6
Part, 274
Parts, compass of, 300
— extreme, inner, 313
Partita, 988, 1059
Part-song, 1075
Passacaglia, 1064

Passing notes, 528-38
— — figuring of, 546
Pause, 214
Pedal, right, 242
— left, 243
Pedal-note, 648-57
— double, 655
— inverted, 654
— point, 1054
Per recte et retro, 1032
Perfect intervals, 185, 186, 205
— consonances, 204
Period, 791
Phrase, 791
— length of, 791
— responsive, 792, 820
— to find end of, 802
Phrasing marks, 803
Pitch, 1, 151
— philosophical, 151
— relative, 152
— standard, 151
Plain song, 1075, p. 262, n.
Polonaise, 881
Polymorphous canon, 1042
Polyphonic music, 985
Praller, or Pralltriller, p. 85, n.
Prefix to a melody, 835
Preparation of dissonant notes, 415, 427
— of suspensions, 492
Prima volta, 211
Principal subject of rondo, variations in, 974, 981
Programme music, p. 385, n. 1
Proportion in form, 868
Quadruple time, 47, 807
Quadruplet, 74
Quality of intervals, 182-7, 193-4
— of inverted intervals, 202
— of sound, 156, 158
Quarter-notes, 30
Quartet, 885, 1020
Quaver, 29
Quintet, 885
Quintuplet, 75
R. H., 241
Recapitulation, 930-9
— inversion of subjects in, 937
— irregularity of key of first subject, 93*
— keys used in, 931-5
— modification of subjects in, 939
— shortening of subjects in, 938
Recitative, 1066-7
Related keys, 472-4, 853-5, 948
Relative major, 129
— minor, 128
— scales, 127
Repeat marks. 210-13
Repetition; importance in form, 858, 860, 862
— of cadence, 827
— of figures, 984
— of group of notes, 222
— sequential, 830
Reprise, 930
— i.e. episode, p. 373, n. 2
Resolution, 374, 380
— of suspensions, 492 3
— ornamental, 387, 405, 425, 519-20
Resonance, 157

INDEX

Responsive phrase, 792
Resta, 34
— dotted, 36, 72
— use of, 68-9, 70-2
Retardations, 545
Retrograde imitation, 1032
Reversed accents, 1030
Rhythm, 247, 787, 852
— in dance tunes, 988
Ricercare, Ricercata, p. 400, n. 1
Riddle canon, 1040
Ritornello, 871
Rondo form, 970-83
— a movement of contrast, 973
— bridge passages in, 976
— compared with three-part form, 971, 979
— defined, 971
— length of P. S., 979
— modern, 981-3
Rondos which are not in rondo form, 980
Root of chord, 276
— double, 631
— to find, 565
Round, 1043
Sarabande, 1062
Scale, 100, 117, 118
— arbitrary chromatic, 176
— chromatic, 174, 623-8
— degree of, p. 38, n.
— diatonic, 101
— harmonic chromatic, 175
— how to write the chromatic, p. 60
— major, 102
— minor, 119-124
— natural, 109
— with flats, 112
— with sharps, 106
Scarlatti form, 1069
Scena, scena ed aria, 1074
Scherzo, 966-8
— as an independent movement, 968
Score, open and short, 302
Second inversions, 337-47
— — in arpeggio, 347
— subject compared with first, 897-900
Seconda volta, 211
Secondary ninths, 574-80
— sevenths and ninths compared, 578
— sevenths, 414
— — and dominant compared, 426
— — in sequence, 424
Seconds, 182
Sections, 812
— comparison of, 821
— of two bars, 846
— to find end of, 813-14
Semibreve, 29
Semidemisemiquaver, 37
Semiquaver, 29
Semitone, 88
— chromatic, 161-164
— diatonic, 160
— mean, 565
Sentence, 791
— ending on half-cadence, p. 311, n. 1
— four-bar, 806
— length of, 811
— with four phrases, 801
— with three phrases, 800

Sentence with two phrases, 791-99
Septet, 855
Sequences, 464-70
Sevenths, 184
— chromatic, 600-7
— dominant, 373-7, 485-8
— secondary, 414
Sextet, 855
Sextuplet, 75
Shake, 232-3, 542
— double, 233
Sharp, 89
— double, 90
Shortening of a sentence, 837-40
Signature, key, 110, 115, 133-4
Simili, 216 (a)
Sixteenth note, 30
Sixths, 183 (a)
Slow movement, form of, 949
— — key of, 948
Slur, 215
Sonata da camera, 988
— da chiesa, 988
— modern, 994
— old, 993-4
— quasi una fantasia, p. 342, n. 2
Sonata form, 883, 887, 889, 890
— — Beethoven's influence on, 997
— — Brahms' influence on, 998
— — coda, 940-3
— — compared with song form, 944
— — development, 910-29
— — exposition, 891-906
— — Haydn's influence on, 996
— — history of, 984-99
— — introduction, 907
— — key of second subject, 895-906
— — modified, 958
— — recapitulation, 930-39
Sonata-rondo, 981
— — with development, 983
Sonatina, p. 340, n. 2
Song cycle, 1073
— form, 853-61
Songs, 1069-74
— in sonata form, 1071
Soprano, 22
— clef, 18
Sordini, con, 242
— senza, 242
Staccato, 216
Stave, 4, 245
— great, 14
Stretto, 1053
String quartet, 1020
Strophic song, 957, 1070
Subdominant, 138
Submediant, 138
Suite, 988, 1060
— dances in, 1062
— form of, 1061
Supertonic, 138
— chromatic common chords, 506
— — ninths, 601
— — sevenths, 611
Suspensions, 489-92
— double, triple, 521
— figuring of, 498, 503, 509-13, 516-7
— of chords, 524

414   *INDEX*

Suspensions, resolution of, 506
— rules for, 500
Suspended fourth, 507-15
— ninth, 495
Symphonic, 1009
Symphony, history of, 1008
— modern, 1009-11
— original meaning of, 1000
— of a song, 871, 874, 885
— form, p 342, n. 1
Syncopation, 79-81
Tempo a cappella, 60
— rubato, 84, 240
Tenor, 22, 246
— C, 28
— clef, 19
Terms, musical, 236-44
Tetrachord, 104
— conjunct and disjunct, 104
Thirds, 183
Thirteenth, the dominant, 587-91
— supertonic and tonic, 617
Thirty-second note, 30
Three-four time, 809
Three-part form, 872-81
— — — summary of, 880
Tie, 33, 215
Tierce de Picardie, 365-6
Timbre, 156, 158
Time, 47, 787
— alternation of, 87, 852
— beating, 66-7
— change of, 84
— common, 48, 59
— compound, 49, 56, 247, 807
— counting, 64
— imperfect, 59
— perfect, 59
— simple, 49
— to change simple into compound, and *vice versa*, 76, 77
— triple, 47
Time-signature, 50-55, 58-60
— correct, 806-11
— double, 78, 852
Time-signatures, table of, p. 21

Tone, 88
— Gregorian, 245
Tonic, 138
— major and minor, 136, 137
— ninths, 615
— sevenths, 605
Transformation of themes, 999
Transposition, 207
Treble, 22, 246
Tre corde, 243
Tremolo, 221
Triad, 277
— augmented and diminished, 640-7, p. 102, n. 2
Tributary subjects, 898
Trill, 232
Trio with minuet, 962
— form of, 962
— key of, 963
Triplet, 73, 76, 249
Tritone, 185
— false relation of, 722
Trochee, 825
Turn, 229-31, 542
— inverted, 230
Tutti, 1012
Two-part form, 857-71
— — — how enlarged, 864, 867
Unaccented bars, 809
— notes at end of phrase, 802 (c)
Una corda, 253
Unessential discords, 547
Unison, 197
Unity in form, 861
Variations, 1021
— methods used in, 1022
— writers of, 1023
Variety in form, 861
Verschiebung, mit, 943
Vocal music, 985, 1066-75
— — form of, 1068-74
Voices, names of, 22, 246
— limits of, 300
Whole-note, 30
Working of a subject, 918
Writing key-signature, 108

II.

List of movements ANALYSED *or* DESCRIBED *in* PART III.

Bach, C. P. E. :
  Rondo II. (3rd set), 974
  Sonatas, p. 380, n. 2
Bach, J. S. :
  English suite I., 1060
  French suite I., 1060
  Fugues, 985
  Passacaglia for organ, 1064
  Violin sonata IV., p. 378, n.
  — (chaconne), 1064
  Wohltemperirtes Clavier, II. 3, p. 397, n. 1
  — — I. 2, p. 399

Beethoven :
  P.F. sonatas
    No. I. (Minuet), 965
     „ I. (Rondo), 982
     „ II. (1st movement), 918
     „ III. (Coda), 941
     „ III. (Development), 928
     „ III. (Scherzo), 967
     „ IV. (Slow movement), 961
     „ VI. (Finale), 1058
     „ VII. (Slow movement), p. 367, n 1
     „ VIII. (Slow movement), 953

INDEX 415

No. X. (1st movement), 900
" XII. (Marcia funebre), 877
" XIII. (Slow movement), 952
" XV. (Slow movement), 979
" XVII. (Slow movement), 958
" XVIII. (Scherzo), 968
" XXVII. (Rondo), 983
" XXIX., p. 382, n. 1
P.F. concerto in E♭, 1014
Overtures, Egmont, 1004 ; Leonora No. 3, 1005
Quartet in G, op. 18, No. 2 (slow movement), 955
Symphony No. IX. (scherzo), 967
Trio for P.F., V. & C. No. 1, 809
Variations in F, op. 34, 390, n. 1
Songs :
  Ah perfido, 1074
  An die ferne Geliebte, 1073
  Kennst du das Land, 1070
  Gott ! welch Dunkel hier, 1074
Bishop, Bid me discourse, 874
Guy Mannering overture, 1006
Brahms' symphony in D, 999
Symphony in E minor, 1064
Clementi, Gradus ad Parnassum, No. 15, 945 ; No. 10, p. 395, n. 1
Corelli, Sonata da camera, op. 2, No. 1, 988
Sonata da chiesa, op. 1, No. 1, 988
— for Violin, IX. (Giga), 992
Couperin, La Favorite, 975
Dussek, P.F. sonatas
  Op. 10, No. 3, p. 341, n.
  Op. 30, No. 2, 951
  Op. 39, No. 1, 977
  Op. 47, No. 1, 980
  Op. 77, p. 395, n. 1
Franz, songs, p. 326, n. 1 ; p. 341, n. 1
Gounod, Canzone di Magali, 852
Handel, Faramondo, 1000
  Judas Maccabæus (march), 993
  — — (overture), 1002
  Lascia ch' io pianga, 873
  Messiah (overture), 1002
    (For behold), 1067
    (There were shepherds), 1067
    (Thy rebuke), 1066
    (Rejoice greatly), 1071
    (Why do the nations), 1069
  Samson (overture), 1002
  Suites, 1064

Haydn, P.F. sonata VII., 952
" " IX., 972
" " XIV., 964
Quartet, Op. 1, No. 1, 860
Symphony in B♭, 957
Hérold, Zampa (overture), 1006
Hummel,[1] P.F. sonata VIII., 849
Kuhnau, Bible sonata I., 993
Mackenzie, Rose of Sharon (Unto my charger), 1071
Mendelssohn :
  Christmas Pieces (VI.), 946
  Concerto (P.F. in G minor), 1014
  " (violin), p. 387, n. 1
  Infelice, 1074
  M.N.D. (overture), p. 384, n. 2
  " (scherzo), 968
  Songs without Words, No. 35, 870
  " " No. 23, 871
Mozart, P.F. sonatas :[2]
  No. VII. in C, 956
  " VIII. in A minor, 909, 928
  " IX. in D, 925, 978
  " XIII. in B♭, 996
Sonata for P.F. and Violin in A, p. 341, n. 1
Concerto for P.F. in C, 983
Fantasia in D minor, 1024
Operas, Die Entführung (overture), 1005
  " " (songs), 1071
  Don Juan (overture), 1005
  " " (Batti, batti), 1072
  Die Zauberflöte (overture), 1005
Rondo in D, 980
String quartet in G, 1059
Symphonies, The Jupiter, 1059
  The Prague, 1011
Purcell, I attempt from love's sickness to fly, 876
Raff, Suite in E minor, Op. 72 1065
Schubert, P.F. Sonata, Op. 120 (slow movement), 961
Die schöne Müllerin, 1073
Schumann, Sonata for P.F. and Violin, Op. 121 (scherzo), 999
E♭ Symphony, 1011
Sullivan, The Window, 1073
Tartini, Il trillo del diavolo, 990
Wagner, Die Meistersinger (overture), 1006
Weber, Rondo in E♭, 983
  Der Freischütz (overture), 1005
  " " (Wie nahte mir der Schlummer), 1074

---

[1] Edition Litolff.   [2] Edition Novello.

www.ingramcontent.com/pod-product-compliance
Lightning Source LLC
Chambersburg PA
CBHW030546300426
44111CB00009B/872